Reader's Digest

OUR ISLAND HERITAGE

OUR ISLAND HERITAGE
was edited and designed by
The Reader's Digest Association Limited
London

First Edition
Copyright © 1988
The Reader's Digest Association Limited
Berkeley Square House
Berkeley Square
London W1X 6AB

Reprinted with amendments **1990**

Copyright © 1988
Reader's Digest Services Pty. Limited
Sydney, Australia

Copyright © 1988
The Reader's Digest Association
South Africa (Pty.) Limited

Copyright © 1988
Reader's Digest Association
Far East Limited

Philippines Copyright © 1988
Reader's Digest Association
Far East Limited

® READER'S DIGEST, The Digest, and the
Pegasus logo are registered trademarks of
The Reader's Digest Association, Inc.
of Pleasantville, New York, U.S.A.

ISBN 0 276 48943 8
Printed in Great Britain

Reader's Digest

OUR ISLAND
HERITAGE

VOLUME TWO

The Stuarts to the Battle of Waterloo

Published by The Reader's Digest Association Limited
London • New York • Montreal • Sydney • Cape Town

Contents

CHAPTERS

From Winston S. Churchill's *A History of the English-Speaking Peoples*

SOCIAL HISTORY SECTIONS

COLOUR SECTIONS

CHAPTER 1
THE UNITED CROWNS

KING JAMES VI OF SCOTLAND was the only son of Mary Queen of Scots. He had been subjected from his youth to a rigid Calvinist upbringing which was not much to his taste. With little money and strict tutors he had long coveted the throne of England, but till the last moment the prize had seemed elusive. The struggle for power between Essex and Robert Cecil might always have provoked Elizabeth, whom he knew only by intermittent correspondence, into some swift decision which would lose him the Crown. But now all appeared settled. Cecil was his ally and skilful manager in the tense days after the Queen died. James was proclaimed King James I of England without opposition, and in April 1603 began a leisurely journey from Holyrood to London.

He was a stranger and an alien, and his qualifications for governing England were yet to be tested. Trevelyan says James was "So ignorant of England and her laws that at Newark he ordered a cut-purse caught in the act to be hanged without a trial at a word from his royal mouth." The execution did not take place. Detesting the political ideas of his Calvinist mentors, James had fixed ideas about kingship and the divine right of monarchs to rule. He was a scholar with pretensions to being a philosopher, and in the course of his life published numerous tracts and treatises, ranging from denunciation of witchcraft and tobacco to abstract political theory. He came to England with a closed mind, and a weakness for lecturing. But England was changing. The habit of obedience to a dynasty had died with the last of the Tudors. Spain was no longer a threat, and the Union of the Crowns deprived foreign enemies of an ally, or even a foothold, in the island. The country gentlemen on whom the Tudors relied to maintain a balance against the old nobility, and on whom they had devolved the whole business of local government, were beginning to feel their strength. England was secure, free to attend to her own concerns, and a powerful class was now eager to take a hand in their management.

Over these deep-cutting issues there loomed a fiscal crisis of the first magnitude. The importation of precious metals from the New World had swelled the rise in prices throughout Europe. Every year the fixed revenues of the Crown were worth less and less. By extreme frugality Elizabeth had postponed a conflict. But it could not be averted, and bound up with it was a formidable constitutional problem. Who was to have the last word in the matter of taxation? Hitherto everyone had accepted the medieval doctrine that "The King may not rule his people by other laws than they assent unto,

James VI of Scotland became James I of England in 1603 when he was thirty-seven. He was well-educated, but introduced policies that alienated people, and thus acquired the nickname of "the wisest fool in Christendom". This portrait by Daniel Mytens can be seen in the National Portrait Gallery.

"Great Britain" is stamped on this coin dating from 1603, when the union of Scotland and England was brought about by James's accession to the English throne.

and therefore he may set upon them no imposition [*i.e.* tax] without their assent." But no one had traced out its implications in any detail. Was it the inalienable birthright of Englishmen, or a concession which might be revoked? Was the King beneath the law or was he not? And who was to say what the law was? The greater part of the seventeenth century was to be spent in trying to find answers, historical, legal, theoretical, and practical, to such questions. Lawyers, scholars, statesmen, soldiers all joined in this great debate. Relief at an undisputed succession gave the new sovereign a loyal, and even enthusiastic, reception. But James and his subjects were soon at odds about this and other topics.

His first Parliament at once raised the question of Parliamentary privilege and Royal Prerogative. In dutiful but firm language the Commons drew up an Apology reminding the King that their liberties included free elections, free speech, and freedom from arrest during Parliamentary sessions. "The voice of the people" they protested, "in the things of their knowledge is said to be as the voice of God." James treated these expressions contemptuously, brushing them aside as personal insults to himself and breaches of good manners. The King indulged his taste for lecturing, and reminded them of his divine right to rule and their solemn duty to supply his needs.

Hitherto James had been straitened; now he thought he was rich. The "beggarly Scotsmen" who had come south with him also enriched themselves. To his surprise James very soon found himself pressed for money. It was an ancient and obstinate belief that the King should "live of his own", and that the traditional revenues from the Crown lands and from the Customs should suffice for the upkeep of the public services. Parliament did not expect to have to provide more money except in emergencies. Fortunately the judges ruled that the ports were under the King's exclusive jurisdiction and that he could impose extra Customs duties as he thought fit. This gave James a revenue that rose with the increasing national wealth and the higher prices. The Commons questioned the judges' ruling, and James made matters worse by turning the argument into a technical one about Royal Prerogative. Here, but only for a time, the matter rested.

The King had decided views on religion. He was greeted upon his accession with a petition from the Puritans. These opponents of the Episcopal State Church hoped that the new King from Calvinist Scotland would listen to their case. But James had had enough of the Kirk. He realised that Calvinism and monarchy would quarrel in the long run and that if men could decide for themselves about religion they could also decide for themselves on politics. In 1604 he held a conference at Hampton Court between the Puritan leaders and those who accepted the Elizabethan system. His prejudice was soon manifest. In the middle of the debate he accused the Puritans of aiming "at a Scottish presbytery which agreeth as well with the monarch as God and the Devil . . . ." James made it clear to them that there would be no changes in the Elizabethan Church Settlement. His slogan was "No Bishop, no King".

All the Puritan demands were rejected, but towards the end of the conference a Puritan divine, Dr John Reynolds, asked seemingly on the spur of the moment, if a new version of the Bible could be produced. This appealed to James. Till now the clergy and laity had relied on a number of different translations – Tyndale's, Coverdale's, the Geneva Bible, the "Bishop's Bible" of Queen Elizabeth. Each party used the version which best suited its own views. Here, thought James, was the chance to rid the Scriptures of propaganda. Within a few months committees or "companies" were set up, two each in Oxford, Cambridge, and Westminster, comprising in all about fifty scholars and divines, selected without regard to their theological or ecclesiastical bias. Each committee was assigned a portion of the text and their draft was to be scrutinised by all the other committees and finally revised by a committee of twelve. The work was accomplished with remarkable swiftness. In an age without an efficient postal service or mechanical methods of copying texts, the committees finished their task in 1609. Nine months sufficed for the scrutiny of the supervisory committee, and in 1611 the Authorised Version of the Bible was produced by the King's Printer. It was an immediate and lasting triumph. It superseded all other versions, and no new revision was deemed necessary for nearly three hundred years. This may well be James's greatest achievement, for the impulse was largely his.

At the accession the Catholics also were anxious and hopeful. After all, the King's mother had been their champion. Their position was delicate. A European controversy was raging about the nature of obedience, and James plunged into the argument. The Jesuits replied with volumes attacking his right to the throne. James, although inclined to toleration, was forced to act. Catholics were fined for refusing to attend the services of the Established Church and their priests were banished.

Disappointment and despair led a small group of Catholic gentry to an infernal design for blowing up James and his whole Parliament while they were in session at Westminster. They hoped that in the confusion a Catholic regime might be re-established with Spanish help. The chief plotter was Robert Catesby, assisted by Guy Fawkes, a veteran of the Spanish wars against the Dutch. One of their followers warned a relative who was a Catholic peer. The story reached Cecil, and the cellars of Parliament were searched. Fawkes was taken on the spot, and there was a storm of excitement in the city. James went down to open Parliament, and made an emotional speech upon what an honourable end it would have been to die with his faithful Commons. The House displayed an incomprehensible indifference, and, turning to the business of the day, discussed the petition of a member who had asked to be relieved of his Parliamentary duties owing to an attack of gout. The conspirators were hunted down, tortured, and then executed. So novel and so wholesale a treason exposed the Catholic

A contemporary engraving shows Guy Fawkes standing third from the right next to the large figure of Robert Catesby, the instigator of the Gunpowder Plot to blow up the Houses of Parliament in 1605.

community to an immediate and severe persecution and to a more persistent detestation. The Thanksgiving Service for the deliverance of November 5 was not removed from the Prayer Book until 1854; and the anniversary is even now celebrated by bonfires and fireworks.

James and his Parliaments grew more and more out of sympathy as the years went by. The Tudors had been discreet in their use of the Royal Prerogative but James saw himself as the schoolmaster of the whole island. In theory there was a good case for absolute monarchy. The whole political development of the sixteenth century was on his side. He found a brilliant supporter in the person of Francis Bacon, the ambitious lawyer who had dabbled in politics with Essex and crept back to obedience when his patron fell. Bacon held a succession of high legal offices, culminating in the Lord Chancellorship. He maintained that the absolute rule of the King with the help of his judges was justified by its efficiency, but his theories were unreal and widely unpopular.

The subsequent conflict centred on the nature of the Royal Prerogative and the powers of an Act of Parliament. The modern view had not yet emerged that an Act of Parliament is supreme and unalterable unless repealed or amended, and the sovereign power of the State can be exercised in no other way. The Tudor statutes had indeed been the instruments of profound changes in Church and State, and there seemed little they could not do. But statutes required both the assent of Parliament and the approval of the King. No Parliament could meet without the summons of the King, or sit after he had dismissed it. Little else but financial necessity could compel the King to call a Parliament. If money could be raised elsewhere he might govern for years at a time without one. Moreover, a certain undefined prerogative power the King assuredly had; the exigencies of government required it. Who was to say what he could and could not do? If the King chose, on grounds of public interest, to make an ordinance dispensing with a statute, who could say he was acting illegally?

At this point the Common Lawyers, headed by Chief Justice Coke, stepped to the forefront of English history. Coke, one of the most learned of English judges, declared that conflicts between Prerogative and statutes should be resolved not by the Crown but by the judges. It was a tremendous assertion, for if the judges were to decide which laws were valid and which were not they would become the ultimate lawgivers in the State. Coke's high claims rested on the ancient tradition that law declared in the courts was superior to law published by the central authority, for it existed already, merely awaiting revelation and exposition. If Acts of Parliament conflicted with it they were invalid. James had a very different view of the function of judges. They might have the duty of deciding between the conflicting claims of statute and Prerogative, but if so they were bound to decide in the Crown's favour. As judges were appointed by the King, they should obey him like other royal servants. James therefore dismissed Coke in 1616.

Five years later Coke entered the House of Commons and found that the leadership of the lawyers was readily accepted. Few of the country gentlemen sitting in the Commons had any deep knowledge of Parliamentary history, or could produce any coherent theory to justify the claims of Parliament. They simply felt a smouldering injustice at the arbitrary conduct and jarring theories of the King. For all its stirring movements, this was an age of profound respect for precedents and constitutional forms. If the whole weight of legal opinion had been thrown into the royal scale the Commons' task would have been much harder. They would have had to break with the past and admit they were revolutionaries. But the adherence of the lawyers freed them from an agonising choice. Coke, Selden, and others, including Pym, who had read law even if he had not practised, formed a group of able leaders who gradually built up a case on which Parliament could claim with conviction that it was fighting, not for something new, but for the traditional and lawful heritage of the English people. Thus were laid the foundations of a united, disciplined opposition.

James had no sympathy with these agitations. It was only the need of money that forced him to deal with Parliament at all. "The House of Commons," he once told the Spanish Ambassador, "is a body without a head. The Members give their opinions in a disorderly manner. At their meetings nothing is heard but cries, shouts, and confusion. I am surprised that my ancestors should ever have permitted such an institution to have come into existence. I am a stranger, and found it here when I arrived, so that I am obliged to put up with what I cannot get rid of."

James's foreign policy perhaps met the needs of the age for peace, but often clashed with its temper. When he came to the throne England was still technically at war with Spain. With Cecil's support hostilities were concluded and diplomatic relations renewed. The main struggle had already shifted from the high seas to Europe. The House of Habsburg, at the head of

A COUNTERBLAST TO TOBACCO

James I was under no illusions about the effects of tobacco, in spite of the commonly held belief that it was good for the health. The sentiments which he expressed in 1604 in his essay entitled A Counterblast to Tobacco *have a surprisingly modern tone.*

Now surely in my opinion, there cannot be a more base and hurtful corruption in a country than is the vile use of taking Tobacco in this Kingdom. Now how you are by this custom disabled in your goods, let the gentry of this land bear witness, some of them bestowing three, some four hundred pounds a year upon this precious stink. Is it not both great vanity and uncleanness, that at table, a place of respect, of cleanliness, of modesty, men should not be ashamed, to sit tossing of tobacco pipes and puffing of the smoke of tobacco one to another, to exhale athwart the dishes, and infect the air, when very often men that abhor it are at their repast? Surely smoke becomes a kitchen far better than a dining chamber, and yet it makes a kitchen also oftentimes in the inward parts of men, soiling and infecting them with an unctuous and oily kind of soot, as hath been found in some great Tobacco takers, that after their death were opened.

Are you not guilty of sinful and shameful lust? That although you be troubled with no disease, but in perfect health, yet can you neither be merry at an Ordinary, nor lascivious in the Stews, if you lack Tobacco to provoke your appetite to any of those sorts of recreation, lusting after it as the children of Israel did in the wilderness after Quails? Mollicies and delicacy were the wrack and

overthrow, first of the Persian, and next of the Roman Empire. Have you not reason then to be ashamed, and to forbear this filthy novelty, so basely grounded, so foolishly received, and so grossly mistaken in the right use thereof?

In your abuse thereof sinning against God, and taking also thereby the marks and notes of Vanity upon you. A custom loathsome to the eye, hateful to the nose, harmful to the brain, dangerous to the lungs, and in the black stinking fume thereof, nearest resembling the horrible Stygian smoke of the pit that is bottomless.

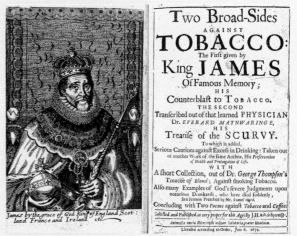

James I considered it his duty as a ruler to purge the country of what he termed its "popular errors, diseases and corruptions." It is no accident that his essay condemning tobacco should be published with a Dr Mainwaring's treatise on scurvy.

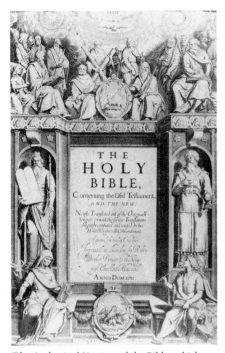

The Authorised Version of the Bible, which was first published in 1611, is still linguistically the most beautiful of all translations. It has provided a model of English style for writers in all subsequent centuries.

the Holy Roman Empire, still dominated the Continent from Vienna. The territories of the Emperor and of his cousin the King of Spain now stretched from Portugal to Poland, and their power was backed by the proselytising fervour of the Jesuits. The Commons and the country remained vehemently hostile to Spain, but James was unmoved. Learning nothing from Tudor experiences, James proposed not merely an alliance with Spain, but a Spanish match for his son.

His daughter however was already in the opposite camp. The Princess Elizabeth had married one of the Protestant champions of Europe, Frederick, the Elector Palatine of the Rhine. Habsburg attempts to recover for the Catholic faith those areas in Germany which the law of the Empire had recognised as Protestant provoked the vehement opposition of the Protestant princes. The storm centre was Bohemia, where a haughty, resolute Czech nobility obstructed the centralising policy of Vienna both in religion and politics. In the fifteenth-century days of John Huss they had set up their own Church and fought both Pope and Emperor. Now they defied Emperor Ferdinand. In 1618 their leaders flung the Imperial envoys from the windows of the royal palace in Prague. This action, later known as the Defenestration, started the war which was to ravage Germany for thirty years. The Czechs offered Frederick the throne of Bohemia. Frederick accepted, and became the recognised leader of the Protestant revolt.

The Elector Frederick was soon driven out of Bohemia, and his hereditary lands were occupied by Habsburg troops. So short had been his reign that he is known to history as "the Winter King". The House of Commons clamoured for war. Private subscriptions and bands of volunteers were raised for the defence of the Protestants. James however contented himself with academic discussions upon Bohemian rights with the Spanish ambassador. To pose as Protestant champion in the great war now begun might gain a fleeting popularity with his subjects, but would also deliver him into the hands of the House of Commons. Parliament would assuredly demand some control over the expenditure of the money it voted for arms, and was unlikely to be generous. James seems genuinely to have believed in his mission as the peacemaker of Europe, and he also had a deep-rooted nervous dislike of fighting, founded in the tumultuous experiences of his youth in Scotland. He ignored the demand for intervention, and continued his negotiations for the Spanish match.

In the midst of these turmoils Sir Walter Raleigh was executed to please the Spanish Government. Raleigh had been imprisoned at the beginning of the reign for conspiring to supplant James by his cousin, Arabella Stuart. This charge was probably unjust, and the trial was certainly so. Raleigh's dream of finding gold on the Orinoco River, which had cheered his long confinement, ended in disaster in 1617. This last expedition of his, for which he was specially released from the Tower, had merely affronted the Spanish governors of South America. The old capital sentence was now revived against him. His death on October 29, 1618 was intended to mark the new policy of appeasement and prepare the way for good relations with Spain. This deed of shame sets a barrier forever between King James and the English people. There are others.

James's attention to handsome young men resulted in a noticeable loss of respect for the monarchy. After the death of his wise counsellor, Robert Cecil, the Court had been afflicted by a number of odious scandals. One of his favourites, Robert Carr, was implicated in a murder by poison, of which his wife was undoubtedly guilty. James at first paid little attention to the storm raised by this crime; but even he found it impossible to maintain Carr in high office. He was succeeded in the King's regard by a good-looking, quick-witted, extravagant youth, George Villiers, soon ennobled as Duke of Buckingham. This young man quickly became all-powerful at Court. He formed a deep and honourable friendship with Charles, Prince of Wales. He accepted unhesitatingly the royal policy of a Spanish marriage, and in 1623 staged a romantic journey to Madrid for the Prince and himself to view the bride. Their unorthodox behaviour failed to impress the ceremonious Court of Spain. Moreover, the Spaniards demanded concessions for the English Catholics, which James knew Parliament would never grant.

When the news spread through the country that Prince Charles was safely back at Portsmouth, unwedded to the Infanta, unseduced from the Protestant faith, a surge of joy arose among all classes. The overpowering wish and potent will of England was to resist, and if necessary to fight, Spain and all that Spain meant. The deadly sin of Papist idolatry, as they conceived it, terrified their souls. Streets were crowded with waggons carrying faggots for the bonfires. The red glow of rejoicing was reflected in the London sky.

Buckingham and Charles were now eager for war. James at first wavered. He was, he said, an old man who once knew something about politics. Now the two beings he loved best in the world urged him upon a course directly contrary to his judgment and past action. In this sharp pinch Buckingham with remarkable agility turned himself from a royal favourite into a national, if short-lived, statesman. While using all his personal address to over-persuade the sovereign, he sought and obtained the support of Parliament and people. He took a number of steps which recognised, in a manner unknown since the days of the House of Lancaster, Parliamentary rights and power. Whereas all interference by Parliament in foreign affairs had been repelled by the Tudors, and hitherto by James, the minister-favourite now invited Lords and Commons to give their opinion. The answer of both Houses was prompt and plain. It was contrary, they said, to the honour of the King, to the welfare of his people, and to the terms of his former alliances to continue the negotiations with Spain. Upon this Buckingham did

James I's daughter, Elizabeth of Bohemia, was known as "the Winter Queen" because her reign lasted only three months. She was the grandmother of George I, and thus the founder of the Hanoverian dynasty.

Prince Charles's affectionate welcome home from Spain, unwedded to the Spanish Infanta, is celebrated in this woodcut taken from a pamphlet or broadside, in the Collection of the Society of Antiquaries.

George Villiers, the favourite of James I, was promoted to the post of Royal Cupbearer, Gentleman of the Bedchamber and eventually Duke of Buckingham. He was also appointed Lord High Admiral, although he knew nothing whatsoever about the navy.

not conceal that he differed somewhat from his master. He said bluntly that he wished to tread only one path, whereas the King thought he could walk two different paths at once. He would not be a mere flatterer; he must express his convictions or be a traitor.

At these developments Parliament was delighted. But now came the question of raising funds. Parliament urged a naval war with Spain. Suspicious of the King's intentions, the Commons voted less than half the sum for which he asked, and laid stringent conditions on how it should be spent.

Buckingham trimmed his sails and for the moment preserved his new Parliamentary prestige. This he used to break his rival, Lord Treasurer Cranfield. The Treasurer, now Earl of Middlesex, was one of the outstanding "new men" in the kingdom. He was a merchant who had risen to great wealth and high office. He was now dismissed and imprisoned by the new Parliamentary engine of "impeachment". This weapon had already been used against Bacon, who was found guilty of corruption in 1621, dismissed from the Chancellorship, fined, and banished. It was never to be laid aside until many great issues had been settled once and for all.

No sooner was the Spanish match broken off than Buckingham turned to France for a bride for Charles. When he and the Prince of Wales had passed through Paris on their way to Madrid, Charles had been struck by the charm of Henrietta Maria, sister of Louis XIII and then in her fourteenth year. A marriage with a Protestant princess would have united Crown and Parliament. But this was never the intention of the governing circle. A daughter of France seemed to them the only alternative to the Infanta. The old King ratified the marriage treaty in December 1624. Three months later the first King of Great Britain was dead.

CHAPTER 2

THE MAYFLOWER

The tobacco plant established Virginia's prosperity. Smoking had been popular with the American Indians for centuries; Hawkins and Raleigh had brought the habit to the Elizabethan Court.

THE STRUGGLE WITH SPAIN had long absorbed the energies of Englishmen, and in the last years of Queen Elizabeth few fresh enterprises had been carried out upon the oceans. For a while little was heard of the New World. Hawkins and Drake in their early voyages had opened up broad prospects for England in the Caribbean; Frobisher and others had penetrated deeply into the Arctic recesses of Canada in search of a northwest passage to Asia; but the lure of exploration and trade had given way to the demands of war. The novel idea of founding colonies also received a setback. Humphrey Gilbert, Raleigh, and Grenville had been its pioneers. Their bold plans had come to nothing, but they left behind them an inspiring tradition. Now after a lapse of time their endeavours were taken up by new figures, less glittering, more practical and luckier. Piecemeal and from many motives the English-speaking communities in North America were founded.

The steady rise in prices had caused much hardship to wage-earners. Though the general standard of living improved during the sixteenth century, a wide range of prices rose sixfold and wages only twofold. The medieval system of craftsmen's guilds, which was still enforced, made the entry of young apprentices harsh and difficult. The squirearchy, strong in its political alliance with the Crown, owned most of the land and ran all the local government. The march of enclosures which they pursued drove many English peasants off the land. The whole scheme of life seemed to have contracted and the framework of social organisation had hardened. There were many without advantage, hope, or livelihood in the New Age. Colonies, it was thought, might help to solve these distressing problems and trade with lively colonies promised an increase in the Customs revenue on which the Crown heavily depended. Merchants and the richer landed gentry saw new opportunities across the Atlantic for profitable investment, and an escape from the general decline of European trade during the religious wars. Raleigh's experiments had demonstrated the ill-success of individual effort, but a new method of financing large-scale trading enterprises was evolving in the shape of the joint stock company. In 1606 a group of speculators acquired a royal charter creating the Virginia Company.

A plan was carefully drawn up in consultation with experts, but they had little practical experience and underestimated the difficulties of the profoundly novel departure they were making. After all, it is not given to many to start a nation. It was a few hundred people who now took the first step. A settlement was made at Jamestown, in the Chesapeake Bay, on the Virginian coast, in May 1607. By the following spring half the population was dead from malaria, cold and famine. After a long and heroic struggle the survivors became self-supporting, but profits to the promoters at home were very small. Captain John Smith, a military adventurer, became the dictator of the tiny colony, and enforced harsh discipline. The marriage of his lieutenant John Rolfe with Pocahontas, the daughter of an Indian chief, caused a sensation in the English capital. But the London Company had little control, and the administration of the colony was rough-and-ready. The objects of the directors were mixed and ill-defined. Some thought that colonisation would reduce poverty and crime in England. Others looked for profit to the fisheries of the North American coast, or hoped for raw materials to reduce their dependence on the exports from the Spanish colonies. All were wrong, and Virginia's fortune sprang from a novel and unexpected cause. By chance a crop of tobacco was planted, and the soil proved benevolent. Tobacco had been introduced into Europe by the Spaniards and the habit of smoking was spreading fast. Profits on the Virginia tobacco crop were high, and the colony began to stand on its own feet. As it grew and prospered its society came to resemble the mother country, with rich planters in the place of squires, but they were not long in developing independence of mind and a sturdy capacity for self-government.

Meanwhile beneath the drab exterior of Jacobean England, with favouritism at Court and humiliation in Europe, other and more vital forces were at work. The Elizabethan bishops had driven the nobler and tougher Puritan spirits out of the Established Church. But though they destroyed the organisation of the party small illegal gatherings of religious extremists continued to meet. There was no systematic persecution, but petty restrictions and spyings obstructed their peaceful worship. A congregation at Scrooby, in Nottinghamshire, led by one of their pastors, John Robinson, and by William Brewster, the Puritan bailiff of the manor of the Archibishop of York, resolved to seek freedom of worship abroad. In 1607 they left England and settled at Leyden, hoping to find asylum among the tolerant and industrious Dutch. For ten years these Puritan farmers struggled for a decent existence. Out of place in a maritime industrial community, barred

Pocahontas's mantle is made from four pieces of tanned buckskin decorated with shells and can be seen in the Ashmolean Museum, Oxford. The daughter of an Indian chief, Pocahontas married John Rolfe, a lieutenant of Captain John Smith, and came to live in London, where she gave birth to a son and died shortly afterwards of smallpox.

John White's watercolour of a Huron Indian was painted at Roanoake, in Virginia, in 1595. It bears this inscription in his fine Italic hand: "The manner of their attire and painting themselves when they goe to their generall huntings or at theire Solemne feasts".

by their nationality from the guilds of craftsmen, without capital and without training, the only work they could get was rough manual labour. The authorities had been sympathetic, but in practice unhelpful. The Puritans began to look elsewhere.

Emigration to the New World presented itself as an escape. There they might gain a livelihood unhampered by Dutch guilds, and practise their creed unharassed by English clerics. As one of their number records, "The place they had thoughts on was some of those vast and unpeopled countries of America, which are fruitful and fit for habitation; being devoid of all civil inhabitants; where there are only savage and brutish men, which range up and down little otherwise than the wild beasts of the same."

Throughout the winter of 1616-17, when Holland was threatened with a renewal of war with Spain, there were many discussions among the anxious community. To the peril of the unknown, to famine, and the record of past failures were added gruesome tales of the Indians; how they flayed men with the shells of fishes and cut off steaks which they broiled upon the coals before the eyes of the victims.

They realised it was impossible to venture out upon their own. Help must come from England. They accordingly sent agents to London to negotiate with the only body interested in emigration, the Virginia Company. One of its members was an influential Parliamentarian, Sir Edwin Sandys. Supported by the London backers of the Company, he furthered the project. Here were ideal settlers, sober, hardworking, and skilled in agriculture. Sandys and the emissaries from Holland went to see the King. James was sceptical. He asked how the little band proposed to support itself. "By fishing," they replied. This appealed to James. "So God have my soul," he exclaimed in one of his more agreeable remarks, "'tis an honest trade! It was the Apostles' own calling."

The Leyden community was granted a licence to settle in America, and arrangements for their departure were hastened on. Thirty-five members of the Leyden congregation left Holland and joined sixty-six West Country adventurers at Plymouth. There, in September 1620, they set sail in the *Mayflower*, a vessel of one hundred and eighty tons.

After two and half months of voyaging across the winter ocean they reached the shores of Cape Cod, and thus, by an accident, landed outside the jurisdiction of the Virginia Company. There they founded the town of Plymouth. The same bitter struggle with nature that had taken place in Virginia now began. There was no staple crop. By toil and faith they survived, but the financial supporters in London reaped no profits. In 1627 they sold out and the Plymouth colony was left to its own resources. Such was the founding of New England.

For ten years afterwards there was no more planned emigration to America; but the tiny colony of Plymouth pointed a path to freedom. As friction grew between Crown and subjects, so opposition to the Anglican Church strengthened, and many people of independent mind began to consider leaving home to find freedom and justice in the wilds.

Just as the congregation from Scrooby had emigrated in a body to Holland, so in 1629 another Puritan group in Dorset, inspired by the Reverend John White, resolved to move to the New World. After an unhappy start this venture won support in London and the eastern counties. After the precedent of Virginia a chartered company was formed, eventually named

"The Company of the Massachusetts Bay in New England". News spread rapidly and there was no lack of colonists. An advance party founded the settlement of Salem, to the north of Plymouth, and in 1630 the Governor of the Company, John Winthrop, followed with a thousand settlers. He was the leading personality in the enterprise. The uneasiness of the time is reflected in his letters, which reveal the reasons why his family went. "I am verily persuaded," he wrote about England, "God will bring some heavy affliction upon this land, and that speedily; but be of good comfort . . . . If the Lord seeth it will be good for us, He will provide a shelter and a hiding place for us and others . . . . Evil times are coming when the Church must fly into the wilderness." The wilderness that Winthrop chose lay on the Charles River. Here from modest beginnings arose the city of Boston, which was to become in the next century the heart of resistance to British rule and long remain the intellectual capital of America.

The Massachusetts Bay Company was by its constitution a joint stock corporation, organised entirely for trading purposes, but by accident or intent there was no mention in the charter where the Company was to hold its meetings. Some of the Puritan stockholders realised that there was no obstacle to transferring the Company, directors and all, to New England. A

THE VOYAGE OF THE MAYFLOWER

On Wednesday, September 6, 1620, the Pilgrim Fathers sailed to America from Plymouth in the Mayflower. *The following extract is written by William Bradford who was one of the emigrants and became second governor of the new Plymouth colony.*

And I may not omit here a special work of GOD's Providence. There was a proud and very profane young man, one of the seamen; of a lusty able body, which made him the more haughty. He would always be contemning the poor people in their sickness, and cursing them daily with grievous execrations, and he did not let to tell them, That he hoped to help to cast half of them overboard before they came to their journey's end; and to make merry with what property they had. And if he were by any gently reproved, he would curse and swear most bitterly.

But it pleased GOD, before they came half the seas over, to smite this young man with a grievous disease; of which he died in a desperate manner. And so he was himself the first that was thrown overboard. Thus his curses lighted on his own head; and it was an astonishment to all his fellows; for they noted it to be the just hand of GOD upon him.

After they had enjoyed fair winds and weather for a season, they were incountered many times with cross winds; and met with many fierce storms; with which the ship was shrewdly shaken, and her upper works made very leaky. . . . In sundry of these storms, the winds were so fierce and the seas so high, as they could not bear a knot of sail: but were forced to hull for divers days together.

And in one of them, as they thus lay at hull, in a mighty storm, a lusty young man, called JOHN HOWLAND, coming upon some occasion above the gratings, was with the seel [sudden heeling over] of the ship thrown into the sea: but it pleased GOD that he caught hold of the top sail halliards,

This replica of the Mayflower *was built in 1970 to celebrate the three hundred and fiftieth anniversary of the voyage of the Pilgrim Fathers.*

which hung overboard and ran out at length; yet he held his hold, though he was sundry fathoms under water, till he was hauled up, by the same rope, to the brim of the water; and then, with a boathook and other means, was got into the ship again, and his life saved.

general court of the Company was held, and this momentous decision taken. From the joint stock Company was born the self-governing colony of Massachusetts. Between 1629 and 1640 the colonists rose in numbers from three hundred to fourteen thousand. The resources of the Company offered favourable prospects. In England life for farm labourers was often hard. Here in the New World there was land for every newcomer and freedom from all restrictions upon the movement of labour and such other medieval regulations as oppressed and embittered the peasantry at home.

The leaders and ministers who ruled in Massachusetts however understood toleration as little as the Anglicans, and disputes broke out about religion. By no means all were rigid Calvinists, and recalcitrant bodies split off from the parent colony. Some of them moved to the valley of the Connecticut River, and founded the town of Hartford near its banks. Other exiles from Massachusetts, some of them forcibly banished, founded the town of Providence in 1636, which became the colony of Rhode Island.

By 1640 five main English settlements had thus been established in North America: Virginia, technically under the direct rule of the Crown, and administered, somewhat ineffectually, by a standing committee of the Privy Council since the Company's charter was abrogated in 1624; the original pilgrim settlement at Plymouth, which, for want of capital, had not expanded; the flourishing Massachusetts Bay colony, and its two offshoots, Connecticut and Rhode Island.

The last four were the New England colonies. In spite of religious divergences they were much alike. All were coastal settlements, bound together by trade, fisheries, and shipping, and soon forced to make common cause against their neighbours. For the French were already reaching out from their earlier bases in Canada, having ousted an adventurous band of Scotsmen who had been ensconced for a time on the upper reaches of the St Lawrence. By 1630 the river was entirely in French hands. The only other waterway, the Hudson, was ruled by the Dutch, who had established at its mouth in 1621 the colony of New Netherland, later to become New York.

Two other ventures, both essentially commercial, established the English-speaking peoples in the New World. Since Elizabethan days they had often tried to get a foothold in the Spanish West Indies. In 1623, on his way back from a fruitless expedition to Guiana, a Suffolk gentleman named Thomas Warner deposited a few colonists on St Christopher, one of the less inhabited West Indian islands, and hurried home to get a royal patent for a more extensive enterprise. This achieved, he returned to the Caribbean, and, though much harassed by Spanish raids, he established the English in this disputed sea. By the 1640s Barbados, St Christopher, Nevis, Montserrat, and Antigua were in English hands and several thousand colonists had arrived. Sugar assured their prosperity, and the Spanish grip on the West Indies was shaken. There was much competition and warfare in the succeeding years, but for a long time these island settlements were commercially much more valuable to England than the colonies in North America.

Another settlement of this period was sponsored by the monarchy. In theory all land settled by Englishmen belonged to the King. He had the right to grant such portions as he chose either to recognised companies or to individuals. Just as Elizabeth and James had granted industrial and commercial monopolies to courtiers, so now Charles I attempted to regulate colonial settlement. In 1632 Lord Baltimore, a Roman Catholic courtier who had

Lord Baltimore, Governor of Maryland, is seen here with his grandson and an African slave. Baltimore was the son of a Catholic courtier who, in 1632, had applied for a patent to settle in Virginia. He was given leave to settle a new colony named Maryland in honour of the Queen, Henrietta Maria.

long been interested in colonisation, applied for a patent for settling in the neighbourhood of Virginia. It was granted after his death to his son. The terms of the patent resembled the conditions under which land was already held in Virginia. It conferred complete proprietary rights over the new area, and tried to transport the manorial system to the New World. The government of the colony was vested in the Baltimore family. Courtiers and merchants subscribed to the venture, and the new colony was named Maryland in honour of Charles's Queen, Henrietta Maria. Although the proprietor was a Roman Catholic there was a tolerant flavour about its government from the beginning, because Baltimore had only obtained his patent by proclaiming the religion of the Established Church as the official creed of the new settlement. The aristocratic nature of the regime was much modified in practice, and the powers of the local administration set up by Baltimore increased at the expense of his paper rights.

In these first decades of the great emigration, over eighty thousand English-speaking people crossed the Atlantic. Saxon and Viking had colonised England. Now, one thousand years later, their descendants were taking possession of America. Many different streams of migrants were to make their confluence in the New World and contribute to the manifold character of the future United States. But the British stream flowed first and remained foremost. From the beginning its leaders were out of sympathy with the Government at home and during the critical years of settlement and consolidation the mother country was paralysed by civil war. When England again achieved stability it was confronted with self-supporting, self-reliant communities which had evolved traditions and ideas of their own.

CHAPTER 3

CHARLES I AND BUCKINGHAM

OF THE MANY DESCRIPTIONS OF CHARLES I at the beginning of his reign none is more attractive than the cameo which we owe to the German historian, Ranke. He was, he says, "in the bloom of life: he had just completed his twenty-fifth year. He looked well on horseback: men saw him govern with safety horses that were hard to manage: he was expert in knightly exercises: he was a good shot with the crossbow, as well as with the gun, and even learned how to load a cannon. He was hardly less unweariedly devoted to the chase than his father. He could not vie with him in intelligence and knowledge, nor with his deceased brother Henry in vivacious energy and in popularity of disposition. . . . In moral qualities he was superior to both. He was one of those young men of whom it is said that they have no fault. His strict propriety of demeanour bordered on maiden bashfulness: a serious and temperate soul spoke from his calm eyes. He had a natural gift for apprehending even the most complicated questions, and he was a good writer. From his youth he showed himself economical; not profuse, but at the same time not niggardly; in all matters precise." He had however suffered from infantile paralysis and spoke with a stammer.

A great political and religious crisis was overhanging England. Already in King James's time Parliament had begun to take the lead, not only in levying taxes but increasingly in the conduct of affairs, and especially in

Charles I at the age of twenty-eight, painted by Gerard Honthorst, three years after his accession. Painters depicted Charles sitting down at a desk or on horseback because his legs were weak. Charles was the most artistic of the Stuarts, and the paintings he gathered were the beginning of today's royal collection.

The House of Lords in the time of Charles I. The King is enthroned, with the Lords Spiritual and Temporal seated round him in their robes of office. The lower picture represents the House of Commons; on the table is the Mace.

foreign policy. It is remarkable to see how far-reaching was the interest shown by the educated part of the English nation in Europe. Events in Prague seemed as important to Englishmen as what happened in York or Bristol. The frontiers of Bohemia, the conditions in the Palatinate, ranked as high as many domestic questions. This wide outlook was no longer due, as in the days of the Plantagenets, to dynastic claims. The English people now felt that their survival and salvation were bound up forever with the victory of the Reformed Faith, and they watched with straining, vigilant eyes every episode which marked its advance or misfortune. An intense desire for England to lead and champion the Protestant cause wherever it was assailed drove forward the Parliamentary movement with a force far greater than would ever have sprung merely from the issues which were now opening at home.

The secular issues were nevertheless themselves of enormous weight. Tudor authority had been accepted as a relief from the anarchy of the Wars of the Roses, but had now ceased to fit either the needs or the temper of a continually growing society. Men looked back to earlier times. Great lawyers like Coke and Selden had directed their gaze to the rights which they thought Parliament possessed under the Lancastrian kings. Ranging farther, they spoke with pride of the work of Simon de Montfort, of Magna Carta, and even of still more ancient rights in the mists of Anglo-Saxon monarchy. From these studies they derived the conviction that they were the heirs of a whole structure of fundamental law inherent in the customs of the island, from which the Crown was threatening to depart. But the Crown also looked back, and found many precedents of a contrary character, especially in the last hundred years, for the most thorough exercise of the Royal Prerogative. Both King and Parliament had a body of doctrine upon which they dwelt with sincere conviction. This brought pathos and grandeur to the coming struggle.

A society more complex than that of Tudor England was coming into existence. Trade, both foreign and internal, was expanding. Coal-mining and other industries were rapidly developing. In the van stood London, with its thousands of lusty, free-spoken prentices and its wealthy City guilds and companies. Outside London many of the landed gentry, who supplied numerous members to Parliament, were acquiring close connections with new industry and trade. In these years the Commons were not so much seeking to legislate as trying to prevent all this recent growth from falling under the Crown's autocratic grip.

The men at the head of this strenuous and, to our time, invaluable movement were notable figures. Coke had unearthed an armoury of precedents, and set many to work upon their furbishing and sharpening. Two country gentlemen stand with him: one from the west, Sir John Eliot, a Cornishman; the other, Thomas Wentworth, a Yorkshire squire. Both these men possessed the highest qualities of force and temper. For a time they worked together; for a time they were rivals; for a time they were foes. By opposite paths both reached the extremity of sacrifice. Behind them, lacking nothing in grit, were leaders of the Puritan gentry, Denzil Holles, Arthur Hazelrigg, John Pym. Pym was eventually to go far and to carry the cause still farther. He was a Somerset man, a lawyer, strongly anti-High Church. Here was a man who understood every move in the political game, and would play it out remorselessly.

The Parliaments of James, and now those of Charles, were for war and intervention in Europe. They knew well, among other things, that the stresses of war would force the Crown to come to them. Their power would grow with the adoption of their policy, which was also their faith. The pacifism of James I, often ignominious, had upon the whole avoided this trap. But King Charles and Buckingham were high-spirited men in the ardour of youth. The King, affronted by the manner in which his father's overtures for a Spanish match had been slighted was for war with Spain. He at once carried through his marriage with the French princess, Henrietta Maria. Her arrival at Dover surrounded by a throng of French Papists and priests was the first serious shock to Charles's popularity. The new Parliament granted supplies against Spain; but their purpose to review the whole question of indirect taxation was plain when they resolved that the Customs duties of tonnage and poundage without which the King could not live, even in peace, should for the first time for many reigns be voted, not for the King's life, but only for one year. This restriction galled Charles, but did not deter him from the war. Thus at the very outset of his reign he was placed in a position of exceptional dependence upon Parliament, while resenting its increasing claims.

Princess Henrietta Maria of France married Charles I in 1625 when she was fifteen. She never understood the political situation in England and heightened Charles's troubles by her championship of English Catholics. This picture by Van Dyck shows her as an expectant mother in 1633.

The war with Spain went badly. Buckingham led an expedition to Cadiz in an attempt to emulate the feats of Queen Elizabeth's days, but it accomplished nothing. On his return Parliament resolved to unseat the glittering, incompetent minister. "We protest," the Commons told Charles, "that until this great person be removed from intermeddling with the great affairs of State any money we shall or can give will through his misemployment be turned rather to the hurt and prejudice of this your kingdom than otherwise." Buckingham was impeached, and to save his friend the King hastily dissolved Parliament.

A new complication was now added to the scene. Charles had hoped to conclude an alliance with France against the Habsburg rulers of Spain and the Empire. But France showed no desire to fight for the recovery of the Palatinate, and the breach was widened by the cause of the Huguenots. The new, powerful French minister, Cardinal Richelieu, was determined to curb the independence of the Huguenots in France, and in particular to reduce their maritime stronghold of La Rochelle. English sympathies naturally lay with these French Protestants whom they had helped to sustain in the days of Henry of Navarre, and the two countries drifted into war. In 1627 a considerable force was dispatched under Buckingham to help the Rochelais. It landed off the coast in the Ile de Ré, failed to storm the citadel, and withdrew in disorder. Thus Buckingham's military efforts were once more marked by waste and failure. At home the billeting of soldiers brought an acute grievance into thousands of cottage homes. This was aggravated by the arbitrary decisions of martial law, which was used to settle all disputes between soldiers and civilians.

The King was torn between the grinding need of finding money for the war and the danger that Parliament would again impeach his friend. In his vexation, and having the war on his hands, he resorted to dubious methods of raising money. He demanded a forced loan; and when many important persons refused to pay he threw them into prison. Five of these prisoners, known as the Five Knights, appealed against these proceedings. However, King's Bench ruled that habeas corpus, no imprisonment without trial, could

STUART STYLES

I N THE REIGN OF QUEEN ELIZABETH I a visitor to England said of the English that they dressed "in elegant, light and costly garments, but they are inconsistent and desirous of novelties, changing their fashions every year, both men and women". Clearly this observation applied only to the rich and powerful, and it might equally have been made about much of the Stuart period, in spite of strong Puritan objections to such signs of display. Thus, a courtier of James I could be described by the poet John Donne as "a silken painted fool . . . a many colour'd peacock", while another well-known writer, Anthony Wood, damned the early years of Charles II's reign as "a strange effeminate age, when men strive to imitate women in their apparel, *viz.* long periwigs, patches on their faces, painting, short wide breeches like petticoats, muffs and their clothes highly scented, bedecked with ribbons of all colours".

There were many changes in the fashions of the seventeenth century, but there was usually a note of extravagance. This was apparent in Jacobean furniture also, elaborate but solid, and in the ornate multi-chimneyed new buildings that housed it. Inigo Jones, designer of lavish Court masques for Charles I, dreamt of constructing vast complexes of magnificent buildings, more in a continental than an English style. Charles II, for his part, modestly believed that "God will never damn a man for allowing himself a little pleasure," and his court fully sustained that belief. His mistresses were unusually expensive, and he left at least fourteen illegitimate children.

Pleasures were of many kinds. Dancing was one. Smoking was another. "He that will refuse to take a pipe of tobacco among his fellows . . . is accounted peevish and no good company," James I complained. In Izaak Walton's *The Compleat Angler* (1653), which dealt with a simple pleasure still to retain its appeal today, the fisherman Piscator speaks fondly of "a pipe of tobacco which is always my breakfast".

LAVISH CARVING, *with scrollwork, mouldings, inlaid panelling, balusters, "ear-pieces" and turned legs, was a characteristic of Stuart oak furniture. It was so substantial that much of it has lasted. This mid-seventeenth century chair is in the Victoria and Albert Museum.*

HATFIELD HOUSE, HERTFORDSHIRE, *(above) combines English and Renaissance styles. The symmetrical wings of brick, with their turrets, balustrades and patterned chimneys, are typically Jacobean; the loggia in the centre demonstrates the influence of the Italian architect, Palladio. Gardens were formal, as in Tudor times, but on a grander scale. There was an increasing interest in plants which led to the foundation of the first botanical garden in Oxford in the year 1617.*

WHITEHALL'S BANQUETING HOUSE *was a royal commission for Inigo Jones in 1619. The classically proportioned throne room (right) with its fine painted ceiling by Rubens, reveals a Renaissance influence. The stage design below was sketched for Ben Jonson's Masque of Queens. The six-sided building with relief sculptures resembles a Roman triumphal column.*

BOSOM-REVEALING FASHIONS were shocking to the Puritans. A Royalist lady at her toilette demonstrates the Stuart love of pearls, off-the-shoulder silk dresses, and smooth ringlets surrounding hair drawn into a knot near the nape of the neck. The illustration comes from The Genteel Habits of England, *by Marmion, the Royalist author, published in 1640.*

MASQUES WERE THEATRICAL PRODUCTIONS which were very popular in the sixteenth and early seventeenth centuries. They were usually based on myth, or allegory. Costumes and theatrical effects tended to assume more importance than the acting. The exotic design (above) was made by Inigo Jones for Ben Jonson's Masque of Blackness *and is an example of audiences' love of spectacle.*

not be used against imprisonments "by special command of the King".

Forced loans could not suffice to replenish the Treasury, and having secured a promise that the impeachment of Buckingham would not be pursued the King agreed to summon Parliament. The country was now in a ferment. The election returned men pledged to resist arbitrary exactions. Parliament wished to support the war, but it would not grant money to a King and minister it distrusted. The King used the threat of despotic action. He must have "such supply as to secure ourselves and save our friends from imminent ruin. . . . Every man must now do according to his conscience, wherefore if you (which God forbid) should not do your duties in contributing what this State at this time needs I must . . . use those other means which God hath put into my hands to save that which the follies of other men may otherwise hazard to lose."

It must not be supposed that all the wrongdoing was on one side. Parliament, which had approved the wars, was playing an artful game with the King, confronting him with the shame to his princely honour of deserting the Huguenots, or else yielding the Prerogative his predecessors had so long enjoyed. They offered no fewer than five subsidies, amounting to £300,000, all to be paid within twelve months. Here was enough to carry on the war; but before they would confirm this in a Bill they demanded their price.

The following four resolutions were passed unanimously: that no freeman ought to be restrained unless some lawful cause was expressed; that the writ of habeas corpus ought to be granted to every man restrained, even though it might be at the command of the King or of the Privy Council; that if no legal cause for imprisonment were shown the party ought to be set free or bailed; that it was the ancient and undoubted right of every freeman to have a full and absolute property in his goods and estate, and that no tax, loan, or benevolence ought to be levied by the King or his ministers without common consent by Act of Parliament.

At Coke's prompting the Commons now went on to frame the Petition of Right. Its object was to curtail the King's Prerogative. The Petition complained against forced loans, imprisonment without trial, billeting, and martial law. These and others of the King's proceedings were condemned "as being contrary to the rights and liberties of the subject, and the laws and statutes of the nation". Unless the King accepted the Petition he would have no subsidies, and must face the wars to which Parliament had incited him as best he could. Charles, resorting to manoeuvre, secretly consulted the judges, who assured him that even his consent to these liberties would not affect his ultimate Prerogative. He was none too sure of this; and when his first evasive answer was delivered in the House of Lords a howl went up, not only from the Commons, but from the great majority of all assembled. He therefore fell back upon the opinion of the judges and gave full consent while making mental reservation.

"Now," said the King, "I have performed my part. If this Parliament have not a happy conclusion the sin is yours. I am free of it." On this there was general rejoicing. The Commons voted all the subsidies and believed that a definite bargain had been struck.

We reach here, amid much confusion, the main foundation of English freedom. The right of the Executive Government to imprison a man, high or low, for reasons of State was denied; and that denial, made good in painful struggles, constitutes the charter of every self-respecting man at any

Henrietta Maria's eldest brother was the powerful Louis XIII of France. A contemporary engraving of the monarch on horseback glorifies his achievements in crushing the Protestant town of La Rochelle.

time in any land. Trial by jury of equals, only for offences known to the law, if maintained, makes the difference between bond and free. But the King felt this would hamper him, and no doubt a plausible case can be advanced that in times of emergency dangerous persons must be confined.

At the back of the Parliamentary movement in all its expressions lay a deep fear. Everywhere in Europe they saw the monarchies becoming more autocratic. In France, the States-General, which had met in Paris in 1614, had not been summoned again; it was not indeed to be summoned until the clash of 1789. The rise of standing armies, composed of men drilled in firearms and supported by trains of artillery, had stripped alike the nobles and the common people of their means of independent resistance.

Both sides pressed farther along their paths. The King, having got his money, dwelt unduly upon the assurances he had received from the judges that his Prerogative was intact. The Commons came forward with further complaints against the growth of Popery and Arminianism—the form of High Church doctrine most directly opposed to Calvinism—about the mismanagement of the war, about injury to trade and commerce from naval weakness in the Narrow Seas, and about Buckingham, asking the King whether it was consistent with his safety, or the safety of the realm, that the author of so many calamities should continue to hold office. Charles dismissed the Houses hoping that before he had need of them again he and his cherished minister would present them with a military or diplomatic result in which all could rejoice. A King who had delivered La Rochelle could surely claim the right to exercise indulgence even to Papists in his own land. This was not a discreditable position, but Fate moved differently.

Buckingham himself was deeply conscious of the hatreds of which he was the object, and it is clear that in putting himself at the head of a new expedition to La Rochelle he hoped to win again for himself some national backing, which would at least divide his pursuers. But at the moment when his resolves were at their highest, as he was about to embark at Portsmouth, he was stabbed to death by John Felton, a fanatical naval lieutenant.

The death of Buckingham was a devastating blow to the young King. At the same time it immensely relieved his public difficulties, for much of the anger of the Parliament died with the favourite; and it brought for the first time a unity into his married life. Hitherto he had been morally and mentally dominated by "Steenie", the beloved friend of his boyhood and youth, to whom he confided his inmost thoughts. For three years he had lived in cold estrangement from the Queen. It was even said that the marriage had never been consummated; and he had distressed her by dismissing all her French attendants. The death of Buckingham was the birth of his love for his wife. Little but storm lay before them, but henceforth they faced it together.

Though the Commons had granted the five subsidies, they still held tonnage and poundage in reserve. When the year lapsed for which this had been voted the Parliamentary party throughout the country were angered to find that the King continued to collect the tax, as had been the custom for so many reigns. Distraint and imprisonment were used against those who refused to pay. In all this was seen the King's contempt for the Petition of Right. When copies of the Petition were printed, it was found that the King's first evasive answer was appended and not his later plain acceptance in the ancient form. The expedition to La Rochelle, which had sailed under another commander, miscarried. Cardinal Richelieu succeeded in

Cardinal Richelieu, Louis XIII's capable minister, enabled the king to rule without recourse to the States-General, but weakened Louis's power by taking decisions independently. His reputation was high throughout Europe.

maintaining the boom he had built against the English ships, and eventually the Huguenots in despair surrendered the city to the King of France. This collapse caused shock and grief throughout England.

Thus when Parliament met again at the beginning of 1629 there was no lack of grievances. It was upon questions of religion that the attack began. The Commons showed themselves to be in a most aggressive mood, and worked themselves into passion by long debates upon the laxity with which the laws against Popery were enforced. This brought the great majority of them together, joined with the patriots who were laying the foundations of English freedom.

In a comprehensive resolution the Commons declared that whoever furthered Popery, whoever collected or helped to collect tonnage and poundage before it was granted, or even paid it, was a public enemy. All this was embodied in a single Remonstrance directed against the King. The Speaker, who had been gained to the King's side, announced on March 2 that the King adjourned the House till the 10th, thus frustrating the carrying of the Remonstrance. A wave of wrath swept through the assembly. When the Speaker rose to leave he was forced back and held down on his chair by two resolute and muscular members, Holles and Valentine. The doors were barred against Black Rod, and the Remonstrance, recited from memory by Holles, was declared carried by acclamation. The doors were then opened and the members poured forth tumultuously. It had become plain to all that King and Commons could not work together on any terms. The next week Parliament was dissolved and the period of King Charles's personal rule began.

CHAPTER 4

THE PERSONAL RULE

THE PERSONAL RULE OF THE KING was not set up covertly or by degrees. Charles openly proclaimed his intention. "We have showed," he said, "by our frequent meeting our people, our love to the use of Parliaments; yet, the late abuse having for the present driven us unwillingly out of that course, we shall account it presumption for any to prescribe any time unto us for Parliaments, the calling, continuing, and dissolving of which is always in our own power. . . ."

This policy required other large measures. First, there must be peace with France and Spain. Without the support of Parliament Charles had not the strength to carry on foreign wars. It was not difficult to obtain peace. The second condition was the gaining of some at least of the Parliamentary leaders. In those days there were few men who did not seek the favour of the Crown. Some sought it by subservience, and others by opposition. Sir Henry Savile and Thomas Digges were deemed serviceable acquisitions, but Wentworth was the man of all others most worth winning. In the debates upon the Petition of Right, behind the fierce invective of the Parliamentarian he had shown a certain willingness not to exclude the other side of the argument. His abilities were of the first order, and so were his ambitions.

To Wentworth therefore the King turned and found him more than willing. He was a born administrator; all he wanted was scope for his

Thomas Wentworth, Earl of Strafford, was eventually impeached for misusing his position as Lord Lieutenant of Ireland. His biographers have questioned the justice of this, seeing him as a scapegoat for his enemies in Parliament.

endeavours. In December 1628 he became Lord President of the Council of the North and a member of the Privy Council. From this moment Wentworth not only abandoned all the ideas of which he had been the ablest exponent, but all the friends who had fought at his side. This was the reason why a hatred centred upon Wentworth different from that which even incompetence attracted to other ministers. He was "the lost Archangel", "the suborned traitor to the cause of Parliament". No administrative achievements, no eloquence, could atone to his former friends for his desertion.

Savile and Digges also accepted office. Other leaders of the Parliamentary movement either suffered ill-usage at the royal hands or, like Holles, Hazelrigg, and Pym, were allowed to brood and fume in obscurity. Eliot, Wentworth's rival, languished to his death in the Tower.

But the third and least sentimental condition of the personal rule was dominant—money. How to get the money? First, an extreme frugality must be practised by the executive—no wars, no adventures of any kind, no disturbances; all State action reduced to a minimum. These were the inevitable rules of King Charles's new system. The Crown had to make shift with what it could scrape from old taxes.

The wealth gained by national toil now fructified in the pockets of the people. Peace reigned throughout the land. The King, with his elegant, dignified Court, whose figures are portrayed by Van Dyck, whose manners and whose morals were an example to all, reigned on the smallest scale. He was a despot, but an unarmed despot. He sincerely believed, and his people found it difficult to deny, that he was ruling according to many of the old customs of the realm. It is a travesty to represent this period of personal rule as a time of tyranny in any effective sense. In later years, under the yoke of Cromwell's major generals, all England looked back to these placid thirties as an age of ease and tranquillity. But man has never sought tranquillity alone.

The prerogative of the Crown offered a wide and vaguely defined field within which taxes could be raised. The King, supported by his judges, strained all expedients to the limit. He not only persisted in levying tonnage and poundage, but he raised or varied the rates upon certain articles. He profited greatly by exercising the Crown's rights of wardship over the estates of heirs who were minors. He mulcted all persons who had not obeyed the summons to receive knighthood at his coronation. Their attendance had long been regarded as a mere form; their absence now opened a source of revenue. He organised into a system the sporadic monopolies in which Queen Elizabeth and his father, to the resentment of Parliament, had indulged. This was in practice a system of indirect taxation farmed out through deeply interested tax-gatherers. Large sums of money were paid for each concession, and a handsome due was yielded upon each year's

Inigo Jones's design for the classically proportioned new Palace at Whitehall is now in the collection of Worcester College, Oxford.

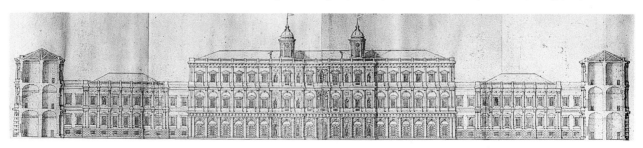

The Sovereign of the Seas, *built in 1637, was England's first one-hundred-gun battleship. When Charles insisted that the cost of the navy, paid by a tax known as "Ship Money", should be shared by all, some people objected. John Hampden, a former Member of Parliament, was tried for his refusal to pay and his case contributed to the outbreak of Civil War.*

trading. London, with its suburbs, numbered a quarter of a million people. The plague lurked in their congested habitations, and public opinion had supported strict rules against new buildings. Nevertheless many had built houses and the King's commissioners now came along with the hard alternative, demolish or ransom. In some cases the poor, ill-housed society tore down the structures it had raised; in most they paid the fine.

Meanwhile Wentworth, now Lord Lieutenant of Ireland, had, by a combination of tact and authority, reduced that kingdom to a greater submission to the British Crown than ever before or since. He assuaged internal feuds; he established order and prosperity; and he produced an Irish army and a substantial Irish subvention for the upkeep of Charles's Crown. His repute in history must rest upon his Irish administration. At the end of seven years he stood at the head of a country which he had disciplined and exploited, but which, without any apparent violent measures or bloodshed, lay docile in his hands.

By all these means King Charles managed to do without a Parliament. Yet hungry forces still lay in shadow. All the ideas which they cherished and championed stirred in their minds, but they had no focus, no expression. Many who would have been vehement if the chance had come their way were content to live their life from day to day. The land was good; springtime, summertime, autumn, had their joys; in the winter there was the yule log and amusements. Agriculture and fox-hunting cast their compulsive or soothing balms upon restless spirits. Harvests were now abundant and the rise in prices had almost ceased. The Poor Law was administered with exceptional humanity. Ordinary gentlefolk might have no share in national government, but they were still lords on their own estates. In quarter sessions they ruled the shires, and as long as they paid their taxes they were left in peace. It required an intense effort by the Parliamentary party to rouse in them under such conditions a national feeling and concern for the State. So the malcontents looked about for points which would inflame the inert forces of the nation.

Presently Charles's lawyers drew attention to an anomaly which had grown with the passage of years. According to the immemorial laws of England, the whole land should pay for the upkeep of the fleet. However, for a long time only the maritime counties had paid. Yet was not this navy the shield of all the peace and freedom which thrived in Britain? Why should not all pay where all benefited? There never was a juster demand. But the abuse of letting the inland counties go untaxed had grown into a custom not broken even in the days of the Armada. So when, in August 1635 the King levied "Ship Money" upon the whole country, John Hampden, a Buckinghamshire gentleman and a former Member of Parliament, stood forth among many others and refused to pay. Upon the principle that even the best of taxes could be levied only with the consent of Parliament he faced the distraint and imprisonment which were the penalties of contumacy. His refusal was selected by both sides as a test case. The Parliamentarians, who had no other means of expression, welcomed a martyr whose sacrifice would disturb the public tameness. The Crown, on the other hand, was encouraged by the logic of its argument. The case of Hampden therefore became famous at once and forever. The Crown prevailed. But the grievance ran far and wide. Ninety per cent of Ship Money was eventually collected for the year 1637, but only twenty per cent for 1639. Everywhere persons of property looked up from their pleasant life and began to use again the language of the Petition of Right.

Yet the constitutional issue alone would not have sufficed to rouse the country. The Parliamentary party therefore continued to foster religious agitation as the surest means of waking England from its apathy. Here emerges the man who of all others was Charles's evil genius—William Laud, Archbishop of Canterbury. He was a convinced Anglican, wholehearted in his opposition both to Rome and to Calvinism. But he had an itch for politics. He stepped with untimely vigour from an academic career at Oxford into national politics and the King's Council at a time when religious affairs were paramount.

Among Laud's innovations was the railing off of the altar. Thus to considerable resentment, the gulf between clergy and congregation was widened and the role of authority visibly enhanced. Laud also found a new source of revenue for the Crown. Under the statutes of Elizabeth everyone was obliged to go to church; they might think as they liked, but they must conform in public worship. This requirement had fallen into widespread disuse, but now all over England men and women found themselves haled before the justices for not attending church and fined one shilling a time. The Puritans regarded this as persecution; the Parliamentary agitation which had been conducted during all these years with so much difficulty gained a widespread accession of strength.

Yet the prosecutions that followed, of Prynne and other Puritan writers, and the pillorying, branding, and cropping of ears which they suffered in punishment, were isolated blots upon a regime mild and good-natured compared with that of other countries in the recent past. Indeed it is by no means certain that, left to herself, England would have broken into revolt.

Archbishop William Laud imposed several innovations on the Church of England. His opponents regarded this as a step towards Roman Catholicism which added to Charles I's unpopularity and sent thousands of emigrants to settle in the new American colonies.

The Arch-Prelate of St Andrewes in Scotland reading the new Service-booke in his pontificalibus assaulted by men & women, with Crickets stooles Stickes and Stones.

The introduction of a new Prayer Book aroused a storm of protest in Scotland, as this broadsheet demonstrates.

It was in Scotland, the home of the Stuarts and Charles's birthplace, that the torch was lighted which began the vast conflagration. Laud was dissatisfied with the spiritual conditions prevailing in the northern kingdom, and he moved the King to make some effort to improve them. The Scots must adopt the English Prayer Book, and enter broadly into communion with their English brethren.

Besides the desire for uniformity in religious ceremonies, King Charles had practical and secular aims. His father had re-established bishops in Scotland with the aim of disciplining the outspoken Presbyterian ministers. James had also adroitly backed the Scottish nobles in their resistance to the pretensions of the Kirk. Charles however on his accession had alienated the nobles by an Act which sought to take away from them the Church lands they had acquired since the Reformation. Furthermore, he was determined to reform the system of collecting tithes, which had largely fallen into their hands. Charles's plans for reinforcing episcopacy in Scotland thus drove the Scottish nobles into opposition.

The bishops, as agents of the distant King, found themselves increasingly disliked. In order to strengthen their hands a new exposition of Canon Law was framed emphasising the position of the Crown, and a new Prayer Book or Liturgy was drawn up in London for Scotland. These books were promulgated in the year 1636. No one appears to have foreseen the stormy consequences.

Charles and his advisers had no thought of challenging doctrine, still less of taking any step towards Popery. They desired to assert the Protestant High Church view, with new stress on the royal supremacy and especially in the sacrament of the Lord's Supper, a somewhat more elaborate ritual. Thus in their course they affronted at the same time the property interests of the powerful, the religious convictions of all classes, and the independent spirit of the Scottish nation. The Scottish people believed, and were told by their native leaders to believe, that they were to be forced to take the first fatal steps towards Roman Catholicism. Every word of the new Prayer Book was scanned with profound suspicion. Was not the King married to a Popish wife, who practised idolatry in her private chapel? Were not

Papists tolerated throughout England in a manner increasingly dangerous to the Protestant faith?

When in July 1637 the dignitaries of Scottish Church and State were gathered in St Giles's Church in Edinburgh for the first solemn reading of the new Prayer Book, an outburst of fury and insult overwhelmed the Dean. A woman even threw her footstool at the wolf in sheep's clothing now revealed in their midst. A great surge of passion swept the ancient capital before which both the episcopal and royal authorities trembled.

King Charles was startled by the news. He tried to reassure his Scottish subjects and professed himself willing to amend the new Prayer Book. But this was vain: only the immediate withdrawal of the offensive book could have availed. Instead a long argument on minor points began, with repeated concessions on the part of the King and growing anger throughout Scotland. The Scots, shrewdly advised by their men of law, cast their resistance into the form of a petition, a Grand Supplication, under the pressure of which the new Prayer Book was withdrawn. But too late. A tempest was blowing which bore men forward. Respect and loyalty were still professed to the King; the blast beat upon the bishops. At length the whole original policy of the King was withdrawn. It had served only to raise a counter-movement, a union which challenged existing conditions both in Church and State.

At the beginning of 1638 the petition was abandoned for the signing of a Covenant. There was little new in it. Much of it merely repeated the confession of faith agreed upon by all fifty years before under King James VI. But the Covenant now became the solemn bond of a whole nation. All who signed pledged themselves to "adhere to and defend the aforesaid true religion, and forbear the practice of all novations in the matter of the worship of God till they be tried and allowed in free Assemblies and in Parliaments." On February 28, 1638, the Covenant was read in Greyfriars churchyard in Edinburgh. The Earl of Sutherland, the first to sign his name thereto, was followed by a long list of notables who felt themselves borne forward upon what is described as the "demoniacal frenzy" of the populace. Many cut a vein for their ink, and copies were taken for signature to nearly every town and village. The Covenant embodied the unalterable resolve of a whole people to perish rather than submit to Popery. Nothing of this sort had ever been intended or dreamt of by the King; but this was the storm he had aroused.

He met it by a fresh semblance of concessions. The Marquis of Hamilton, an experienced Scottish statesman, was sent to the north as lay commissioner, with the supreme aim of making friends again. Hamilton fought for nothing more than some show of dignity to cover the temporary royal retreat. He was expostulating with a whirlwind. It was agreed that a General Assembly should be convoked and when it met in St Mungo's Cathedral in Glasgow was found to be dominated by the religious convictions of the northern kingdom, supported by a formidable lay element, who, surrounded by fervent adherents of all classes, sat armed with sword and dagger in the middle of the church.

The King was confronted with a hostile and organised Assembly now led by armed lay elders, whose aims were definitely political and whose demand was the actual abolition of the episcopacy. He ordered its dissolution. It declared itself resolved to continue in permanent session. The refusal of the General Assembly of Scotland in November 1638 to dissolve upon

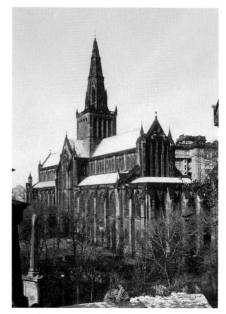

St Mungo's Cathedral in Glasgow where the Scottish General Assembly met stands on the historic site of the church built by the city's founder in 543.

the demand of the King's commissioner has since been compared to that of the French National Assembly in 1789, when for the first time they resisted the royal will. The circumstances no doubt were different; but both events led to the same end, namely, the solemn beheading of a king.

Hamilton now declared himself in favour of drastic measures. The matter was long debated in the King's Council. On the one hand, it was asked, why draw the sword upon a whole people who still proclaimed their love and reverence for the Crown? And how to levy war upon them without money or armed forces and without the support of a united England? Yet, Charles's ministers could not fail to see the deadly recoil of the Scottish revolt upon the English situation, so outwardly calm, so tense and brittle. If this succeeded where would it stop? The royal authority had reigned, not without challenge, but effectually for ten years without a Parliament. Here in the north was open defiance. Laud in England and Wentworth in Ireland were in constant correspondence, and to stamp it out while time remained was the mood of both. That mood prevailed, and both King and Covenanters looked about for arms and means of war.

The King's Council turned its eyes to Wentworth's troops in Ireland, and even to Spain. There was talk of hiring two thousand Spanish infantry to form the nucleus around which the well-affected in Scotland, of whom there were many, might gather. But the Covenanters had far better resources overseas. In the Thirty Years' War Scots brigades and Scottish generals had already played a famous part in Germany. Alexander Leslie had risen to the rank of field marshal. He felt himself called upon to return and fight on his native soil. To him and his warriors it was but a flanking operation in the vast conflict of the Protestants with the Catholic Church. Back they flowed in thousands: trained officers and men, experienced in many harsh campaigns. They became instantly the core of a disciplined army, and in a few months Scotland had the strongest armed force in the island. It had more: it was inspired with earnest, slowly roused, and now fanatical religious passion. The preachers, sword at side, carbine in hand, aided the drill sergeants with their exhortations. The soldiers stood ranked in humble supplication, chanting their psalms. They still had reverence for the King, but their banners displayed the motto "For Christ's Crown, and the Covenant". In May 1639 this army, about twenty thousand strong, stood upon the Scottish border opposite the weaker, ill-disciplined, and uncertain forces which Charles and his advisers had gathered.

It was clear from the first that in the King's camp there was no united desire to make war upon the Scots; on the contrary parleys were set on foot in a good spirit, and on June 18 the so-called "Pacification of Berwick" was agreed. The Scots promised to disband their army and restore the royal castles, which they had seized. The King agreed to the summoning in the following August both of a General Assembly and of a Parliament; that these should henceforth be regularly summoned, and that one should have the decision of ecclesiastical and the other of temporal affairs. Charles however thought of the Pacification as a device to gain time, and the Covenanters were soon convinced of this. The spirit of independence was now aroused throughout Scotland. Wrath was expressed at the restoration of the royal fortresses, and fears at the dispersal of the Scottish army.

Hamilton, returning to Scotland, found himself in a world of rising antagonism. The Scottish Parliament, which met in Edinburgh at the end

This woodcut of about 1640 satirises the rapacity of English soldiers raised for service in Ireland.

KING AND COMMONWEALTH

The years of King Charles I and Cromwell's Commonwealth were scarred by conflict, but there was also a remarkable burst of creative energy as the British adapted European ideas to form their own distinctive style.

"CHARLES I" BY VAN DYCK, NATIONAL GALLERY, LONDON

CHARLTON HOUSE, GREENWICH, GREATER LONDON, *(above) is the oldest of a group of seventeenth-century buildings that make this village overlooking the Thames unique. Built in 1612 for Sir Adam Newton, tutor to the Prince of Wales, it is constructed largely of brick like the Elizabethan mansions, yet it also illustrates the growing interest in neo-classical symmetry.*

THE QUEEN'S HOUSE, GREENWICH, GREATER LONDON, *designed in 1618 by Inigo Jones, introduced the Palladian style of architecture into Britain. This is reflected in the classical design of the buildings, as viewed from the river (right), and of the interior (far right). The house is flanked by the Royal Naval College, begun by John Webb but mostly the work of Wren and his successors, Hawksmoor and Vanbrugh.*

THE "NOVEMBER AND DECEMBER" TAPESTRY, *Victoria and Albert Museum, London, (above) is a fine example of the work of Britain's best-known seventeenth-century tapestry workshop, at Mortlake. It* illustrates *the traditional rural labours of November and December, beating the flax and slaughtering the pigs. The zodiac signs of Sagittarius and Capricorn can be seen on the borders of the tapestry.*

THE BANQUETING HOUSE, WHITEHALL, LONDON, *(below) is all that remains of Whitehall Palace. It was from this magnificent building, commissioned by his father, James I, from Inigo Jones, that Charles I walked out to the scaffold in 1649.*

WILTON HOUSE, WILTSHIRE, (above) is the supreme monument to the age of Charles I. Rebuilt to the design of its greatest architect, Inigo Jones, Wilton was established by the owner, the Earl of Pembroke, as so influential a centre for learning and artistic excellence that the King himself went there every summer. The great Double Cube Room—60ft × 30ft × 30ft—(left) was redesigned to hold Van Dyck's portraits of the Pembrokes and of the King's three eldest children (above the fireplace): the future Charles II, James II, and the mother of William III.

KNOLE, KENT, is one of the largest private houses in Britain, owned by the Sackville family since 1603, when Thomas Sackville remodelled the interior in the grand manner. The wooden staircase (left), and the magnificent "Spangle" bedroom (below) are typical of those parts of a seventeenth-century house that were designed in order to impress visitors. The family itself lived in far simpler accommodation on the ground floor.

"THE SALTONSTALL FAMILY", Tate Gallery, London, (above) was painted by David Des Granges in about 1636. In the seventeenth century much stress was laid on the authority of husbands over wives and of parents over children. The grouping of the figures here emphasises both the authority of the father, and the hazards of childbirth in an age when few infants survived for long, and when death in childbed was a commonplace occurrence.

MILTON'S COTTAGE, CHALFONT ST GILES, BUCKINGHAMSHIRE, *(above and right)* was the poet's home at the time he was completing Paradise Lost. He moved there from London to escape the Plague in 1665. As Latin Secretary to the Council of State in 1649, he had been responsible for a number of anti-Royalist publications. Although disgraced at the Restoration, he was allowed to work on at his poetry until his death in 1674. As well as first editions of his work, the cottage contains armaments used in the Civil War.

CULROSS, FIFE, *is a splendidly pre-*
served seventeenth-century harbour
town. The town's prosperity was
founded on its coalmines. The red-
tiled Dutch-style gabled houses,
lining the narrow streets which con-
verge on the Mercat (market) Cross
in the cobbled square, (above) are
evidence of a once-thriving trade
with the Lowlands.

DRUMLANRIG CASTLE, DUMFRIES AND
GALLOWAY, *(left) designed in 1645*
by Sir William Bruce, was one of
the first great Renaissance buildings
in Scotland. Horrified by its cost,
its owner, the Duke of Queensbury,
occupied it for only one day.

"THE QUEEN MOTHER PLUM", *Ashmo-*
lean Museum, Oxford, (above) is
from the sketchbook of one of Bri-
tain's finest botanists, John Trade-
scant (1608–62), after whom the
plant tradescantia is named.

THE OLD GRAMMAR SCHOOL, MARKET
HARBOROUGH, LEICESTERSHIRE, *(right)*
was the gift of Robert Smyth, a
poor local boy who became a rich
London merchant. The timbers still
carry the biblical quotations on
which the founder insisted. Lessons
continued there until 1892, with a
butter market held below.

KEW PALACE, GREATER LONDON, *is the most modest of palaces. A simple charming family house, it was built in 1631 in the fashionable Dutch style by a London merchant of Dutch extraction. A century later the "Dutch House" was bought by that least pretentious of monarchs, George III. Now, as Kew Palace, it stands picturesquely between its own restored herb gardens and the Royal Botanic Gardens.*

of August 1639, claimed forthwith that the King's Privy Council should be responsible to it, and that the King should follow its advice in appointing commanders of troops, and especially of fortresses. Hamilton could only at first temporise by adjournments, and finally by a prorogation until June 1640. Before the Assembly dispersed it left in full authority a powerful and representative committee, which was in fact the Government of Scotland. By the end of 1639 Charles thus saw himself confronted with an independent State and Government in the north, which, though it paid formal homage to him as King, was resolved to pursue its own policy both at home and abroad. It challenged not only the King's Prerogative, but the integrity of his dominions. He felt bound to fight. But how?

Hamilton, back from Scotland, posed the hard question, "If the Kingly way be taken, how money may be levied, and if that be feasible without a Parliament?" Wentworth was now summoned from Ireland to strengthen the Council. His repute at Court stood high. He believed himself capable of enforcing upon Scotland, and later upon England, the system of autocratic rule which had brought him success in the sister island. He now threw his weight upon the side of war with Scotland. He hoped, once fighting started, to arouse the old antagonism of the English against the Scots. He dreamt of a new Flodden; and he was fully prepared to use his Irish army of eight thousand men in Scotland whenever it might be necessary.

At this decisive moment England's monarchy might well have conformed to the absolutism which was becoming general throughout Europe. Events however took a different turn. Wentworth saw clearly enough that the royal revenues were not sufficient to support the cost of the campaign. He concluded therefore that Parliament must be summoned. In his over-confidence he thought that the Commons would prove manageable. He was wrong. But a momentous step was taken. After nearly eleven years of personal rule the King issued writs for a new Parliament, and elections were held throughout England. This opened the world-famous struggle of Parliament against the King.

The Parliamentary forces, though without public expression, had been neither impotent nor idle. They had established a strong control of local government in many parts of the country. When suddenly elections were held they were immediately able to secure a Parliament which began where its predecessor had left off. More than this, they presented the issues of 1629 with the pent-up anger and embitterment of eleven years of gag and muzzle. Charles had now to come back cap in hand to those very forces which he had disdainfully dismissed. Parliament met on April 13, 1640. Only a quarter of the former members reappeared. Eliot was dead in the Tower; Wentworth was now Earl of Strafford, and the King's First Minister. But of the old lot one man stood forth, competent, instructed, and avenging. From the moment when the new, afterwards called the Short, Parliament met, Pym was the central figure. "He had observed the errors and mistakes in government", his contemporary Clarendon wrote of him, "and knew well how to make them appear greater than they were." In a long, majestic oration he restated the main case. Charles and his chief counsellors, Strafford and Laud, were met by such a temper that by an act of extreme imprudence the new assembly was dissolved on May 5 after a few days. Its calling had only served to excite and engage the whole of England in the controversy.

The expedient of calling Parliament had clearly failed. The Scottish army

John Pym, a Parliamentary leader and a fine orator, is shown in this engraving by J. Houbraken. Public-speaking skills were crucial for seventeenth-century politicians. Charles I, who stammered, was at a disadvantage.

During the era of Parliament's growing power, Roman Catholics were persecuted for their faith and had to worship in secret. Catholic households had cunning hiding places for priests in case of intruders. This priest's hole at Sawston Hall, Cambridgeshire, dates from the mid-seventeenth century.

was on the Border, and only weak, ill-disciplined forces could be mustered against it. To place armed men in the field both money and a cause were needed. Neither could be found. Many of the great nobles gave or loaned money to the King for the defence of the realm. Catholic England, silent, banned, but still grateful, made its contribution, secretly given and received. But what did these poor sums avail for a war?

Strafford wished to bring over his Irish troops, but fear of the reactions which this step might provoke paralysed the Council. As Lord President of the North he harangued the nobility at York in rugged, violent terms. The reception was cool and disappointing. Presently the Scots crossed the Tweed in good order. The cavalry stood upstream to break the current while the foot waded across. They were met with no opposition until they reached the Tyne. Then, as before the Pacification of Berwick, the two hosts faced one another. The Scottish leaders were encouraged in their invasion by the Parliamentary and Puritan movements throughout England, and in the centre of this combination stood Pym. For some days little happened, but one morning a Scottish horseman, watering his horse in the river, came too near the English outposts. Someone pulled a trigger; the imprudent rider was wounded; all the Scots cannon fired and all the English army fled. A contemporary wrote that "Never so many ran from so few with less ado." Arriving swiftly before the gates of Newcastle, the Scots generals declared that they stood for the liberties of England, and appealed for aid from all who agreed with the Parliamentary cause. Meanwhile Strafford at York was frantically striving to form a front against the invasion, vainly hoping that the insult to English soil would produce the longed-for revival of the national spirit, trying without success to gain a majority upon the Council for the importation of Irish troops.

At this time many of the lords who were now meeting in London pressed on the King the proposal to summon a Magnum Concilium, which was an assembly of the Peers without the Commons. Centuries had passed since it had been convoked, but was not here a crisis which demanded it? Charles agreed, but this antique body could only recommend that Parliament should be called. Only Parliament could save the land from what had now become an act of Scottish aggression. At this moment King Charles's moral position was at its worst. He had plumbed the depths of personal failure. His enemies, while finally achieving his destruction, now built for him a party and a cause for which any man could die.

CHAPTER 5

THE REVOLT OF PARLIAMENT

THE INVADING SCOTTISH ARMY now had possession of Durham and Northumberland. Their leaders were in close correspondence with the Parliamentary and Puritan party in England. They put forward not only demands which affected the northern kingdom, but others which they knew would reverberate in the south. They were careful that the supply of sea-coal to London should not fail for a single day; but at the same time their marauding bands lay heavy on the occupied counties. The King could not prevail against them. Strafford believed that he could hold Yorkshire, but that was all. The Privy Council addressed itself to making a truce with the Scots, who demanded forty thousand pounds a month to maintain their army on English soil until their claims should be met. By haggling this was reduced to £850 a day. Thus the two armies, facing each other with sheathed swords, were each to be maintained during an indefinite period of negotiation at the cost of the Crown, which was penniless. The so-called "Bishops' War" was over; the real war had yet to begin.

There now arose from all quarters a cry that Parliament should be summoned. A group of lords, headed by the Earl of Bedford, who was in close touch with Pym, waited on the Privy Council and called for a Parliament. It was even implied that if the King would not issue the writs himself a Parliament would be convened without him. The Queen and such counsellors as were with her wrote urgently to Charles that they saw no other course. The King had himself arrived at the same conclusion and now recognised that his theory of monarchy must be modified. In summoning the new Parliament he accepted a different relationship between the people and the Crown.

The calling of Parliament relieved for a space the severe tension, but it was only after long begging, supported by the very lords who were opposing the King, and on their personal security, that the City of London consented to advance £50,000, pending the meeting of Parliament, to keep the Scottish army in the north of England and the English army from mutiny.

There is no surer way of rousing popular excitement than the holding of General Elections in quick succession. Passions ran high; beer flowed. The leaders of the popular party hastened from county to county exhorting their adherents. The King too appealed, not without response, to the great lords who stood by him. In some places four or five rival candidates appeared; but the tide ran strong against the Court. Three-fifths of the members of the Short Parliament, two hundred and ninety-four out of four hundred and ninety-three, were returned, and nearly all the newcomers were opponents of the Government. The King found that he could count on less than a third of the House.

Thus on November 3, 1640, was installed the most memorable Parliament that ever sat in England. It derived its force from a blending of political and religious ideas. It was upborne by the need of a growing society to base itself upon a wider foundation than Tudor paternal rule. It used for tactical purposes the military threat of the invaders from Scotland. Scottish commissioners and divines arrived in London, and were hailed as the deliverers of England. They found themselves outpaced in their hostility to the bishops by some of their English Parliamentary allies. Demands in both kingdoms for far-reaching changes in the civil and religious government were pooled and set forth again with combined force. The accession of James I had involved the union of the Crowns of England and Scotland; but now in a manner very different from what James or his son had conceived there was a union of the dominant political parties in both countries, and they strove together for a common cause. Here then was an explosive charge, directed upon King Charles and those who were his trusted ministers.

Of these the first and most obnoxious was Strafford. Pym and Hampden, the leading figures in the new House of Commons, were immediately in command of a large and indignant majority. The rage of the Parliamentary

"The Scots holding their young kinges nose to the grindstone" is a satirical drawing aimed at the King's extravagant dress, as well as at the Scots' love of the spoils of war, and the tenacity of the Presbyterian ministers.

A seating plan of both the Lords and the Commons in Westminster Hall. This contemporary engraving was made during the impeachment of Thomas Wentworth the Earl of Strafford, in 1641.

party, all the rancour of old comradeship forsworn, and all that self-preservation dictated, concentrated upon "the wicked Earl".

On the morning of November 11 the doors of St Stephen's Chapel were locked; the key placed upon the table; no strangers might enter, no member might leave. Late in the afternoon Pym and Hampden, attended by three hundred members, carried the articles of Strafford's impeachment up to the House of Lords. At the King's request Strafford had come to London. In the morning he had been greeted with respect by the peers. Hearing what was afoot, he returned to the Chamber. But now all was changed. Shouts were raised that he should withdraw while the issue was being debated. He was forced to do so. In less than an hour the powerful minister found himself to his own and the general surprise kneeling at the Bar to be deprived of his sword and taken into custody by Black Rod. As he went through the crowd on his journey to Black Rod's house the hostility of the populace was terrible.

The proscription extended to all the ministers of the King. Archbishop Laud, impeached in the Lords, was removed by water to the Tower. Some ministers escaped to the Continent. All this was done by the fierce anger of the Commons, supported by the Londoners and by the distant military forces of Scotland, and accepted by the peers.

Yet the main feature of the Puritan Revolution for our generation is its measured restraint. The issues were fought out with remorseless antagonism, not only in Parliament, but also in the streets of London. Yet respect for law and for human life nevertheless prevailed and physical violence was long held in check.

The Commons however were harassed by fears and rumours. They had been careful to pay the Scottish army for invading England; it was the English troops who had gone short. There were tales of mutinies and military plots. Pym, with cold-blooded skill, played upon these alarms, which indeed needed but a tremor of Parliamentary weakness to become real. The Scots, now so influential in London and masters in the north, sought to establish the Presbyterian system of Church government. This was indeed turning the tables. A petition signed by fifteen thousand was presented to the House, and caught up by the majority, seeking to extirpate the rule of bishops, the Episcopate, "root and branch".

But now for the first time effective counter-forces appeared. A second petition signed by seven hundred clergymen hostile to the principles of the King and the Archbishop proposed the restriction of the bishops' power to spiritual matters, and limited them at certain points in these. It was known that the King regarded the Episcopate, based upon the apostolic succession, as inseparable from the Christian faith. In the religious field the quarrel was between men who were all Protestants, but who were divided upon the method of Church government. On this they were prepared to proceed to extremes against each other; but whereas in politics the opposition to personal rule was at this moment overwhelming, on the Church question the balance was far more even. Pym realised this and decided to delay a full debate. Both petitions were therefore sent to a committee.

Strafford's appearance rapidly aged as he faced his enemies. This portrait was made shortly before his execution, when he was forty-eight.

Meanwhile the trial of Strafford had begun. The Commons at once found difficulty in establishing a case against the hated Minister. That he was the arch-enemy of all that the majority championed, and indeed of the rights and liberties of the nation, was apparent. But to prove him guilty of the capital offence of treason was not possible. Within Westminster Hall the leaders of the nation assembled. One-third of the floor was thronged with the public. The King and Queen sat daily in their special box, hoping by their presence to restrain the prosecution. Strafford defended himself with magnificent ability. Each morning he knelt to the Lord Steward and bowed to the lords and to the assembly. Each day by logic and appeal he broke up the heads of accusation. He drove home the massive doctrine of English liberty, "No law, no crime." What law had he broken? With every art of the orator, he wrought not only upon the minds but upon the sentiments of the audience. The King worked night and day upon the peers. There was nothing he would not concede to save Strafford. He had assured him on his kingly word that he should not suffer in liberty or life. The sympathy not only of the galleries, crowded with the wives of all the leading men, but of the peers themselves, was gradually gained. The prisoner's hopes stood high. The Commons, baffled, trooped back to St Stephen's Chapel and again locked their doors. Was this enemy of English rights to escape by legal processes? They knew he was their foe, and they meant to have his blood. They would dispense with a trial and have him declared guilty by Act of Parliament.

The Bill of Attainder passed the House of Commons on April 21, 1641, by two hundred and four votes to fifty-nine. Among the minority was Lord Digby, who had come to Parliament as one of the leading opponents of the Crown. With all his gifts, which were exceptional, he pleaded against his own party. He gained nothing but the suspicion of being a renegade. The names of the fifty-nine were spread abroad as traitors defending a traitor. The aspect of the multitude which daily beset the approaches to Parliament became more than ever threatening. The peers deemed to be favourable to Strafford were cowed by the frenzy they saw around them. When Oliver St John urged the case for the Attainder, the seizure of property and loss of

Edward Bowyer's "portrait of a young cavalier" in Dunster Castle demonstrates the flamboyant style of dress adopted by royalist supporters.

rights, in a great conference between the Houses, he used arguments not of law but of revolution. It had been said that where no law was there could be no transgression. But that plea could not avail for the man who had desired to overthrow all laws. "It was never accounted either cruelty or foul play," said St John, "to knock foxes and wolves on the head because they be beasts of prey."

When Strafford heard this harsh cry for vengeance he raised his hands as if to implore the mercy of Heaven, knowing that all was lost on earth. Only half the lords who had been present at the impeachment dared to vote upon the Bill of Attainder, and these in great preponderance sent Strafford to his doom. As the Earl of Essex, the discontented son of Queen Elizabeth's favourite, brutally observed, "Stone-dead hath no fellow."

There were however other chances. The King tried to gain control of the Tower and of the prisoner. But the Governor, Sir William Balfour, closed his gates and also spurned an immense bribe offered him by Strafford. The cry for "Justice!" rang through London streets. A mob of several thousand, many of them armed, appeared before the palace roaring for Strafford's head. In Parliament it was bruited that they would now impeach the Queen.

This was the agony of Charles's life, to which none of his other sufferings compared. He appealed to the bishops, who, with two exceptions, advised him that he must separate his feelings as a man from those of a sovereign. But his real release came from Strafford himself. In a noble letter, written before the vote in the Lords, he had urged the King not to let any promise to him endanger the monarchy or the peace of the realm. At last Charles made the surrender which haunted him to the last moment of his life. He gave his assent to the Bill of Attainder.

An immense concourse of persons crowded to the place of execution. Strafford died with fortitude and dignity. He was beyond doubt a man conscious of commanding gifts, impelled by high ambition and a desire to rule. He had sought power by the path of Parliament. He had found it in the favour of the Crown. The circumstances of his trial and of the Attainder threw odium upon his pursuers. They slaughtered a man they could not convict. But that man, if given his full career, would have closed perhaps for generations the windows of civic freedom upon the English people.

In the crash of the Strafford trial and execution the King let various matters slip. The Triennial Bill providing for the summoning of Parliament at least once in three years, if necessary in spite of the Crown, put a final end to the system of personal rule over which Charles had so far presided. The grant of tonnage and poundage for one year only was accompanied by a censure upon the exaction of Ship Money, and reparation to all who had suffered for their resistance to it. The King perforce subscribed to all this. But he must have been completely broken for the moment when he assented on the same day as the Bill of Strafford's Attainder, to a measure designed "to prevent inconvenience that may happen by the untimely prorogation or dissolving of this present Parliament" except by its own consent. It was in fact a law making this Parliament, since called the Long Parliament, perpetual. Many other changes were made. The judges, whose tenure had hitherto been dependent upon the pleasure of the Crown, now held office on good behaviour. The Court of Star Chamber was abolished. So was the Court of High Commission, which had striven to impose religious uniformity. The jurisdiction of the Privy Council was strictly and narrowly defined. The principles of the Petition of Right about personal liberty were now finally established. Charles endorsed these great decisions. He had realised that in his trusteeship of the rights of monarchy he had grasped too much.

Everything was now fluid, and in that strong-willed England, men without regard to their former actions, looked about them for sure foothold. From the day when Strafford's head fell beneath the axe there began a conservative reaction. Charles found himself increasingly sustained by strong and deep currents of public feeling. The excesses and fanaticism of the Puritan party, their war upon the Church, their confederacy with the Scottish invaders, roused antagonisms of which the hitherto helpless Court was but a spectator, but from which the Crown might by patience and wisdom emerge secure.

Charles now felt that his hope lay in a reconciliation with Scotland. He resolved to go to Scotland himself and open a Parliament in Edinburgh. Pym and his adherents could hardly object to this. Moderate opinion welcomed the plan. In Scotland Charles accepted everything he had most abhorred. He strove to win the hearts of the Covenanters. He listened devoutly to their sermons and assented to the establishment of total Presbyterianism in Scotland. But all was in vain. Charles was accused of complicity in an ill-starred attempt of royalist partisans to kidnap the Scottish leader, the Marquis of Argyll. The King returned to England crestfallen.

Upon this melancholy scene a hideous apparition now appeared. The execution of Strafford liberated all the elemental forces in Ireland which his system had so successfully held in restraint. The Irish Parliament in Dublin, formerly submissive, had hastened to voice their complaints against his rule. At the same time a Roman Catholic Celtic people regarded the English Protestantism with the utmost aversion. Strafford's disciplined Irish army was disbanded and the passions of the hungry, downtrodden masses, bursting from all control, were directed upon the gentry, the landowners, and the Protestants. In the autumn of 1641, the propertied classes, their families and dependants, fled to the few garrisoned towns. Cruelties unspeakable were reported on all sides, and the Government struck back without mercy. A general slaughter of males and a policy of devastation were proclaimed throughout large parts of the countryside. As the tale of these atrocities crept home to England it gave a shock to men's minds which deeply harmed the King's interests. The Puritans declared they saw in the Irish outrage the fate to which they would be consigned if the Popish tendencies of the bishops were armed with the sword of an absolute sovereign.

The mere fact of his absence from London, which had left the Parliamentary forces to their full play, had served the King's interests better than the closest attention to English affairs. During September and October conservative reaction had become a tide. Who could accuse the Court of army plots when the English and Irish armies had both been disbanded? Englishmen, irrespective of religious and constitutional convictions, were ill-disposed to be taxed for the upkeep of invading Scottish troops. Presbyterianism made little appeal to the bulk of the English people, who, so far as they were not satisfied with the Elizabethan Church tradition, sought spiritual comfort or excitement in the more vehement sects which had sprung up in the general turmoil of the Reformation, or in the Puritan body itself; such as Anabaptism and Brownism, both of which were as opposed to Presbytery as to bishops. In the Commons Pym and his supporters

Parliament supporters, like Thomas Luttrell of Dunster Castle, dressed simply and wore their hair short. A few extremists cropped their hair and thus earned the nickname of "Roundheads".

Atrocities in Ireland against Protestants followed Strafford's death and the disbanding of his army in 1641. It was in vengeance for the Protestant martyrs that Cromwell slaughtered all the inhabitants of the Catholic towns of Wexford and Drogheda in 1649-50.

were still dominant, although there was an opposition equally resolute. The Lords were now at variance with the Commons, and a large majority sided with the King. From being the servants of the national cause the Puritans had become an aggressive faction. Men felt their hands itching to grasp the swords by which alone it seemed their case could be urged.

It was in this stormy weather that Pym and Hampden sought to rally their forces by bringing forward what was called the "Grand Remonstrance". This long document was in fact a party manifesto. It was intended to advertise all that had so far been accomplished by Parliament in remedying old grievances, and to proclaim the future policy of the Parliamentary leaders. Pym's hope was to re-establish the unity of his diverse followers, and so the more extreme demands for religious reform were dropped. The power of bishops was to be curtailed, but not abolished. Nevertheless the growing body of Conservatives, or "Episcopalian Party", as they were sometimes named, did not like the way that Pym was going. They wanted "to win the King by the sweeter way of concealing his errors than by publishing of them". Pym however was preparing to carry the struggle further; he would appeal to the people and win complete control for Parliament over the King's ministers. In a message about the Irish rebellion, he demanded that the King "employ such counsellors and ministers as shall be approved by his Parliament". If this were not conceded he threatened that Parliament would take Irish affairs into its own hands.

Here was a sweeping challenge to royal authority. But the King now had at his side very different counsellors from those of a year before. Many of his former opponents, chief among them Digby and his father, the Earl of Bristol, were hostile to Pym. Bishop Williams, foremost of Laud's critics, now stood against Laud's accusers. Falkland and Colepeper ranged themselves against the violence of the majority and were soon to take office in the King's Government. Edward Hyde, later famous as the historian Clarendon, opened the debate by insisting that the aim must now be peace: if the Remonstrance as a whole were carried, and especially if it were published, the disputes would be embittered and prolonged.

The debate was long and earnest, vehement with restrained passion. At last at midnight the Remonstrance, somewhat amended, was put to the vote. When Parliament had met a year earlier the King's party could not count on a third of its members. Now the Grand Remonstrance was carried only by eleven votes. A motion was put forward by the majority that it should be printed forthwith. On this the Commons rose to a clash of opposing wills. About one o'clock in the morning a lawyer of the Middle Temple, Mr Geoffrey Palmer, demanded that the clerk should record the names of all who protested. A great crowd rose to their feet with the cry, "All! All!" Plumed hats were waved, men laid their hands upon their swords, some even drew them and rested their hands upon the pommels. "I thought", wrote a member, Philip Warwick, of this moment in the crowded, dimly lighted room of the chapel, "we had all sat in the Valley of the Shadow of Death, that we, like Abner's and Joab's young men, had catched at each other's locks and sheathed our swords in each other's bowels." Only Hampden's suave, timely intervention prevented a bloody collision. But here the pathway of debate was broken, and war alone could promise further stepping-stones.

A hitherto little-noticed member for Cambridge, Oliver Cromwell, rather rough in his manners, but an offshoot of Thomas Cromwell's line, said to Falkland as they left the House, "If the Remonstrance had been rejected I would have sold all that I had next morning, and never have seen England anymore; and I know there are many honest men of the same resolution."

The King, who, in spite of his failure in Scotland and the Irish catastrophe, had been conscious of ever-gathering support, was now drawn into various contradictory blunders. At one moment he sought to form a Ministry dependent upon the majority faction which ruled the House of Commons. A dozen of the Opposition lords were sworn members of the Privy Council. But when in a few weeks it was found that these noblemen began to speak of the King in terms of undue respect the London factions howled upon them as backsliders. Still seeking desperately for a foothold, Charles invited Pym himself to become Chancellor of the Exchequer. Such a plan had no contact with reality. Colepeper took the post instead, and Falkland became Secretary of State. Next, in violent revulsion, Charles resolved to prosecute five of his principal opponents in the Commons for high treason. Upon this wild course he was impelled by Queen Henrietta Maria. She taunted him with cowardice, and exhorted him, if he would ever see her again, to lay strong hands upon those who spent their nights and days seeking his overthrow and her life. He certainly convinced himself that Pym meant to impeach the Queen.

Thus goaded, Charles, accompanied by three or four hundred swordsmen—"Cavaliers" we may now call them—went down to the House of Commons. It was January 4, 1642. Never before had a king set foot in the Chamber. When his officers knocked at the door and it was known that he had come in person, members of all parties looked upon each other in amazement. All rose at his entry. The Speaker, William Lenthall, quitted his chair and knelt before him. The King, seating himself in the chair, after professing his goodwill to the House, demanded the surrender of the five indicted Members—Pym, Hampden, Holles, Hazelrigg, and Strode. But a treacherous message from a lady of the Queen's Bedchamber had given

Van Dyck's charming picture of the royal children in 1640 gives no hint of the political troubles of the age. The picture of the future Charles II, his sister Mary and brother James with their younger sisters and dogs suggests a carefree and harmonious family life.

A coach labelled "Commonwealth" crushes Charles I under its wheels. It is driven by Satan whose horses, named Republican Tyranny, Presbytery and Moderation, trample Liberty, Loyalty and Episcopacy beneath their hooves.

Pym a timely warning. The accused members had already embarked at Westminster steps and were safe amid the trainbands (militia) and magistrates of the City. Speaker Lenthall could give no information. "I have only eyes to see and ears to hear as the House may direct," he pleaded. The King cast his eyes around the assembly. "I see that the birds are flown," he said and departed at the head of his disappointed adherents. But as he left the Chamber a low, long murmur of "Privilege" pursued him.

Upon this episode the wrath of London became uncontrollable. The infuriated mobs who bellowed outside the palace caused Charles to escape from the capital to Hampton Court. He never saw London again except to suffer trial and death. Within a week of his intrusion into the House the five members were escorted back to Parliament from the City. Their progress was triumphal. Over two thousand armed men accompanied them up the river, and on either bank large forces, each with eight pieces of cannon, marched abreast of the flotilla. Henceforth London was irretrievably lost to the King. By stages he withdrew to Newmarket, to Nottingham, and to York. Here he waited during the early months of 1642, while the tireless antagonisms which rent England apart slowly rebuilt him an authority and an armed force.

There were now two centres of government. Pym, the Puritans, and what was left of the Parliament ruled with dictatorial power in London in the King's name. The King, round whom there gathered many of the finest elements in Old England, freed from the bullying of the London mob, became once again a prince with sovereign rights. About these two centres there slowly assembled the troops and resources for the waging of civil war.

CHAPTER 6

THE GREAT REBELLION

THE NEGOTIATIONS BETWEEN KING AND PARLIAMENT which occupied the early months of 1642 served to emphasise their differences while both were gathering their forces. The question of the Roundheads, as the militant section of the Parliamentary party was now called, was whether the King should govern as a god by his will, and the nation be governed by force like beasts; or whether the people should be governed by laws made by themselves and live under a government derived from their own consent.

On June 1, 1642, Parliament presented nineteen propositions to the King. In brief, the King was invited to surrender his whole effective sovereignty over Church and State. But underlying the apparently clear-cut constitutional issue was a religious and class conflict. The Puritans were predominant in Parliament, High Churchmen at Court. The new classes of merchants and manufacturers and the substantial tenant farmers in some counties were claiming a share of political power, which had hitherto been almost monopolised by the aristocracy and the hereditary landlords.

Yet when the alignment of the parties on the outbreak of the Civil War is surveyed, no simple divisions are to be found. Brother fought against brother, father against son. Against loyalty to Parliament the Royalists invoked loyalty to the Crown; against Puritan ardour Anglican unity. They preferred the ancient light of divinely blessed authority to the distant glimmer of democracy. "God saith, 'Touch not Mine anointed'," wrote a Cavalier knight as he reluctantly girded on his sword for the battle. On both sides men went into the fight doubtfully, but guided by their belief in high-souled ideals. On both sides were others—dissolute courtiers, ambitious politicians spoiling for a fight, out-of-work mercenaries; but, broadly, the contest now became a tragic conflict of loyalties and ideals.

The arrogant tone and ever-growing demands of the Parliamentary party shaped the lines of the struggle and recruited the forces of the King. The greater part of the nobility gradually rallied to the Royalist cause; the tradesmen and merchants generally inclined to the Parliament; but a substantial section of the aristocracy were behind Pym, and many boroughs were devotedly Royalist. The counties nearer London generally inclined to Parliament, while the north and west remained largely Royalist. Both sides fought in the name of the King, and both upheld the Parliamentary institution. The Roundheads always spoke of "King and Parliament". The orders given to their first commander in chief, the Earl of Essex, directed him to "rescue" the King and princes from the evil counsellors into whose power they had fallen. Behind all class and political issues the religious quarrel was the driving power. In Cromwell's words, "Religion was not the thing at first contested for, but God brought it to that issue at last; . . . and at last it proved that which was most dear to us."

For more than seventy years absolute peace had reigned in England. Except for a few officers who had seen service on the Continent, no one knew anything about military matters. At first the Cavaliers, trained in fencing, inured to the chase, had a military advantage over the Roundheads. From York the King looked to Hull, where the weapons of his disbanded army against the Scots had been stored. The Prince of Wales and the Duke of York, who were but boys aged twelve and nine, paid a visit to Hull and were courteously received, but when the King himself sought entry the Governor, Sir John Hotham, closed the gates against him. As he had only a few thousand local levies or trainbands, the King had to accept what was a heavy blow. Arms were vital. At Nottingham, where town and county alike had proclaimed devotion, Charles set up his standard on August 22 and called his loyal subjects to his aid. This was the ancient signal for feudal duty, and its message awoke memories throughout the land.

The King had only eight hundred horse and three hundred foot, and at

These carved wooden soldiers stand on the newel posts of the staircase at Cromwell House, Highgate, London. The house was built in 1630 when the Thirty Years' War was raging in Europe. The soldiers wear the uniforms of the hero of the hour—the Swedish king, Gustavus Adolphus. Some English soldiers who subsequently fought in the Civil War had gained experience in European armies.

Prince Rupert of the Rhine learnt the art of warfare in the Thirty Years' War. He was the son of Charles's older sister, Elizabeth of Bohemia, wife of the Protestant champion, Frederick, Elector Palatine. His portrait, after Van Dyck, was painted in 1637, four years before his debut in England as Charles's Commander of the Cavalry in the Civil War.

first it seemed doubtful whether any royal army could be raised. But the violence of Parliament served him well. By the end of September he had with him two thousand horse and six thousand foot. A few weeks later their numbers were more than doubled, and other forces were raised for him all over the country. The Queen, who had found refuge in Holland, sent arms and trained officers, procured by the sale of the Crown jewels. But the navy, which Charles had quarrelled with his subjects to sustain, adhered to Parliament and the blockade was hard to run. The great nobles supplied the King with money. The Marquis of Newcastle is said to have spent nearly a million pounds upon the Royalist cause, and the Marquis of Worcester seven or eight thousand. The University of Oxford melted their plate, and this example was followed in many a hall and manor. Meanwhile the Roundheads, sustained by ample funds from the wealth and regular taxation of London, levied and trained an army of twenty-five thousand men under Essex. As on the Royalist side, most of the regiments were raised personally by prominent people. But whereas the King could give only a commission to raise a regiment or a troop, Parliament could provide the equipment as well.

The King, skilfully avoiding Essex's army, now moved west to join his Welsh reinforcements, and then struck south for the Thames valley and London. There was a panic in the capital when this became evident. An address was hastily dispatched to the King, proposing that he should return to his Parliament, and at the same time Essex was enjoined to overtake him. Charles did not dare to be caught between the troops in London and those who followed hard upon him. At Edgehill, in Warwickshire, on October 23 the royal army turned on its pursuers and attacked them. The battle was marked by abundant ignorance and zeal on both sides. Prince Rupert of the Rhine, the King's nephew, who, with his younger brother, Prince Maurice, both fresh from the European wars, had hastened to his side and taken command of the cavalry, charged and overthrew all the Parliamentary horse on their left wing. Carried away by his own ardour or the indiscipline of his troopers, he pursued the Roundheads into the village of Kineton, where he plundered the baggage train. Meanwhile the King and the royal infantry, unsupported by any cavalry of his own, had to withstand a strong Parliamentary assault. The royal standard was for a time taken, and its bearer, Sir Edmund Verney, was cut down. But the approach of the Parliamentary rearguard under Hampden drove Rupert and his cavalry from the baggage train. They returned to the battlefield in time to avert defeat and both sides retired to their morning positions. At least five thousand Englishmen lay upon the field; twelve hundred were buried by the vicar of Kineton.

Edgehill, which might so easily have ended the war in the King's favour, was judged a drawn battle. Essex resumed his march to cover London, and the King occupied Banbury. In triumph he entered Oxford, which now became his headquarters and remained so to the very end.

It has often been asked whether Charles could have reached London before Essex, and what would have happened when he got there. It seems probable that the royal army would have been involved in heavy fighting with the Londoners, while Essex, still himself superior in numbers, came steadily in upon them. But now the advance was made from Oxford and the King contented himself with dispersing the local forces that stood in the way. At the same time the Parliamentary envoys were presenting a new address to the King, and negotiations were in progress. While Essex's leading regiments were rapidly approaching the capital, Rupert attacked them at Brentford, on the Thames, and routed and pursued them with great severity. Each side accused the other of treachery. Parliament declared that their innocent men had been fallen upon while parleys were proceeding. The Royalists pointed to the military fact that Essex was hourly effecting his junction with the London forces.

A few days later, at Turnham Green, a few miles west of London, the King found himself confronted with the combined forces of Essex's field army and the London garrison. He was outnumbered by more than two to one. After a cannonade he withdrew towards Oxford, being, as some held, lucky in getting clear.

Throughout angry England, divided in every shire, in every town, in every village, all eyes had been fixed upon the clash and manoeuvre of the two main armies. The hopes of both sides were that these would give a decision, and thereafter peace. When it was seen that nothing of the kind would happen, and that a long, balanced struggle lay ahead, all suspended antagonisms started into action. The constitutional issue, the religious quarrel, and countless local feuds combined in a surge of party hatred.

Before the Battle of Edgehill in Warwickshire in October, 1642, Prince Rupert's headquarters were above this gatehouse.

From the beginning of 1643 the war became general. The ports and manufacturing centres mostly adhered to the Parliament; what might be called Old England rallied to Charles. In the north and the west the King's cause prospered. Braving the blockade, Queen Henrietta Maria brought a considerable shipload of cannon and munitions to Bridlington, on the Yorkshire coast. The Parliamentary warships were hard upon her wake. Coming as close inshore as the ebb tide would permit, they fired their guns upon the house where she was sleeping. In barefoot haste she sheltered from the whistling shot in the village. This personal cannonade upon the Queen by the Parliamentary admiral was deemed unwarrantable and indecent in an age where sex, rank, and chivalry still counted.

Henrietta Maria entered York amid intense rejoicing. Enormous crowds of loyal people cheered the imposing train of cannon which followed behind her. She brought with her a spirit as indomitable as Margaret of Anjou.

At first the decisive action was not in the north. Parliament was already in some doubts about the capacity of Essex as a general. The fancy of those who wanted all-out war was Sir William Waller, now sent to command the Parliamentary army in the west. The Cornishmen, however, showed a lively devotion to the royal cause and uncommon nimbleness and courage in fighting. Here also the most sagacious and skilful of the Royalist generals, Sir Ralph Hopton, commanded. Three fierce battles on a small scale were fought by Hopton and Waller. A warm personal friendship subsisted between them, but, as Waller wrote to his opponent, "each had to bear his part in a matter of honour and fidelity". At Lansdowne, outside Bath, Hopton's Cornishmen stormed Waller's position. The feature of Waller's army was the London cavalry. These were so completely encased in armour that they were called by both sides "the Lobsters". The Lobsters were charged uphill by the Royalists, who wrought great havoc among them. Waller was defeated, but Hopton's losses were so severe that he took refuge in Devizes. His horsemen, under Prince Maurice, ran away. But the Prince, returning by a rapid march with fresh cavalry from Oxford, found Waller

England loyal to
the King at the
end of 1643

Throughout the war, London was in the possession of Parliament. The nearest Charles came to attacking the capital was at Turnham Green, in the autumn of 1642.

drawn up to receive him on Roundway Down. The Royalists attacked and drove the Lobsters headlong down the steep slopes, while Hopton moved out from the town and completed the victory with his infantry.

Fired with these successes, Rupert, with the Oxford army joined to Hopton's forces, summoned, assaulted, and procured the surrender of the city of Bristol. This was the second city in the kingdom, and on the whole its inhabitants were Royalist. The warships in the port declared for the King, and hope dawned of a royal squadron which could command the Bristol Channel. King Charles's cause had also prevailed in Yorkshire. Here Lord Fairfax and his son, Sir Thomas, led the Parliamentary forces. Sir Thomas besieged York; but the Marquis of Newcastle, rich, corpulent, proud, but entirely devoted, led his territorial retainers, the valiant "white-coats", to its relief, and later in the summer overwhelmed the Fairfaxes at Adwalton Moor, along with numbers of peasants armed with scythes or bludgeons. The defeat left Parliament with Hull as their only stronghold in the north. Now in Hull Governor Hotham, hitherto so steadfast for the Roundheads, was converted to the royal side, in part by the persuasions of one of his captives, Lord Digby, and also, no doubt, by the King's successes. Eighteen months before, when Hull and its munitions might have been decisive, he could have delivered all with ease. But he had built up a spirit of resistance among the townsfolk, who did not change with him. He and his son were arrested and carried by sea to London. Meanwhile in the Midlands also the Royalists made headway.

Charles had not that intense clarity of view and promptitude to act which are the qualities of great commanders, but he possessed a certain strategic comprehension, and he was brave in action. From the beginning of 1643 his design was for a general advance on London. Hopton from the west, Newcastle from the north, himself from Oxford, would converge on the capital. Till midsummer the results of the fighting seemed to favour this decisive plan; but the King had neither the resources nor the authority for so large a combination. The heavy fighting in the west had cost him his best adherents. Hopton's little army marched steadily east through Hampshire and Sussex, and was checked, while the western Royalists, who ought to have reinforced it, were content to sit down before Plymouth, whose Parliamentary garrison had been raiding far and wide. Indeed, the loyalty to Parliament of a single town in a generally Royalist region made it hard for the King to draw off local troops for a national campaign. Newcastle could not be dissuaded from a land attack upon Hull so the Queen and other counsellors urged a single-handed advance on London. The sole stronghold remaining to the Parliament between Bristol and York was Gloucester; thus the King, in the zenith of his military fortune, resolved to besiege it. Accordingly on August 5 the city was invested.

Meanwhile in London, Pym, the master of the Parliament, was in grievous straits. As head of the Government he was obliged to raise money for an increasingly unpopular war by methods as little conformable to the principles he championed as those which Charles had used against the Scots in 1640. Forced loans and direct taxation of almost everyone were among his devices. Strong currents of Royalism now flowed in the capital. The Common Council of the City was unyielding; but Royalist opinion was too strong to be silenced. At one time seventy merchants were in prison for refusing to pay taxes which they judged illegal. The House of Lords, consisting now of fewer than twenty sitting peers, carried a precise and solemn resolution for peace negotiations. Even the Commons agreed to the Lords' propositions. Pym's life was ebbing to its close. He had cancer. His greatest colleague, Hampden, had died of wounds early in the year after a clash with Rupert's cavalry at Chalgrove Field. The ruin of his cause and the approach of death seemed to be the only reward of Pym's struggles. Undaunted, he bore up against all; and the last impulse of his life may well have turned the scale. All the Puritan forces in London were roused to repudiate peace. The preachers exhorted their congregations, and warlike crowds beset Westminster.

The Earl of Essex had fallen into just disrepute as a general, and was suspected of political lukewarmness. Although ever faithful to the cause he had espoused, he sought a peaceful settlement. Now however he was ordered to relieve Gloucester. He accepted the duty, perhaps hoping this would give him strength to stop England tearing herself to pieces. The London trainbands clamoured to march in a surge of resolve, and they departed through cheering crowds.

At Gloucester Governor Massey, who was believed to be ready to change sides, had failed the King. The violent Puritanism within his walls left him no choice of treacheries. The King's resources, indeed the art of war in England at this time, afforded no satisfactory method of making a siege. Compared with the gigantic systematised operations of later times the sieges of the English Civil War were feeble and primitive. A few batteries of cannon, with scanty powder and ball, tried to make a hole in the wall in which both sides could fight with sword and musket until food ran short or the inhabitants in fear of sack forced a capitulation. The King had made no progress against Gloucester when, in the early days of September, Essex and the London army drew near in superior numbers. There was no choice but to raise the siege and retire upon Oxford.

"When Did You Last See Your Father?" This celebrated nineteenth-century painting by Cedric Yeames, now in the Walker Art Gallery, Liverpool, depicts the way in which Parliamentary officials were thought to have carried out their stringent inquiries.

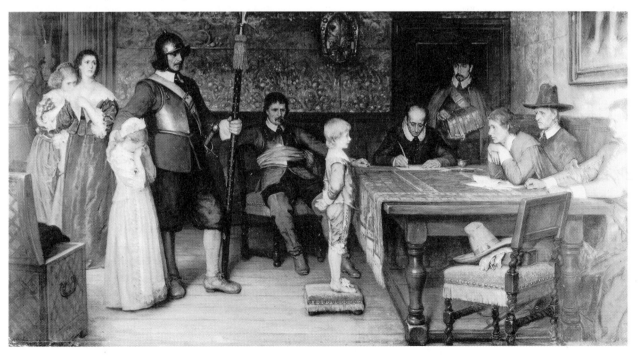

These substitute coins were minted at Oxford during the King's exile from London in the Civil War. Traces of the highly decorated metal dinner plates from which they were made can be seen in the finished coins.

Essex entered Gloucester in triumph, but found himself immediately short of supplies and food, with a formidable enemy between him and home. Both armies headed for London, and on September 20 they clashed at Newbury, in Berkshire. There was a long and bitter conflict. Once again Rupert's cavalry beat their opponents; but they could make no impression on the London pikemen and musketeers. A third of the troops were casualties, and on the Royalist side many nobles fell, among them Lord Falkland. The battle was undecided when darkness fell. Essex had no choice but to renew it at dawn; but the King withdrew, stricken by the loss of so many personal friends, and short of powder. The London road lay open to the Roundheads.

The King's large plan for 1643 had failed. Nevertheless the campaign had been very favourable to him. He had gained control of a great part of England. His troops were still, on the whole, better fighting-men than the Roundheads. Much ground lost at the beginning of the war had been recovered. A drift of desertion to the royal camp had begun. All could see how even were the forces which rent the kingdom. On both sides men's thoughts turned to peace. Not so the thoughts of Pym; by substantial money payments he induced a Scots army of not less than eleven thousand men to intervene. Then on December 8 Pym died, uncheered by success, but unwearied by misfortune. He had neglected his private affairs in the public cause, and his estate would have been bankrupt had not Parliament, as some expression of their grief and gratitude, paid his debts. He remains the most famous of the old Parliamentarians, and the man who more than any other saved England from absolute monarchy and set her upon the path she has since pursued.

There was a lull during the winter. Charles was encouraged by the death of the great French minister, Richelieu, which restored power to his Queen's brother, Louis XIII, and by the friendly aid of the King of Denmark. In Ireland the Earl of Ormonde, Lord Lieutenant, had made a truce with the Catholics, who, in spite of all atrocities committed and suffered, still accepted the monarchy. The Royalist camp even considered bringing Irish Papists into England, and rumours of this did harm to the King's cause. But the "Cessation" in Ireland, as it was called, enabled Irish Protestant regiments and other royal troops to be brought to England.

Charles had never dissolved the Parliament which was warring against him, because in so doing he would have invalidated his assent to many laws which counted with his own supporters. Declaring therefore that the Parliament at Westminster was no longer a free Parliament, he summoned all who had been expelled or who had fled from it to a counter-assembly. The response was remarkable. Eighty-three peers and a hundred and seventy-five Members met in Oxford on January 22, 1644.

But these advantages were overwhelmed by the arrival in England of a Scottish army of eighteen thousand foot and three thousand horse, who crossed the Tweed in January. For this succour the London Parliament paid £31,000 a month and the cost of equipment. But the Scots, though in a sense hired, had other objects besides money. They now aspired to outroot the Episcopacy and impose by armed force the Presbyterian system of Church government upon England. Now no longer were the Scots defending their own religious liberties; they sought to compel the far larger and stronger English nation to conform to their ideas.

CHAPTER 7

MARSTON MOOR AND NASEBY

T HE KING AT THE BEGINNING OF 1644 had the larger part of the country behind him and a considerable Parliament of his own which met in Oxford. Military victory in England seemed within his grasp. The Scots reversed the balance. As their army advanced southward they stormed the city of Newcastle, and sent the bill to Westminster. Their commissioners arrived in London with three principal aims: first, the imposition of Presbyterianism upon all England; secondly, a share in the government of England by means of the Committee of Both Kingdoms; thirdly, the maintenance of the monarchy. They liked to see a Scottish line on the English throne.

Grim as were the straits to which the cause of the dead Pym and Hampden was now reduced, these transactions did not pass without protest. The Parliamentary taxpayers resented the expense of the Scottish army. The House of Lords, or what was left of it at Westminster, resisted the plan for the Committee of Both Kingdoms as subverting their constitutional rights. But the most serious difference was on religion. It was now that Oliver Cromwell came into prominence. The Member for Cambridge, who had trained the troops of the Eastern Counties Association, was deemed the best officer on the Parliamentary side, though he had not yet held a supreme command. His regiment had a discipline and quality surpassing, as it seemed, any formation on either side. The rise of Cromwell to the first rank of power during 1644 sprang both from his triumphs on the battlefield and his resistance to the Presbyterians and the Scots at Westminster. All the obscurer Protestant sects saw in him their champion.

There was a formidable division between the Presbyterians and the Congregationalists or Independents. The Congregationalists were but a seventh of the Westminster Assembly, but their zeal and valour made them powerful in the army. They rejected all forms of ordination by the laying on of hands. These, they declared with some logic, savoured of episcopacy. The Reformation could only be fulfilled by going back to the original institution of independent churches. Presbyterian discipline was as abhorrent to them as episcopacy. The Scottish divines were shocked by such doctrines of spiritual anarchy, but neither they nor their English colleagues could afford to quarrel with Cromwell. They thought it better for their army to penetrate deeply into England and become involved in the war before dealing with these "dissenting brethren" as they deserved. Thus not for the first or last time theology waited upon arms.

In the north the Marquis of Newcastle had now to contend with the Scottish army on one side and the two Fairfaxes on the other. In the spring he marched north against the Scots and left Lord Bellasis to ward off the Roundheads. Bellasis was overwhelmed at Selby on April 11 by the Fairfaxes. Newcastle's rear was thereby exposed, and he could do no more than maintain himself in York, where he was presently vigorously besieged. The loss of York would ruin the King's cause in the north. Charles therefore sent Prince Rupert with a strong cavalry force to relieve the city. Rupert fought his way into Lancashire, striking heavy blows on all sides, and on

Samuel Cooper's miniature of Oliver Cromwell is now in the National Portrait Gallery. Both portrait and frame reflect plainness and strength, the fundamental characteristics of the Protector.

Henry Ireton (1611-51) was Cromwell's second-in-command in Ireland where he continued the policy of settling the country with English Protestants. The portrait above is attributed to Robert Walker and can be seen in the National Portrait Gallery.

Parliament (to which the royal assent may be desired) for our indemnity and security in all such services." Even after Marston Moor and Naseby the victorious Ironsides did not feel sure that anything counted without the royal authority. Here is the salient fact which distinguishes the English Revolution from all others: that those who wielded irresistible physical force were throughout convinced that it could give them no security. Law in the King's name was the sole foundation on which they could build.

The Parliamentary leaders received the officers' petition with displeasure. They ordered each regiment to proceed to a different station in order that they might be separately disbanded. The reply of the Army was to concentrate at Newmarket. There they made a Solemn Engagement not to disband until their desires were met. As the balance between authority and physical force seemed fairly even both sides sought allies. The Presbyterians in Parliament looked to the Scots and the Army leaders looked to the King. The generals—Cromwell, Ireton, and Fairfax, commander in chief, to put them in their order of power—saw themselves about to be reduced to something lower than the venomous faction-politicians, who thought the victory was their own property. Up to this point the Army, generals, officers, and men were at one.

Cromwell and Ireton felt that if they could get hold of the King physically, and before Parliament did so, it would be much. If they could gain him morally it would be all. Ireton was already secretly in touch with the King. Now in early June on his and Cromwell's orders Cornet Joyce, with near four hundred Ironside troopers, rode to Holmby House, where the King was agreeably residing. The colonel of his Parliamentary guard fled.

Cornet Joyce intimated with due respect that he had come to remove the King. Charles made no protest. He walked out onto the terrace and eyed the solid buff and steel array with an almost proprietary air. "Mr Joyce," said the King, "tell me, where is your commission? Have you anything in writing from Sir Thomas Fairfax?" Cornet Joyce was embarrassed. Finally he said, pointing to the regiment, "Here!" "Indeed," said the King, with the compulsive smile and confidence of sovereignty and Divine Right. "It is one I can read without spelling: as handsome and proper a company of gentlemen as I have seen this many a day. . . . Where next, Mr Joyce?"

The Cornet and those who had sent him thought only of studying the King's wishes so long as they had him in their power. Off they all rode together, and for three days the King lay at Childerley, near Newmarket. Cambridge University flocked out with loyal addresses, which had been lacking in the Civil War. Soon arrived Cromwell, Ireton, and Fairfax. The royal captive was removed to Hatfield, thence to Hampton Court, where the officers of the household were astonished to see the King walking up and down the garden conversing and laughing with the rebel generals. Eventually the following royal message was framed: "His Majesty, having seen the Proposals of the Army . . . believes his two Houses will think with him that they very much more conduce to the satisfaction of all interests and may be a fitter foundation for a lasting peace than the Propositions now tendered by Parliament. He therefore propounds (as the best way in his judgment in order to peace) that his two Houses would instantly take into consideration those Proposals."

Behind all this was a great political and personal deal. No one has probed its precise details. There was a religious compromise which the nation could have stomached. There was a Constitution where power was balanced between Parliament and Crown. There was substantial indemnity and reward for the Army when disbanded. There is the outline of a Cromwell, Earl and Knight of the Garter, quelling, as Viceroy, the Irish disorders. At this moment there was at fingertips a settlement in the power of the English people and near to their hearts' desire. But of course it was too good to be true. Charles was never wholly sincere in his dealings with the Army leaders; he still pinned his hopes on help from the Scots. Parliament for their part rejected the military and royal proposals. They too hoped that the Scots might be brought to put down the warriors who had saved them in their need. Here were checks. But another came from the Army itself.

Hitherto the generals had held the officers, and the officers had held the men; but all was surging upward upon religious passion. The generals wished to make a good arrangement for the country, for the King, and for themselves. The rank and file had deeper-cutting convictions. They looked upon the King as "the Man of Blood", and were astonished that their leaders should defile themselves by having truck with him. The generals saw themselves in danger of losing control over the soldiers.

The Presbyterian party in the House of Commons now realised they could not quell the Ironsides. But the City of London, its apprentices and its mob, as yet unconvinced, held them to their duty. They were forced by riot and violence to rescind the conciliatory resolutions which they had offered to the Army. In fear of the mob, the Speaker and fifty or sixty members resorted to Army headquarters at Hounslow, claiming the protection of Cromwell. This was granted. On August 6, the Army marched on London, occupied Westminster, entered the City, and everything except their own problems fell prostrate before them.

JOHN AUBREY AT AVEBURY RING

John Aubrey, who wrote Brief Lives, *short and racy biographies of notable sixteenth- and seventeenth-century figures, was also a distinguished archaeologist. He discovered a ring of pits at Stonehenge, now known as the Aubrey Holes. He was twenty-three when he first saw Avebury Ring on the Marlborough downs. He recorded his impressions in* The Natural History of Wiltshire, *published by the Wiltshire Archaeological Society two centuries later.*

Salisbury-plaines and Stonehenge I had known from eight years old: but I never saw the country round Marleborough till Christmas 1648. The morrow after twelf day Mr Charles Seymour and Sir William Button of Tokenham, baronet, mett with their packs of hounds at the Grey-Wethers. These downes look as if they were sowen with great stones, very thick, and in a dusky evening they look like a flock of sheep: from whence they take their name: one might fancy it to have been the scene where the Giants fought with great stones against the Gods. 'Twas here that our game began and the chase led us (at length) through the village of Aubury [Avebury], into the closes there: where I was wonderfully surprised at the sight of those vast stones, of which I had never heard before, as also at the mighty bank and graffe [ditch] about it. I observed in the enclosure some segments of rude circles made with these stones, whence I concluded they had been in the old time complete. I left my company a while, and then (steered by the cry of the hounds) I overtook the company and went with them to Kynnet, where was a good hunting dinner provided. Our repast was cheerful, which being ended, we remounted and beat over the downes with our greyhounds.

The poet, John Milton, was an ardent Cromwellian supporter. This portrait by an unknown artist in 1629 was painted shortly after his student days at Christ's College, Cambridge, when his beauty earned him the nickname of "The Lady". His famous poem, "Paradise Lost" focuses on "man's first disobedience" and the punishment which followed the eating of the forbidden fruit by Adam and Eve in the Garden of Eden.

That autumn a military Parliament or Army debating society was formed. The regiments elected delegates. These wrestled with one another and with their ideas long and earnestly for weeks. They set a secretary to record their proceedings; his records eventually found their way to an Oxford college, and the nineteenth century was presented with a window on the vivid scene. All sorts of new figures sprang up: Sexby, Rainborow, Wildman, Goffe the preaching colonel. These spoke with fervour and power: "The poorest he that is in England hath a life to live as the greatest he . . . " and "A man is not bound to a system of government which he hath not had any hand in setting over him." The ideas of these "Levellers", promoted by John Lilburne, and published in their *Agreement of the People*, were soon abreast of those of the Chartists in the nineteenth century—manhood suffrage at twenty-one, equal electoral districts, biennial Parliaments, and much more in prospect. Cromwell heard all this and brooded over it. He thought such claims would lead to anarchy. When orators raised the cheers of the assembly for the day when King, lords, and property would all be cast down together his thoughts wandered back to his landed estate. Apart from all this political talk, Cromwell had to think of discipline. He still held power. He used it without delay. He carried a resolution that the representatives should be sent back to their regiments. He replaced the General Council of the Army by a General Council of his officers.

Late in this autumn of 1647 Cromwell and Ireton came to the conclusion that even with the pay and indemnity settled they could not unite King and Army. They could not carry the troops. Religious notions which Pym and Hampden would have detested, a Republicanism which the Long Parliament had persistently eschewed, seethed in the conclaves of the soldiers. It remained only to find occasion to break the dangerous, glittering contacts which had been made. There was no difficulty. Royalist England still lived and breathed, watching for its chance. Parliament continued to formulate its solidly based political aims. The Scots, imbued with religious fervour and personal cupidity, hung on the Border. Charles, aware of these movements, began to look elsewhere. Under these stresses the combination between the defeated King and the victorious generals finally splintered.

In November the King, convinced that he would be murdered by the soldiery, whom their officers could no longer restrain, rode off in the night, and by easy stages made his way to Carisbrooke Castle, in the Isle of Wight. Here he dwelt for almost a year, defenceless, sacrosanct, a spiritual King, an ultimate sacrifice. There still resided in him a principle which must be either exploited or destroyed; but in England he no longer had the power to make a bargain. There remained the Scots. With them he signed a secret Engagement by which Royalism and Presbyterianism were to be allied. From this conjunction there shortly sprang the Second Civil War.

How near to the verge both Cromwell and Charles had pushed their effort to agree was meanwhile to be shown. The Army was about to revolt. A plot was made to arrest or murder the generals. Colonels talked of impeaching Cromwell. On December 15 the generals faced their men. Some of the regiments submitted at once; but those of Robert Lilburne and Thomas Harrison were mutinous. They appeared on the field with copies of the *Agreement of the People* stuck in their hats. Harrison's regiment was soon brought to submission but Lilburne's was not in so compliant a mood. Cromwell, seeing that persuasion alone would not avail here, rode along

Carisbrooke Castle, Isle of Wight, in which Charles I and his youngest children were imprisoned during 1648 and the spring of 1649. The house in the inner courtyard is now a museum.

the ranks, sharply ordering the men to tear the papers from their hats, and on finding no signs of obedience dashed among the mutineers with his sword drawn. There was something in his stern face and resolute action which compelled obedience. The instincts of military discipline revived, and the soldiers tore the papers from their hats and craved for mercy. The ringleaders were arrested, and three of them condemned to death. The three were, however, allowed to throw dice for their lives, and the loser was shot in the presence of his comrades. Thus at the cost of a single life discipline was restored, without which the Army would have dissolved into chaos.

The Second Civil War was very different in cause and conditions from the first. The King and his Prerogative were now seen, not as obstacles to Parliamentary right, but as the repository of ordinary English freedom. The Scots, formerly so exacting against the King, were now convinced that their peril lay in the opposite quarter. Wales was solid in its Royalism. London, formerly the main prop of Pym and Hampden, was now deeply inclined to a restoration of the royal authority. The apprentices, who had hounded Charles out of the capital, still rioted in their exuberance; but now they insulted the soldiery and cried "Long live the King!" Half the navy mutinied in Charles's favour. Most of the ships involved sailed off to Holland and entreated the Prince of Wales to become their admiral. All the Royalist forces, smarting, bleeding in pocket and in person, outraged in sentiment and social interest, were eager to draw the sword. Prisoner at Carisbrooke, Charles was now more truly King than he had ever been in the palmiest days of the personal rule.

The story of the Second Civil War is short and simple. King, Lords and Commons, landlords and merchants of the City and the countryside, bishops and presbyters, the Scottish army, the Welsh people, and the English fleet, all now turned against the New Model Army. The Army beat the lot. Fairfax, Cromwell, Ireton, were now once again united to their fierce warriors. A mere detachment sufficed to quell a general rising in Cornwall and the west. They broke the Royalist forces at Colchester; and here the Royalist commanders, Lucas and Lisle, contrary to all previous conventions,

The philosopher Hobbes's book Leviathan, *warned of the danger of tyrannical authority but said that without government life would be "nasty, brutish and short". Leviathan was a monster with one head; it represented all the wishes of the people.*

were by Fairfax's order shot outside the walls after the surrender. Cromwell, having subdued the Welsh rising, moved swiftly to the north, picked up his forces and fell on the Scottish army as it was marching through Lancashire. The invaders were cut off, caught, and destroyed at Preston. The fleet could do little against this all-mastering, furious army which stalked the land in rags, almost barefoot, but with bright armour, sharp swords, and sublime conviction of its wrongheaded mission.

By the end of 1648 all was over. Cromwell was Dictator. The Royalists were crushed; Parliament was a tool; the Constitution was a figment; the Scots were rebuffed, the Welsh back in their mountains; the fleet was reorganised, London overawed. King Charles, at Carisbrooke Castle, was left to pay the bill. It was mortal.

We must not be led into regarding this triumph of the Ironsides and of Cromwell as a kind of victory for democracy and the Parliamentary system. It was the triumph of some twenty thousand military fanatics over all that England has ever willed or ever wished. Long years and unceasing irritations were required to reverse it. Thus the struggle, in which we have in these days so much sympathy, begun to bring about a constitutional and limited monarchy, had led only to the autocracy of the sword.

Plainly the fruit of the victory that could most easily be gathered was the head of the King. True, he had never moved from Carisbrooke, but was he not the pivot upon which all public opinion turned? At a moment of great hesitancy in matters of government, when everything was fluid and uncertain, here was a supreme act upon which the Army could unite. The execution of Charles Stuart, "the Man of Blood", could alone satisfy the soldiers and enable their leaders to hold their obedience.

One stormy evening, with the rain beating down, it was noticed that many boat-loads of Ironside soldiery were being rowed across the Solent and landed in the Isle of Wight. The King's friends urged flight, but Charles, who was deep in new and hopeful negotiations with Parliament, had enough confidence in the strength of his position to reject the opportunity. It was his last. A few days later he was brought to the mainland and confined in Hurst Castle. Here the new severities of the Second Civil War marked the rules to which he was subjected. With scarcely a personal attendant, he found himself shut in the candleless gloom of a small tower prison. There was still a further interlude of negotiations; they were nothing but parleyings with a doomed man. After some delay he was during the Christmas season brought towards London. At first he feared that Colonel Harrison, the officer who fetched him, would be his assassin; but nothing of the kind was intended. The Army meant to have his blood in the manner which would most effectively vindicate their power and their faith. Cromwell, who had nothing else to give his burning legions, could at least present them with an awful and all-dominating scene of expiation. To Colonel Harrison, one evening, on the journey to the capital, Charles put a blunt question: "Are you come to murder me?" "It is not true, sir," said the Colonel. "The law is equally bound to great and small."

Charles slept in peace. By law he was inviolable.

It must have been a vivid contrast with the privations of Hurst Castle when the King rested for nearly a week at Windsor. Here all again was respect and ceremony. A nucleus of the staff and household were in attendance. The King dined every night in ancient state, served on the knee.

The Parliamentary officers joined him at table, saluted, and quitted him with the deepest bows. A strange interlude! But now forward to London; "Will Your Majesty graciously be pleased to set forth?"

London lay locked under the guard of the Army. Some Parliamentary timeserver had stood by Colonel Pride, when the members sought to take their seats in the House of Commons, and had ticked off all those not likely to obey the Army's will. Forty-five members who tried to enter were arrested, and out of a total of over five hundred, three hundred did not take their seats again. This was "Pride's Purge".

The great trial of "the Man of Blood" was to be presented to the nation and to the world. English law and precedent were scoured from the most remote times, but no sanction or even cover for such a proceeding could be found. The slaying of princes had many examples: Edward II at Berkeley Castle, Richard II at Pontefract, had met terrible fates; but these were deeds disavowed by authority, covered at the time by mystery or the plea of natural causes. Here the victorious Army meant to teach the English people that henceforward they must obey; and Cromwell now saw in the King's slaughter his only chance of supremacy and survival. In vain did Fairfax point out that the stroke which killed the captive King would make his son the free possessor of all his rights.

No English jurist could be found to frame the indictment or invent the tribunal. A Dutch lawyer, Isaac Dorislaus, who had long lived in England, was able to deck what was to be done in the trappings of antiquity. The language of the order convening the court had no contact with English history; it looks back to the classical age, when the ruin of tyrants was decreed by the Senate or the Praetorian Guard.

An ordinance passed by the docile remnant of the Commons created a court of a hundred and thirty-five Commissioners, of whom barely sixty would serve, to try the King. The carpenters fitted Westminster Hall for its most memorable scene. This was not only the killing of a king, but the killing of a king who at that time represented the will and the traditions of almost the whole British nation.

The more detail in which the famous trial has been described the greater is the sense of drama. The King, basing himself upon the law and Constitution he had exploited in his years of prosperity, confronted his enemies with an unbreakable defence. He eyed his judges "with unaffected scorn". He refused to acknowledge the tribunal. To him it was a monstrous illegality. The overwhelming sympathy of the great concourse gathered in Westminster Hall was with the King. When, on the afternoon of the final sitting, after being refused leave to speak, he was conducted from the Hall, it was amid a low, intense murmur of "God save the King". But the soldiers, primed by their corporals, and themselves in high resolve, shouted, "Justice! Justice! Execution! Execution!"

Personal dignity and convenience were consulted to the last. Every facility was accorded the King to settle his temporal affairs and to receive the consolations of religion. This was not a butchery, but a ceremony, a sacrifice. On the morning of January 30, 1649, Charles was conducted from St James's, to Whitehall. Snow fell, and he had put on his warm under-clothes. He walked briskly amid the Ironside guard, saying, "Step out now," across the half-mile which led him to the Banqueting House. There, no attempt was made to interfere with his wishes so far as they did not conflict

Charles I did not want the crowds who flocked to his execution to mistake his possible trembling from cold as a sign of fear. He therefore wore two shirts. This one can still be seen in Carisbrooke Castle Museum in the Isle of Wight. Personally brave, Charles was unprepossessing in appearance, and was only about 5'4" tall. His wife, Henrietta Maria, was also tiny.

with what had been resolved. But most of those who had signed the death warrant were aghast at the deed of which they were to bear the weight, and the ultimate vengeance. Cromwell had found great difficulty in holding together enough of his signatories. Fairfax, still commander in chief, was outraged. He had to be mastered. Ireton and Harrison remained in the building with the doomed King.

At one o'clock in the afternoon Charles was informed that his hour had come. He walked through a window of the Banqueting House onto the scaffold. Masses of soldiers, many ranks deep, held an immense multitude afar. The King looked with a disdainful smile upon the cords and pulleys which had been prepared to fasten him down. He was allowed to speak as he chose. His voice could not reach beyond the troops; he therefore spoke to those who gathered on the scaffold. He said that "he died a good Christian, he had forgiven all the world, yea, chiefly those who had caused his death (naming none). He wished their repentance and that they might take the right way to the peace of the kingdom, which was not by way of conquest. He did not believe the happiness of people lay in sharing government, subject and sovereign being clean different. And if he would have given way to an arbitrary Government and to have all laws changed according to the sword he need not have suffered, and so he said he was a martyr to the people."

He resigned himself to death, and assisted the executioner in arranging his hair under a small white satin cap. He laid himself upon the block, and upon his own signal his head was struck off at a single stroke. His severed head was shown to the people, and someone in the crowd cried, "This is the head of a traitor!"

An incalculable multitude had streamed to the spot, swayed by intense though inarticulate emotions. When they saw the severed head "there was such a groan by the thousands then present" wrote a contemporary diarist, "as I never heard before and desire I may never hear again."

A strange destiny had engulfed this King of England. None had resisted with more untimely stubbornness the movement of his age. He had been in his heyday the convinced opponent of all we now call our Parliamentary liberties. Yet as misfortunes crowded upon him he increasingly became the physical embodiment of the liberties and traditions of England. His mistakes and wrong deeds had arisen not so much from personal cravings for arbitrary power as from the conception of kingship to which he was born,

Charles I's death warrant carried as much civil authority as the Republic could amass. Cromwell's signature on this official-looking document is third from the left.

and which had long been the settled custom of the land. In the end he stood against the Army which had destroyed all Parliamentary government, and was about to plunge England in a tyranny at once more irresistible and more petty than any seen before or since. He did not flinch in any respect from the causes in which he believed. He cannot be claimed as the defender of English liberties, nor wholly of the English Church, but nonetheless he died for them, and by his death preserved them not only to his son and heir, but to our own day.

CHAPTER 9

THE ENGLISH REPUBLIC

THE ENGLISH REPUBLIC, OR COMMONWEALTH, had come into existence even before the execution of the King. On January 4, 1649, the handful of Members of the House of Commons who served the purposes of Cromwell and the Ironsides resolved "that the Commons of England in Parliament assembled, being chosen by and representing the people, have the supreme power in this nation." A new seal was presented, bearing on one side a map of England and Ireland and on the other a picture of the House of Commons, with the inscription, "In the first year of freedom, by God's blessing restored". A statue of Charles I was thrown down, and on the pedestal were inscribed the words, "Exit the tyrant, the last of the Kings." On February 5 it was declared that the House of Lords "is useless and dangerous and ought to be abolished." Thereafter it ceased to meet. Vengeance was wrought upon a number of peers taken prisoner, and Lords Hamilton and Holland, statesmen of high intellectual qualities and long record, were beheaded.

The Levellers advocated major social changes in the 1640s such as universal male suffrage, parliamentary democracy and religious tolerance. This title page from their Manifesto draws a grim prophetic warning; the background contains both fire and the sword.

The country was now to be governed by a Council of State chosen annually by Parliament. Its forty-one members included peers, judges, and Members of Parliament, among them most of the principal regicides. It was found to be fearless, diligent, and incorrupt. The judiciary hung for a time in the balance. Six of the twelve judges refused to continue, but the rest agreed to serve the Commonwealth. The accession of the lawyers to the new regime was deemed essential by the highly conservative elements at the head of the Army, for the defence of privilege and property against the assaults of the Levellers, agitators, and extremists.

It was essential to divide and disperse the Army, and Cromwell was willing to lead the larger part of it to a war of retribution in the name of the Lord Jehovah against the idolatrous and bloodstained Papists of Ireland. It was thought that an enterprise of this character would enlist the fanaticism of the rank and file. Lots were drawn which regiments should go to Ireland, and were drawn again and again until only the regiments in which the Levellers were strongest were cast. At this a pamphlet on *England's New Chains* spread through the Army. Mutinies broke out. Many hundreds of veteran soldiers appeared in bands in support of "the sovereignty of the people", manhood suffrage, and annual Parliaments.

This mood was not confined to the soldiers. The idea of equal rights in property as well as in citizenship was boldly announced by a group led by Gerard Winstanley, which came to be known as "the Diggers". Numbers

During the Protectorate the royal family found refuge with Protestants in the Netherlands. Here, in the lively and informal atmosphere of the Dutch Republic, the future Charles II is seen dancing with his aunt, the "Winter Queen", Elizabeth of Bohemia.

Cromwell was made Lord Lieutenant of Ireland on August 1, 1649. The broadsheet from which this picture is taken lists the one hundred and forty victories obtained by the Parliamentary army during the first eight months of his appointment.

of persons appeared upon the common lands in Surrey and prepared to cultivate them on a communal basis. These "Diggers" claimed that the whole earth was a "common treasury" and that the common land should be for all. They argued further that the beheaded King traced his right to William the Conqueror, with whom a crowd of nobles and adventurers had come into England, robbing by force the mass of the people of their ancient rights in Saxon days. The rulers of the Commonwealth regarded all this as dangerous and subversive nonsense.

No one was more shocked than Cromwell. He cared almost as much for private property as for religious liberty. "A nobleman, a gentleman, a yeoman," he said, "that is a good interest of the land and a great one." The Council of State chased the would-be cultivators off the common land, and hunted the mutinous officers and soldiers to death without mercy. Cromwell again quelled a mutiny in person, and by his orders Trooper William Thompson, a follower of Lilburne, was shot in an Oxfordshire churchyard. His opinions and his constancy have led some to crown him as "the first martyr of democracy". Cromwell also discharged from the Army, without their arrears of pay, all men who would not volunteer for the Irish war. Nominated by the Council as commander, he invested his mission not only with a martial but with a priestly aspect. He joined the Puritan divines in preaching a holy war upon the Irish. This was done as part of a profound calculated policy in the face of military and social dangers which, if not strangled, would have opened a new ferocious and measureless social war in England.

Cromwell's campaign of 1649 in Ireland was equally cold-blooded, and equally imbued with those Old Testament sentiments which dominated the minds of the Puritans. The spirit and peril of the Irish race might have prompted them to unite upon Catholic toleration and monarchy, and on this the Catholics could have made a firm alliance with the Protestant Royalists, who, under the Marquis of Ormonde, had an organised army of twelve thousand men. But the arrival of the Papal Nuncio had aggravated the many forces of incoherence and strife.

Ormonde's army was grievously weakened before Cromwell landed. He had already in 1647 ceded Dublin to a Parliamentary general; but he had later occupied the towns of Drogheda and Wexford and was resolved to defend them. Upon these Cromwell marched with his ten thousand veteran troops. Ormonde hoped that Cromwell would break his teeth upon a long siege of Drogheda, in which he placed a garrison of three thousand men, comprising the flower of the Irish Royalists, and English volunteers. Cromwell saw that the destruction of these men would not only ruin Ormonde's military power, but spread a helpful terror throughout the island. He therefore resolved upon a deed of frightfulness.

Having unsuccessfully summoned the garrison to surrender, he breached the ramparts with his cannon, and at the third assault, which he led himself, stormed the town. There followed a massacre so all-effacing as to startle even the opinion of those fierce times. All were put to the sword and the corpses were carefully ransacked for valuables. The ferreting out and slaughter of those in hiding lasted till the third day.

In Oliver's smoky soul there were some misgivings. He writes of the "remorse and regret" which are inseparable from such crimes. While brazening them out, he offers diverse excuses. By a terrifying example he believed that he had saved far greater bloodshed. But this did not prove true. The war continued in squalid, murderous fashion for two years after he had left Ireland. In his hatred of Popery he sought to identify the Royalist garrison of Drogheda with the Roman Catholic Irish peasantry who had massacred the Protestant landlords in 1641. He ought to have known that not one of them had the slightest connection with that eight-year-old horror.

Even Ireland itself offered a tolerable way of life to Protestants and Catholics alike. Upon these Cromwell's record was a lasting bane. By an uncompleted process of terror, by an iniquitous land settlement, by the virtual proscription of the Catholic religion, by the bloody deeds already described, he cut new gulfs between the nations and the creeds. The Irish across three hundred years, have used as their keenest expression of hatred, "The curse of Cromwell on you", and the consequences of Cromwell's merciless rule in Ireland have distressed and distracted English politics down even to the present day.

At the moment when the axe severed the head of King Charles I from his body, his eldest son became, in the opinion of most of his subjects and of Europe, King Charles II. Within the next six days, as soon as horsemen could bear the tidings northward, the Scottish Estates proclaimed him King of Great Britain, France, and Ireland. Their representatives in London demanded his recognition. The oligarchs who called themselves "Parliament" thereupon expelled the envoys, declaring that they had "laid the grounds of a new and bloody war". Charles II sheltered at The Hague. The predominant settlement in Holland was friendly to him, and shocked by his father's execution. Dorislaus, the Dutch lawyer who had been so helpful in drawing up the regicide tribunal, was murdered by Scottish Royalists as he sat at dinner—a crime which was widely applauded.

Montrose, when his army fell to pieces, had on the advice of the late King quitted Scotland, believing at first that the Whitehall execution robbed his life of all purpose. His spirit now was revived by a priest who preached to him a duty of revenge. With a handful of followers he landed in Caithness, was defeated by the Government forces and betrayed for a paltry bribe into their power. He was dragged through many Scottish towns, and hanged at

The Siege of Drogheda and the slaughter of its residents not only deterred the Irish from rebellion but also wiped out many possible recruits for the army. Oliver Cromwell's drastic solution produced immediate results, but it left a legacy of lasting hatred.

THE ENGLISH REPUBLIC

THE ENGLISH REPUBLIC, or Commonwealth as it became known, was never a republic in the later, strictly anti-royalist, sense. Cromwell himself was ranked as a prince, and his children were given the status of dukes. Nonetheless, religious austerity imposed severe restrictions as a reaction against earlier aristocratic extravagance: London's theatres were closed in 1642, there was no Lord Mayor's Show in 1643, and in 1644 even Christmas celebrations were banned. With some reason, therefore, foreign countries saw the administration as unashamedly Bible-thumping and repressive.

But the Commonwealth was not entirely austere. It proved impracticable, for example, to forbid football or many other outdoor or indoor games. Cromwell ordered wines of quality and also organised public concerts as an entertainment: if music was felt to profane the Sabbath, it still had a place as a secular art. So, while church organ pipes were sometimes destroyed and organ cases given to the poor as firewood, much fine music was published during the years of the Commonwealth.

Cromwell's efficient New Model Army, which had won the Civil War, was understandably more interested in serious radical debate than in music, but the discussions at its headquarters in Putney ranged widely over political and social issues as well as religion. And they came up with radical decisions, too—as, for example, when a group known as the Diggers squatted on manorial common lands, felled feudal trees, and had to be forcibly restrained. A bigger, though less extreme group, the Levellers, threatening mutiny over arrears in army pay, were ruthlessly put down. "Conservative" thinking began with Cromwell himself, who was to be described by a later historian as "the most typical Englishman of all time".

THE PUTNEY DEBATES *were organised within the New Model Army in 1647 in order to thrash out matters of government. Their proposals, later published as* The Agreement of the People *demanded popular government against the tyranny of the King, Parliament and army generals. There were differences of opinion at Putney, however, with the Levellers demanding the vote for every man, regardless of wealth or position. In 1649, however, the Levellers were crushed, and never thereafter recovered their former importance. In the picture above, the young Commander in Chief, Sir Thomas Fairfax, presides over the Debates. He distrusted the Levellers and took his own stand on matters of political importance.*

QUAKERS BELIEVED IN EQUALITY, *and allowed women to preach three centuries before the Church of England did. Founded in 1650 by George Fox, the Quakers maintained that any person could communicate with God without an intermediary—they were a non-violent, classless and anti-ritualistic sect. In the twentieth century the Quakers are known as the Religious Society of Friends.*

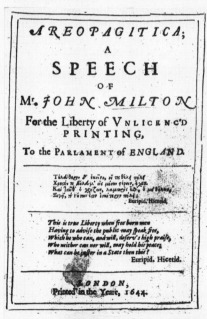

THE BRUTALITY OF CROMWELL'S IRISH POLICY *became evident with his attack on Drogheda, (above) and in the subsequent massacre of all its inhabitants. Cromwell believed that harsh treatment was tactically important in maintaining power, and his victories in Ireland prevented Charles I's son, who later became Charles II, from using the country as a base from which to attack England. He made grievances fester by transferring land from Irish rebels to English soldiers.*

THE NEW MODEL ARMY, *formed by Cromwell in 1645, was the ultimate victor of the Civil War, and the fundamental authority of the Republic was to rest on military might. Unsurprisingly, the English have hated standing armies ever since. The helmet shown below was worn by a trooper in the New Model Army.*

IN JOHN MILTON'S ADDRESS *to Parliament in 1644, the Greek title of which referred to the classical Athenian belief in free speech, he attacked the censorship laws of 1643, limiting the freedom of the press. He argued that censorship had been practised chiefly by the Catholics, whom Parliament detested.*

CROMWELL BECAME MEMBER OF PARLIAMENT *for Huntingdon in 1628. His statue now stands outside the House of Commons. He was no great orator and lived the life of a country landowner until the outbreak of the Civil War revealed his genius for organisation.*

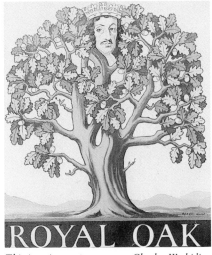

This inn sign commemorates Charles II's hiding place in an oak tree at Boscobel, in Shropshire. A descendant of the original tree survives today and thousands of pubs throughout Britain have been named "The Royal Oak".

Edinburgh on a specially high gallows amid an immense agitated concourse. Yet at the same time that Argyll and the Covenanters inflicted this savage punishment upon an unorthodox Royalist they themselves prepared for war with England in the cause of monarchy and entered into urgent treaty with the new King.

Hard courses were laid before Charles II. If, said the Scottish government, you will embrace the Covenant, all Scotland will march with you into England, where Presbyterians and Royalists alike will join to re-establish the sacred majesty of the Crown against Republicans and regicides. Here at the darkest moment was the proclamation of the continuance of the monarchy. But the price was extortionate and deadly. Charles II must bind himself to destroy the episcopacy and enforce upon England a religious system odious to all who had fought for his father. He was versed in the religious and political controversies of the times. He hesitated long before taking the grim decision of selling his soul to the Devil, as he conceived it, for the interest of the Crown and betraying the cause to save its life.

The fulfilment of the contract was as harsh as the signing. On the ship before the King landed in Scotland the most precise guarantees were extracted. When the King looked out from the windows of the house in which he was lodged at Aberdeen a grisly object met his view. It was the shrivelled hand of Montrose, his devoted servant and friend, nailed to the wall. He found himself virtually a prisoner in the hands of those who had besought him to be their sovereign. He listened to endless sermons, admonitions, and objurgations. We may admire as polished flint the convictions of the Scots government and its divines, but one must be thankful never to have been brought into contact with any of them.

It was the essence of Scottish policy to separate their new war with England from the invasion which had so lamentably failed at Preston two years before and a purge of the army stripped it of three or four thousand of its most experienced officers and men, their places filled with "ministers' sons, clerks, and such other sanctified creatures, who hardly ever saw or heard of any sword but that of the spirit". The unhappy young King was forced, by the need to fight and the desire to win, to issue a declaration in which he desired to be "deeply humbled before God because of his father's opposition to the Solemn League and Covenant; and because his mother had been guilty of idolatry". Charles wondered whether he would dare to look his mother in the face again. On this strange foundation a large Scottish army gathered on the Border.

The menace in the north brought Cromwell back from Ireland. Fairfax, thoroughly estranged from his former colleagues, refused to invade Scotland, and the Council of State at last appointed Cromwell commander in chief in form as he had long been in fact. In his Ironside troops, fresh from their Irish slaughters, he grasped a heavy, sharp and reeking sword. In the Lowlands, the armies manoeuvred against each other. David Leslie was no mean opponent, and his army far more numerous. Cromwell was forced back upon Dunbar, dependent on wind and weather for his daily bread. He might still escape south by sea, picking up supplies at the east coast ports. But this was no culmination to a career of unbroken success.

In the Scottish camp there were two opinions. The first, held by Leslie, was for letting Cromwell go. The second was urged by the six leading ministers of religion; now was the time to wreak the Lord's vengeance upon those guilty ones who would bring spiritual anarchy into the Reformed Church. Bigotry prevailed over strategy. The pious Scottish army closed down upon Cromwell and his saints to prevent their embarkation. Both sides confidently appealed to Jehovah; and the Most High, finding so little to choose between them in faith and zeal, must have allowed purely military factors to prevail. At the first grey light Cromwell, feinting with his right wing, attacked heavily on the left. "Now," he exclaimed, as the sun rose over the sea behind him, "let God arise and let his enemies be scattered." The Scots, finding their right turned, fled, leaving three thousand dead on the field. Nine thousand were prisoners in Oliver's hungry camp, and the army of the Presbyters was broken.

The disaster carried Scots policy out of the trammels of dogma. National safety became the cry. The King was crowned at Scone. The plan of marching south, leaving Cromwell behind in Edinburgh, which he had occupied, and rousing the Royalist forces in England, captivated the majority of the Scots Council.

The inscription above this portrait of Charlotte, Lady Derby, reads, in part: "celebrated for her defences of Lathom House, compelled to surrender Isle of Man". The island was the last Royalist stronghold. Lady Derby's portrait can be seen in the National Portrait Gallery.

A Scottish army now invaded England in 1651 upon a Royalist rather than a Presbyterian enterprise. It is proof of Cromwell's political and military sagacity that he allowed them to pass. His intention was to cut them off from their supplies. The event justified his calculation. The English Royalists, bled white, were found incapable of any fresh response; most of their active leaders had already been executed. Charles II marched in a chilling silence at the head of his troops. But Cromwell could now follow easily upon his track, and his concentration of all the forces of the Commonwealth against the northern invaders was masterly. On his day of fate, September 3, sixteen thousand Scots were brought to battle at Worcester, not only by the twenty thousand veterans of the New Model Army, but by the English militia, who rallied in large numbers against this fresh inroad of the hated and interfering Scots. Leslie, who commanded, lingered in the city with the Scottish cavalry till the day was lost. Charles acquitted himself with distinction. He rode along the regiments in the thick of the fighting, encouraging them in their duty. The struggle was one of the stiffest contests of the civil wars, but it was forlorn, and the Scots and their Royalist comrades were destroyed as a military force. Few returned to Scotland.

To Cromwell this was "the crowning mercy". To Charles II it afforded the most romantic adventure of his life. He escaped with difficulty from the stricken field; a thousand pounds was set upon his head. The land was scoured for him. He hid for a whole day in the famous oak tree at Boscobel, while his pursuers passed by. On every side were men who would have rejoiced to win the price of catching him. But also on every side were friends, secret, silent, unflinching. Nearly fifty persons recognised him, and thus became privy to his escape and liable to grave penalties. The magic of the words "the King, our master", cast its spell upon all classes. "The King is near you and in great distress: can you help us to a boat?" "Is he well?" "Yes." "God be blessed." This was the temper of all who were trusted with or discovered the secret.

Thus after six weeks of desperate peril did the King find himself again in exile. His most faithful surviving supporter, Lord Derby, paid the last forfeit of loyalty on the scaffold. Lady Derby still hoped to keep the royal standard flying in the Isle of Man, the independence of which the Derbys had proclaimed; but Parliamentary ideas and later Parliamentary troops his pricks of conscience about nomination instead of election: "If it were a time to compare your standing with those that have been called by the suffrages of the people, who can tell how soon God may fit the people for such a thing, and none can desire it more than I."

The political behaviour of the Saints was a sad disappointment to their convoker. With breathtaking speed they sought to disestablish the Church and abolish tithes without providing any livelihood for the clergy. In a single day's debate they abolished the Court of Chancery. They reformed taxation in a manner which seemed to weaken the security for the soldiers' pay. This was decisive. The Army bristled. Cromwell saw the Saints as a set of dangerous fools. He afterwards referred to his action in convening them as "a story of my own weakness and folly". The Army leaders, wishing to avoid the scandal of another forcible ejection, persuaded or compelled the more moderate Saints to get up very early one morning before the others were awake and pass a resolution yielding back their power to the Lord General.

Cromwell's high place, for all its apparent strength, depended on the precarious balance of Parliament and Army. He could always use the Army against Parliament; but without a Parliament he felt himself very much alone with the Army. The Army leaders were also conscious of the gulf of military rank and social class which separated them from their formidable rank and file. They too held their position by being the champions of the interests and the doctrines of the soldiery. They must find something to fight against or they would be needed no longer. Thus the whole cluster of these serious, practical, and hitherto triumphant revolutionaries needed to set up a Parliament, if only to have something to pull down. Ireton had died in Ireland, but the Yorkshireman John Lambert and other Army leaders of various ranks drew up an "Instrument of Government", which was in fact the first and last written English Constitution. The executive office of Lord Protector conferred upon Cromwell was checked and balanced by a Council of State, nominated for life, consisting of seven Army leaders and eight civilians. A single Chamber was also set up, elected upon a new

"English Shipping with Cargo on a Quay" by the Dutch artist, Jacob Knyff, depicts a typical port scene with a rowing boat transporting sailors from ship to shore. The mercantile rivalry between the Dutch and the British was soon to lead to naval warfare.

property qualification in the country. The old one had been the possession of a forty-shilling-a-year freehold; the new one was the ownership of personal estate with a capital value of two hundred pounds. All those who had fought against Parliament were disqualified from voting. Cromwell gratefully accepted the Instrument and assumed the title of Lord Protector.

But once again all went wrong with the Parliament. It no sooner met in September 1654 than it was seen to contain a fierce and lively Republican group, which, without the slightest gratitude to the Army leaders or to the Protector, set themselves to tear the new Constitution to pieces. Cromwell at once excluded the Republicans from the House. But even then the remaining Parliamentary majority sought to limit the degree of religious toleration guaranteed by the Instrument, to restrict the Lord Protector's control of the Army, and to reduce both its size and pay. This was carrying the farce too far. At the earliest moment allowed by the Instrument Cromwell dissolved the Commons. Now he was back again at the old and ever-recurring problem. "I am as much for government by consent as any man," he told a critical Republican. "But"—pertinent inquiry—"where shall we find consent?"

Cromwell, although crafty and ruthless as occasion claimed, was at all times a reluctant dictator. He recognised and deplored the arbitrary character of his own rule, but he had no difficulty in persuading himself that his authority sprang both from Above and below. Was he not the new Moses, the chosen Protector of the people of God, commanded to lead them into the Promised Land, if that could indeed be found?

Cromwell only desired personal power in order to have things settled in accord with his vision, not of himself or his fame but of the England of his youthful dreams. He was a giant laggard from the Elizabethan age, still fighting the Spanish Armada, ever ardent to lead his Ironside redcoats against the stakes and faggots of some Grand Inquisitor or the idolatrous superstitions of an Italian Pope. Were these not now ripe for the sickle? In vain did John Thurloe, the able and devoted Secretary to the Council of State, point out that Spain was in decay, and that in the ever-growing power of the united France which Richelieu and Mazarin had welded lay the menace of the future. None of this was apparent to the Master.

Cromwell's successes and failures in foreign policy bore consequences throughout the reign of Charles II. He sought to advance the world interests of Protestantism and the particular needs of British commerce and shipping. In 1654 he ended the sea war against the Dutch which had begun two years earlier. He made ardent proposals for an alliance between England and Holland, which should form the basis of a Protestant League. The Dutch leaders were content to wind up with the least cost to their trading prospects a war in which they knew they were beaten.

Conflict between France and Spain was meanwhile proceeding. In spite of grave arguments to the contrary, Cromwell sent a naval expedition to the West Indies in September 1654 and Jamaica was occupied. This act of aggression led slowly but inevitably to war between England and Spain, and a consequent alliance between England and France. In June 1658 six thousand veteran English soldiers in Flanders under Marshal Turenne defeated the Spaniards at the Battle of the Dunes and helped to capture the port of Dunkirk. The blockade of the Spanish coasts disclosed the strength of Britain's sea power, and one of Blake's captains destroyed a treasure fleet off Tenerife. Cromwell's imperial eye rested long upon Gibraltar. He examined schemes for capturing the marvellous rock. This was reserved for the days of Marlborough, but England retained Jamaica and Dunkirk.

Cromwell found no difficulty in reconciling the predatory aims of the Spanish war with his exertions for a European Protestant League. He was ever ready to strike against the religious persecution of Protestants abroad. When in 1655 he heard that a Protestant sect in the valleys north of Piedmont called the Vaudois were being oppressed and massacred by order of the Duke of Savoy he suspended his negotiations with France and threatened to send the fleet against the Savoyard port of Nice. In the main however Cromwell's foreign policy was more successful in helping British trade and shipping than in checking or reversing the Counter-Reformation. The Mediterranean and Channel were cleared of pirates, foreign trade expanded and the whole world learnt to respect British sea power.

At home military dictatorship had supervened. A Royalist colonel named Penruddock managed to capture Salisbury in March 1655. The rising was easily suppressed. But the outbreak, combined with the discovery by Thurloe, who directed the highly efficient secret service, of a number of abortive plots, convinced the Protector of great danger. "The people," Cromwell had told Parliament, "will prefer their safety to their passions and their real security to forms." He now proceeded to divide England and Wales into eleven districts, over each of which a major general was placed, with the command of a troop of horse and a reorganised militia. The major generals were given three functions—police and public order, the collection of special taxes upon acknowledged Royalists, and the strict enforcement of Puritan morality. For some months they addressed themselves with zeal to their task.

None dared withstand the major generals; but the war with Spain was

THE COMPLEAT ANGLER

Many people during the Protectorate continued their lives and occupations in ignorance of political events. Izaak Walton wrote his popular classic, The Compleat Angler, *in 1653 and lived to be eighty-six, which is a good recommendation for his hobby. In the following extract from his book, he discourses on the art of angling.*

O Sir, doubt not but that angling is an art. Is it not an art to deceive a trout with an artificial fly? a trout that is more sharp-sighted than any hawk you have named, and more watchful and timorous than your high-mettled merlin is bold! and yet I doubt not to catch a brace or two tomorrow for a friend's breakfast. Doubt not, therefore, sir, but that angling is an art, and an art worth learning; the question is rather, whether you be capable of learning it? for angling is somewhat like poetry, men are to be born so—I mean with inclination to it, though both may be heightened by discourse and practise; but he that hopes to be a good angler must not only bring an inquiring, searching, observing wit, but he must bring a large measure of hope and patience, and a love and propensity to the art itself; but having once got and practised it, then doubt not but angling will prove to be so pleasant that it will prove to be like virtue, a reward to itself.

The Compleat Angler or the Contemplative man's Recreation.

costly and the taxes insufficient. Like Charles I, Cromwell was driven again to summon a Parliament. The major generals assured him of their ability to pack a compliant House. But Levellers, Republicans and Royalists were able to exploit the discontent against the military dictatorship, and a large number of members who were known enemies of the Protector were returned. By a strained use of a clause in the Instrument of Government Cromwell managed to exclude a hundred of his opponents from the House, while another fifty or sixty voluntarily withdrew in protest. Even after this purge his attempt to obtain a confirmation of the local rule of the major generals met with such vehement opposition that he was compelled to do without it. Indeed, many of the remaining members "were so highly incensed against the arbitrary acting of the major generals" that they "searched greedily for any powers that will be ruled and limited by law".

It was at this stage that a group of lawyers and gentry decided to offer Cromwell the Crown. "The title of Protector," said one of them, "is not limited by any rule or law; the title of King is." Thus the "Humble Petition and Advice" in 1657 which embodied the proposed Constitution provided not only for the restoration of kingship, but also for the firm re-establishment of Parliament, including a nominated Upper House and a substantial reduction in the powers of the Council of State. Cromwell was not unattracted by the idea of becoming King. But the Army leaders and still more the soldiers showed at once their inveterate hostility to the trappings of monarchy, and Cromwell had to content himself with the right to nominate his successor to the Protectoral throne. In May 1657 he accepted the main provisions of the new Constitution without the title of King.

The Republicans foresaw that this virtual revival of the monarchy opened the way for a Stuart restoration. The terms of the "Humble Petition" allowed the members whom Cromwell had excluded to return to Westminster, while his ablest supporters were taken away to fill the new Upper House. The Republicans could therefore act both inside and outside Parliament against the new regime. Cromwell, in the belief that a hostile design was on foot against him, suddenly, in January 1658, dissolved the most friendly Parliament which he had ever had. He ended his speech of dissolution with the words, "Let God judge between you and me." "Amen," answered the unrepentant Republicans.

The maintenance of all privilege and authority in their own hands at home and a policy of aggression and conquest abroad absorbed the main energies of Cromwell and his Council. They were singularly barren in social legislation. Their treatment of the Poor Law has been called "harshness coupled with failure". Much better conditions were established under the personal rule of Charles I between 1629 and 1640 than under those who claimed to rule in the name of God. They considered that poverty should be punished rather than relieved.

The Puritans concerned themselves actively with the repression of vice. All betting and gambling were forbidden. In 1650 a law was passed making adultery punishable by death, a ferocity mitigated by the fact that nothing would convince the juries of the guilt of the accused. Great numbers of alehouses were closed. Swearing was an offence punishable by a graduated scale of fines: a duke paid thirty shillings for his first offence, a baron twenty shillings, and a squire ten shillings. Common people could relieve their feelings at three shillings and fourpence. Not much was allowed for their money; one man was fined for saying "Upon my life". The feast days of the Church, regarded as superstitious indulgences, were replaced by a monthly fast day. Christmas excited the most fervent hostility of these fanatics. Soldiers were sent round London on Christmas Day to enter private houses without warrants and seize meat cooking in all kitchens. Everywhere was prying and spying.

All over the country the maypoles were hewn down, lest old village dances around them should lead to immorality or at least to levity. Walking abroad on the Sabbath, except to go to church, was punished. Bear-baiting and cock-fighting were effectually ended by shooting the bears and wringing the necks of the cocks. All forms of athletic sports were banned, and laws sought to remove all ornaments from male and female attire.

Behind all this apparatus of cant and malignity stood an army of disciplined sectarians, against whom none could make head. Their generals and colonels soon engrossed to themselves rich landed estates carved out of the Crown lands: Fleetwood became the owner of Woodstock Manor, Lambert of Wimbledon, Okey of Ampthill, and Pride of Nonesuch. To the mass of the nation however, the rule of Cromwell manifested itself in the form of numberless and miserable petty tyrannies, and thus became hated as no government has ever been hated in England before or since. The old kings might have harried the nobles and taxed the rich; but here were personages who had climbed up by lawless, bloody violations, and presumed to order the life and habits of every village and to shift custom from the channels which it had cut in the flow of centuries. What wonder that men dreamt fondly of what they called the good old times and yearned for the day when "the King shall enjoy his own again"?

Religious persecution was a repellent characteristic of Cromwell's rule. The picture above shows a Quaker having his tongue bored through with a hot iron.

The repulsive features fade from the picture and are replaced by colour and even charm as the summit of power is reached. We see the Lord Protector in his glory, the champion of Protestantism, the arbiter of Europe, the patron of learning and the arts. We feel the dignity of his bearing to all men, and his tenderness towards young people. We feel his passion for England. No one can remain unconscious of his desire to find a moral basis for his power, or of his sense of a responsibility to his country and his God. Although Cromwell easily convinced himself that he had been chosen the Supreme Ruler of the State, he was ever ready to share his power with others, provided of course that they agreed with him. But neither his fondlings nor his purgings induced his Parliaments to do his will. Again and again he was forced to use or threaten the power of the sword, and the rule which he sought to make a constitutional alternative to absolutism or anarchy became in practice a military autocracy.

Nevertheless the dictatorship of Cromwell differed in many ways from modern patterns. Although the press was gagged and the Royalists ill-used, although judges were intimidated and local privileges curtailed, there was always an effective vocal opposition, led by convinced Republicans. There was no attempt to make a party round the personality of the dictator, still less to make a party state. Respect was shown for private property, and the process of fining the Cavaliers and allowing them to compound by surrendering part of their estates was conducted with technical formality. Few people were put to death for political crimes, and no one was cast into indefinite bondage without trial.

Liberty of conscience as conceived by Cromwell did not extend to the public profession of Roman Catholicism or Quakerism. He banned open celebration of the Mass and threw hundreds of Quakers into prison. But such limitations to freedom of worship were caused less by religious prejudice than by fear of civil disturbance. Believing the Jews to be a useful element in the civil community, he opened again to them the gates of England, which Edward I had closed nearly four hundred years before. A man who in that bitter age could write, "We look for no compulsion but that of light and reason," and who could dream of a union and a right understanding embracing Jews and Gentiles, cannot be wholly barred from his place in the forward march of liberal ideas.

Although a very passionate man when fully roused, he was frequently harassed by inner doubts and conflicts. He had always been a good and faithful family man, but his strict Puritan upbringing and the soul-stressing of his youth had left him without any certainty as to his own righteousness. This uncertainty about himself reflected itself in his famous utterance, "No man goes so high as he who knows not where he is going." His doubts about political objectives became increasingly marked in his last years. There was ever a conflict in the man between his conviction of his divine right to rule for the good of the people and a genuine Christian humility at his own unworthiness. "Is is possible to fall from grace?" he inquired of his chaplain on his deathbed. On being reassured, he said, "Then I am saved, for I know that once I was in grace."

So, on September 3, 1658, the anniversary of the battles of Dunbar and Worcester and of the siege of Drogheda, in the crash and howling of a mighty storm, death came to the Lord Protector.

If in a tremendous crisis Cromwell's sword had saved the cause of Parliament, he must stand before history as a representative of dictatorship and military rule who, with all his qualities as a soldier and a statesman, is in lasting discord with the genius of the English race. Yet with all his faults and failures he was indeed the Lord Protector of the enduring rights of the Old England he loved against the terrible weapon which he and Parliament had forged to assert them. Without Cromwell there might have been no advance, without him no collapse, without him no recovery. Amid the ruins of every institution, social and political, which had hitherto guided the island life, he towered up, the sole agency by which time could be gained for healing and regrowth.

Cromwell swept away the monarchy, but his attempts to form a totally different system of rule failed. His great seal bears his portrait and the words Protector Olivarius. *By the end of the English Republic he acted as monarch in everything but name.*

CHAPTER 11

THE RESTORATION

IT PROVED IMPOSSIBLE TO FILL THE VOID which the death of the Lord Protector had created. In his last hours Cromwell had in terms "very dark and imperfect" nominated his eldest son, Richard, to succeed him. "Tumbledown Dick", as his enemies nicknamed him, was a respectable country gentleman with good intentions, but without the force and capacity required by the severity of the times. He was at first accepted by the Army and duly installed in his father's seat; but when he attempted to exercise authority he found he had but the form. The first appointment he sought to make in the Army, of which his own brother-in-law, Charles Fleetwood,

Richard Cromwell was Oliver's third son but became his father's heir after the deaths of his older brothers, Robert and Oliver. He changed his name to John Clarke and lived abroad after the restoration of the monarchy but returned to England in about 1680.

Order your Pistoll

Cavalry manuals of the seventeenth century instructed Cavaliers on correct procedures for battle. This illustration shows a flamboyant young officer executing a battle manoeuvre.

was commander in chief, was objected to by the Council of Officers. Richard was made aware alike that the command of the Army was not hereditary, and also that it could not remain unfilled. His brother, Henry, who was both able and energetic, strove like Richard to strengthen the civil power even at the expense of the Protector's office, and upon his advice Parliament was summoned.

It was of course a Parliament from which all Royalists were formally excluded, and one which the ever-active Thurloe made a supreme effort to pack with Protectorate supporters. Nevertheless it immediately raised the large issues of government. After Richard had opened it in due state and delivered his "speech from the throne" the Commons set themselves without delay to restore the principles of the Commonwealth and to control the Army. The Army leaders, determined to preserve their independent power, complained that the "good old cause" was endangered, but the Commons called upon the assembled officers to return to their military duties. "It would fare ill with Parliament", they declared, "if they could no longer order them to return to their posts." They resolved that every officer should pledge himself not to interrupt the sittings and debates of Parliament.

Both sides marshalled their forces; but although at first it seemed that both the Protectorate and Parliament had a proportion of the officers and a number of the regiments at their disposal, the will of the inferior officers and the rank and file prevailed over all. The Commons members who sought to assemble were turned back by the troops. The Army was master, with Fleetwood and Lambert rivals at its head. These generals would have been content to leave Richard a limited dignity, but the spirit of the troops had become hostile to the Protectorate. They were resolved upon a pure republic, in which their military interest and sectarian and Anabaptist doctrines should hold the chief place.

Even in this hour of bloodless and absolute triumph the soldiery felt the need of some civil sanction for their acts. They declared that they recollected that the members of the Parliamentary assembly which sat in April 1653 had been "champions of the good old cause and had been throughout favoured with God's assistance". They went to the house of the former Speaker, Lenthall, and invited him and his surviving colleagues of 1653 to renew the exercise of their powers, and in due course, to the number of forty-two, these astonished Puritan grandees resumed the seats from which they had been expelled six years earlier. Thus was the Rump of the Long Parliament exhumed.

A Council of State was formed in which the three principal Republican leaders, Vane, Hazelrigg, and Scott, sat with eight generals and eighteen other Members of Parliament. Provision was made for Oliver Cromwell's sons, whose acquiescence in the abolition of the Protectorate was desired. Both accepted and lived unharmed to the end of their days. The Army declared that they recognised Fleetwood as their commander in chief, but they agreed that the commissions of high officers should be signed by the Speaker in the name of the Commonwealth. A Republican Constitution based on the representative principle was set up, and all the authorities in the land submitted themselves to it. But the inherent conflict between the Army and Parliament continued. "I know not why," observed General Lambert, "they should not be at our mercy as well as we at theirs."

In the summer of 1659, while these stresses racked the Republican administration, Cavaliers, strangely consorting with Presbyterian allies, appeared in arms in several counties. They were at their strongest in Lancashire and Cheshire, where the Derby influence was lively. Sir George Booth was soon at the head of a large force. Against him Lambert marched with five thousand men. At Winnington Bridge, on August 19, the Royalists were chased from the field, although, as Lambert said in his dispatch, "the horse on both sides fought like Englishmen". Elsewhere the Cavalier gatherings were dispersed by the local militia. The revolt was so swiftly crushed that Charles II, fortunately for himself, had no chance of putting himself at its head.

At this moment Lambert became the most prominent figure. He had returned to London from the victory at Winnington Bridge with most of his troops. When Parliament, offended at his arrogance, sought to dismiss him and his colleagues from their commands, he took the lead in bringing his regiments to Westminster and barred all the entrances to St Stephen's Chapel. Even Speaker Lenthall, who had signed the generals' commissions, was prevented from entering. When he asked "did they not know him" the soldiers replied that they had not noticed him at Winnington Bridge.

Lambert was a man of high ability, with a military record second only to Oliver Cromwell's and a wide knowledge of politics. He did not attempt to make himself Lord Protector. Far different were the ideas that stirred him. His wife, a woman of culture and good family, cherished Royalist sympathies and family ambitions. A plan was proposed for the marriage of their daughter to Charles II's brother, the Duke of York, as part of a process by which Lambert, if he became chief magistrate of the Republic, would restore the King to the throne. This project was seriously entertained on both sides; and the extreme lenience shown to all the Royalists taken prisoner in the recent rising was a part of it. Lambert seems to have believed that he could satisfy the Army, both in politics and religion, better under a restored monarchy than under either the Rump or a Protectorate. Fleetwood's suspicions were aroused, and a deep antagonism grew between these two military chiefs. At the same time the Army began to have misgivings about its violent actions against Parliament.

Sternest and most unbending of the Republican members was Hazelrigg, whose pale face, thin lips, and piercing eyes imparted to all the impression of Brutus-like constancy. Hazelrigg, barred from the Commons, hastened to Portsmouth, and convinced the garrison that the troops in London had done wrong to great principles. This portion of the Ironside Army presently set out for London in order to take a hand in the settlement of affairs.

The schism in the rank and file was beginning to destroy the self-confidence of the troops and put an end to the rule of the sword in England. At Christmas the Army resolved to be reconciled with Parliament. "Let us live and die with Parliament," they shouted. They marched to Chancery Lane and drew up before the house of Speaker Lenthall. Instead of the disrespect with which they had so recently treated him, the soldiers now hailed the Speaker as their general and the father of their country. But obviously this could not last. Someone must produce in England a government which stood for something old or new. It was from Scotland that deliverance was to come.

The Cromwellian commander in Scotland, though very different in temperament from Lambert, was also a man of mark. George Monk, a

Instructions for pikemen are graphically demonstrated in these diagrams from a contemporary instruction sheet. Pikemen were an important section of the New Model Army.

ENGLAND RESTORED

MUCH AS ITS LEADERS might have wished it, the Commonwealth's puritanical restraints failed to turn Britain permanently into a land of saints and a pattern of holiness to the world. Indeed, with the restoration of Charles II, the example set by London and the Court was very different. Extravagance was such that even Charles himself was to complain in 1662 that "men spend much more in their clothes, in their diet, in all expenses than they need to do".

There was a hope in high places that "games, Morris dancing, the Lord of the May, the fool and the hobby horse, Whitsun Lord and Lady . . . carols and wassails at Christmas, with good plum porridge and pies" would provide the people with enough entertainment and harmless activity to keep the country free from unrest or rebellion. And in fact, although there were several conspiracies against Charles during his reign, some led by various of his ministers—the term "cabal" was coined to describe one such group of conspirators—at heart the Restoration was a time of national contentment. Aristocratic manners were worldly, witty and generally self-indulgent, and London life lively.

Samuel Pepys's diaries offer fascinating glimpses into the public and private life of the time, while the plays of contemporary dramatists catch the flavour. The first woman appeared on a public stage when a Mrs Norris played Desdemona in William Shakespeare's *Othello*—until then women's parts had been played by young men or boys. Coffee-houses became popular, and alehouses—condemned by the Puritans as dens of Satan—were reopened.

Not everything was frivolity, however. 1665 was the year of the Great Plague, 1666 the year of the Great Fire of London, which gave a unique opportunity for the architect Christopher Wren to rebuild large parts of a city. King Charles II himself had his own serious side: it was he who founded the Royal Society.

THE STUDY OF SCIENCE *was encouraged by Charles II even though he was no scientist himself. The King was the patron of men like Isaac Newton and the astronomer Edmond Halley, and founded the Royal Society and the* Royal Hospital, Chelsea. The latter's famous *Physic Garden would have pleased Charles as, presumably, did the first pineapple grown in England when it was presented to him by the royal gardener (above).*

THE ARTS FLOURISHED. *The paintings of Sir Peter Lely, Sir Godfrey Kneller and Willem van de Velde, court painters for Charles II, the architecture of Sir Christopher Wren and the music of Henry Purcell won international acclaim. Henry Purcell (above) wrote music for Charles II's band of string players before being appointed royal organist. He also wrote music for the theatre.*

THE PURSUIT OF PLEASURE *was the aim not only of Charles II but also of many of his subjects. The dour austerity of Cromwell's days gave way to a riot of merrymaking. The King, like many of his successors, was an avid patron of the turf—in the picture above he is watching a race at Dorset Ferry, near Windsor. Other Restoration pastimes, such as dancing, skating and hawking, have also remained popular; some, like cockfighting, are now banned.*

PLAYS BY SUCH AUTHORS *as William Congreve and William Wycherley reflected the morals of the Restoration, and many of their comedies were based on sexual intrigues between stock characters—fops, county squires, heiresses, widows and country maidens. For the first time, women's roles were being played by actresses. One of them, popular Nell Gwyn,* became Charles II's mistress and bore him two illegitimate sons. In the romanticised picture above, Nell is shown with her sons portrayed as cherubs. There were women playwrights, too—one was Aphra Behn, possibly the first to make a professional career in letters. From 1663, there has been a theatre on the site of the present Theatre Royal in Drury Lane (left).

General George Monk's wise and humanitarian actions in bringing about the Restoration earned him the Dukedom of Albemarle, an annual pension of £7000 and the appointment as lieutenant-general of the armed forces.

Devonshire gentleman, who had in his youth received a thorough military training in the Dutch wars, was a soldier of fortune, caring more for plying his trade than for causes. He had fought for Charles I in all three kingdoms. After being captured and imprisoned by the Roundheads he went over to their side and supported in turn and at the right moment Parliament, the Commonwealth, and the Protectorate. He brought Scotland, in Oliver Cromwell's day, into complete subjection, but without incurring any lasting animosity. Monk used the watchwords of Parliament and Law; he thus commanded the sympathy of the English Republicans and the complete confidence of the Scots, whose interests he promised to safeguard.

He was one of those gentlemen who understand to perfection the use of time and circumstance. The English are apt to admire men who do not attempt to dominate events or turn the drift of fate; who wait about doing their duty from day to day until there is no doubt whether the tide is on the ebb or the flow; and who then, with the appearance of great propriety and complete self-abnegation, with steady, sterling qualities of conduct if not of heart, move slowly, cautiously, forward towards the obvious purpose of the nation. During the autumn of 1659 General Monk in his headquarters on the Tweed with his well-ordered army of about seven thousand men was the object of passionate solicitations from every quarter. He listened patiently to all they had to urge, and kept them all guessing for a long time what he would do.

At length when patience was exhausted Monk acted. Informed of events in London, he crossed the Tweed from Coldstream on the cold, clear New Year's Day of 1660. The Roundhead veteran Thomas Fairfax now appeared in York, and rallied a large following for a Free Parliament. Monk had promised to be with him or perish within ten days. He kept his word. At York he received what he had long hoped for, the invitation of the House of Commons to come to London. He marched south through towns and counties in which there was but one cry—"A free Parliament!" When Monk and his troops reached London he was soon angered by the peremptory orders given him by the Rump, including one to pull down the City gates in order to overawe the capital. For the City was now turning Royalist and collecting funds for Charles II. Unlike Cromwell and Lambert, Monk decided to tame the Rump by diluting, not by dissolving it. In February he recalled the members who had been excluded by Pride's Purge. These were mainly Presbyterians, most of whom had become at heart Royalists. The restoration of the monarchy now came into sight. On the night of the return of the excluded members Samuel Pepys saw the City of London "from one end to another with a glory about it, so high was the light of the bonfires . . . and the bells rang everywhere." The restored Parliament as their first act declared invalid all Acts and transactions since Pride's Purge in 1648. The interval of twelve years had been filled by events without name of sanction. They declared Monk commander in chief of all the forces. The Long Parliament was dissolved by its own consent. Monk was satisfied that a new Parliament would certainly recall Charles II. He was genuinely convinced after his march from Scotland that it was most plainly the wish of the people that the King should "enjoy his own again". This simple phrase, sprung from the heart of the common folk, also made its dominating appeal to rank and fortune.

There was a vast pother of matters which must first be settled. This was no time for vengeance. If the Parliamentary Army was to bring back the King it must not be by any stultification of their vigorous exertions against his father. Monk sent word to Charles II advising him to offer a free and general pardon, subject only to certain exceptions to be fixed by Parliament; to promise full payment of the soldiers' arrears, and to confirm the land sales. Here was an England where a substantial part of the land, the main source of wealth and distinction, had passed into other hands. These changes could not be entirely undone. The King might enjoy his own again, but not all the Cavaliers.

But sacred blood had flowed. Those living who had shed it were few and identifiable. If everyone else who had profited by the Parliamentary victory could be sure they would not be penalised there would not be much objection on their part to punishing the regicides. The deed of 1649 was abhorrent to the nation. Let those who had done it pay the price. This somewhat unheroic solution was found to be in harmony with that spirit of compromise which has played so invaluable a part in our affairs.

Monk's advice was accepted by Charles's faithful Chancellor, Hyde, who had shared his master's exile and was soon to be rewarded with the Earldom of Clarendon. Hyde drafted Charles's manifesto called the Declaration of Breda. In this document the King promised to leave all thorny problems for future Parliaments to settle. It was largely due to Hyde's lawyerly concern for Parliament and precedent that the Restoration came to stand for the return of good order and the revival of ancient institutions.

While the negotiations reached their final form, the elections for a new Parliament were held. Nominally those who had borne arms against the Republic were excluded, but the Royalist tide flowed so strongly that Presbyterians and Royalists found themselves in a great majority, and the Republicans and Anabaptists went down before them in every county. General Lambert, escaping from the Tower, in which he had been confined, prepared to dispute the quarrel in the field. His men deserted him, and he was recaptured without bloodshed. This fiasco sealed the Restoration. Monk, the bulk of his army, the City militia, the Royalists throughout the land, the great majority of the newly elected House of Commons, the peers, were all banded together, and knew that they had the power. It remained only to complete the three Estates of the Realm by the recall of the King.

Parliament hastened to send the exiled Charles a large sum of money for his convenience, and soon concerned itself with the crimson velvet furniture of his coaches of State. The fleet, once so hostile, was sent to conduct him to his native shores. Immense crowds awaited him at Dover. There on May 25, 1660, General Monk received him with profound reverence as he landed. The journey to London was triumphal. All classes crowded to welcome the King. They cheered and wept in uncontrollable emotion and felt themselves delivered from a nightmare. They now dreamt they had entered a Golden Age. Charles, Clarendon, and a handful of wanderers who had shared the royal misfortunes gazed about them in astonishment. Could this be the same island from which they had escaped so narrowly only a few years back? Still more must Charles have wondered whether he slept or waked when on Blackheath he saw the dark, glistening columns of the Ironside Army drawn up in stately array and dutiful obedience. It was but eight years since he had hidden from its patrols in the branches of the Boscobel oak. The entry to the City was a blaze of thanksgiving. And all around the

The Royal Hospital, Chelsea, was founded by Charles II in 1682 as a home for army pensioners. It was designed by Wren and completed in 1687. This statue of Charles II in the pose and dress of a Roman emperor stands proudly outside the building.

masses, rich and poor, Cavalier and Roundhead, Episcopalian, Presbyterian, and Independent, framed a scene of reconciliation and rejoicing without compare in history. It was England's supreme day of joy.

The wheel had not however swung a full circle, as many might have thought. This was not only the restoration of the monarchy; it was the restoration of Parliament. Indeed, it was the greatest hour in Parliamentary history. The House of Commons had broken the Crown in the field; it had at length mastered the terrible Army it had created for that purpose. It had purged itself of its own excesses, and now stood forth beyond all challenge as the dominant institution of the realm. All the laws of the Long Parliament since Charles I quitted London at the beginning of 1642, all the statutes of the Commonwealth or of the Protectorate, now fell to the ground. But there remained the potent limitations of the Prerogative to which Charles I had agreed. The work of 1641 still stood. Above all, everyone now took it for granted that the Crown was the instrument of Parliament and the King the servant of his people. The idea of the Crown levying taxes without the consent of Parliament had vanished. All legislation henceforward stood upon the majorities of legally elected Parliaments. The victory of the Commons and the Common Law was permanent.

Finance at the Restoration was, as ever, an immediate and thorny subject. Large sums were needed for paying off the Army and the debts contracted by the King in exile. The King relinquished his feudal dues from wardships, knight service, and other medieval survivals. Parliament granted him instead revenues for life which, with his hereditary property, were calculated to yield about £1,200,000. This was keeping him very strait, and in fact the figure proved optimistic, but he and his advisers professed themselves content. The country was impoverished by the ordeal through which it had passed; the process of tax-collection was grievously deranged; a settlement for life was not to be disdained. For all extra-ordinary expenditure the King was dependent upon Parliament, and both he and Clarendon accepted this.

But both Crown and Parliament were to be free of the Army. That force, which had grown to forty thousand men, unequalled in fighting quality in the world, was to be dispersed, and nothing like it was on any account to be raised ever again. "No standing Army" was to be the common watchword of all parties. Everyone, except the soldiers, was agreed about getting rid of the Army; and that this could be done, and done without bloodshed, seemed a miracle. Every hand was turned against the Ironside soldiers. After all the services they had rendered, the victories they had won in the field, the earnest efforts they had made to establish a godly government for the realm, they found themselves universally detested. They were paid their dues, they returned to their homes and their former callings, and within a few months this omnipotent, invincible machine, which might at any moment have devoured the whole realm and society of Britain, vanished in the civil population, leaving scarcely a trace behind.

Such decisions of the united nation, which laid the scalpel on so many festering wounds, could not, however necessary, be received without pain and wincing by those affected. The Cavaliers were mortified that the vindication of their cause brought them no relief from the mulctings of which they had been the victims. And indeed only those who had actually condemned the Royal Martyr were to be punished, and of these a third were dead, a third had fled, and a bare twenty remained. Ironically King Charles strove against his loyal Parliament to save as many as possible, and Parliament, many of whose members had abetted their action, clamoured for retribution. In the end nine suffered the extreme penalty of treason. Nearly all of them gloried in their deed. Harrison and other officers stepped upon the scaffold convinced that posterity would salute their sacrifice.

The numbers of those executed fell so far short of the public demand that an addition was made to the bloody scene. The corpses of Cromwell, Ireton, and Bradshaw were pulled out of their coffins in Westminster Abbey, where they had been buried a few years earlier in solemn state, drawn through the streets on hurdles to Tyburn, hanged upon the three-cornered gibbet for twenty-four hours, their heads spiked up in prominent places, and the remains cast upon the dunghill. Pym and twenty other Parliamentarians were also disinterred and buried in a pit.

Only two other persons in England were condemned to death, General Lambert and Sir Harry Vane. Lambert had imagined himself as the Constable of the Restoration, forestalling Monk. He was a man of limitless audacity and long experience in military revolution. But all just failed. Now he sought mercy from the King. He was pardoned, and lived the rest of his life in Guernsey and Plymouth, consoling himself with painting and botany.

Vane was of tougher quality. He scorned to sue for mercy, and so spirited was his defence that he might well have been indulged. But there was one incident in his past which proved fatal to him. Twenty years before he had purloined, and disclosed to Pym, his father's notes of the Privy Council meeting, alleging that Strafford had advised the bringing of an Irish army into England. If debts were to be paid, this was certainly not one to be overlooked. "He is too dangerous to let live," Charles said, "if we can honestly put him out of the way." He met his death with the utmost alacrity and self-confidence.

Almost the only notable in Scotland to suffer death at the Restoration was the Marquis of Argyll. He came to London to join in the royal welcome, but was immediately arrested. Charles sent him back to Scotland to be tried by his peers and fellow-countrymen. "I am weary of hanging," he said. But the Scottish Parliament made haste to send their former guide and mentor

Lambert K.r of y.e Golden Tulip.

Playing cards relating to the Rump Parliament satirise the representatives who remained after the purge of its best members. The eight of hearts depicts General Lambert as the Knight of the Golden Tulip. The reference is probably to his botanical interests which he pursued during his long retirement.

to the block. In all therefore, through Charles's exertions, and at some expense to his popularity, less than a dozen persons were put to death in this intense Counter-Revolution. By an ironic contrivance which Charles must have enjoyed, they were made to be condemned by some of the principal accessories to their crimes, leading figures of the Parliamentary party, peers and commoners, high officers under the Republic or Cromwell.

CHAPTER 12

THE MERRY MONARCH

THE PARLIAMENT WHICH RECALLED THE KING was a balanced assembly which represented both sides of the nation, and surmounted the grave political difficulties of the Restoration with success. It had, however, no constitutional validity, since it had not been summoned by royal writ. The King, who thought he might well go farther and fare worse, cast his royal authority over the assembly, endorsing retrospectively the action taken in calling them together. But this was felt not to achieve a perfect legality. The House could claim to be only a Convention. At the end of 1660 it was thought necessary to dissolve it. This concession to a newly recovered respect for law prevented all chance of a religious settlement which would embrace the whole nation. The elections expressed the delight of a liberated people. An overwhelming anti-Puritan majority presented itself at Westminster; and from their ruined homes and mutilated estates came the men or their sons who had charged with Rupert.

The longest Parliament in English history now began. It lasted eighteen years. It has been called the Cavalier Parliament. It was composed at first of men well past their prime and when it was eventually dissolved all except two hundred of them had been replaced at by-elections, often by Roundheads or their heirs. From the moment when it first met it showed itself more Royalist in theory than in practice. The many landed gentry who had been impoverished in the royal cause were not blind monarchists. They did not mean to part with any of the Parliamentary rights which had been gained in the struggle. They were ready to make provision for the defence of the country by means of militia, but they took care that the only troops in the country should be under the local control of lieutenants. Thus the repository of force had now become the gentry. Having established this as the result of bitter experiences, the Cavalier Parliament addressed itself to religion and to its own interests.

From the days of Queen Elizabeth down to the Civil War the aim of the monarchy had been the establishment of an all-including national Church, based upon the Prayer Book and episcopacy. There was also the desire to unite the life and faith of England and Scotland. These aims, even extending to Ireland, had been achieved under totally different forms in a brutal fashion by the sword of Cromwell. Against all this, both in Church and State, in Parliament and the Court, there was now a profound reaction.

Since Clarendon as Lord Chancellor was the chief minister, his name is identified with the group of Acts which re-established the Anglican Church and drove the Protestant sects into enduring opposition. Charles would have preferred the way of toleration, Clarendon that of comprehension.

Charles II's mocking glance and sensual smile are brilliantly captured in white marble by the sculptor, Honore Pellé.

He had hoped for union between Church and State, inspired by the heart-melting of the Restoration. But the zeal of the Cavalier Parliament, of the followers of Laud, now returned from exile, and of some recalcitrant Presbyterian leaders, baffled them both. Parliament recognised that there were religious bodies definitely outside the national Church, and determined, if not to extirpate them, at least to leave them under grievous disabilities. In so doing it consolidated Nonconformity as a political force with clear objectives: first, toleration, which was secured at the Revolution of 1688; and thereafter the abolition of the privileged status of the Church. But this latter was only attained, and that partially, when in the nineteenth century the vote of the commercial and industrial middle class became a decisive factor in political combinations. Perhaps a comprehensive Church with wide terms of subscription would best have served the cause of religion. But it is also possible that the variety of religious thought which Nonconformity provided could have been contained within a State Church however broadly based, and that the Three Bodies, as they came to be called—Presbyterians with their rationalism, Congregationalists with their independence, Baptists with their fervour—were expressions of deeply seated and divergent tendencies of the English mind.

For good or ill, the "Clarendon Code" was a parting of the ways. It destroyed all chance of a united national church. The episcopacy, unconsciously perhaps, but decidedly, accepted the position not of the leaders of a nationwide faith but of "the established sect". Outside were all the forms of dissent or nonconformity. The Cavalier Parliament accepted the schism, and rejoiced in belonging to the larger, richer, and more favoured section. They built upon their system not a nation but a party. The country gentlemen and landowners who had fought for God and King should have their own Church and bishops, as they now had their own militia and their own Commission of the Peace.

The Clarendon Code consisted of a series of statutes. The Corporation Act of 1661 required all persons holding municipal office to renounce the Solemn League and Covenant—a test which excluded many of the Presbyterians; to take the oath of non-resistance—which excluded Republicans; and to receive the Sacrament according to the rites of the Church of England—which excluded Roman Catholics and some of the Nonconformists. The object of this Act was to confine municipal office to Royalist Anglicans. The Act of Uniformity of 1662 imposed upon the clergy the Prayer Book of Queen Elizabeth, with some excisions and certain valuable

The Clarendon Building, Oxford, was built largely from the proceeds of the Earl of Clarendon's History of the Great Rebellion, *published in 1702-04. It now forms part of the University.*

Charles II's triumphal return from Portsmouth to Hampton Court with his bride, Catherine of Braganza, is celebrated in this engraving of 1662.

additions. It required from them a declaration of unfeigned assent and consent to all and everything contained in the Prayer Book and exacted from them and from all teachers in schools and universities a declaration "to conform to the Liturgy of the Church of England as it is now by law established". One-fifth of the clergy, nearly two thousand ministers, refusing to comply, were deprived of their livings. The Conventicle Act of 1664 sought to prevent the ejected clergy from preaching to audiences of their own, and the Five-Mile Act of 1665 forbade them to go within five miles of any "City or Town Corporate or Borough or any parish or place where they had preached or held a living".

The echoes of this Code divide the present-day religious life of England. It potently assisted the foundation of parties. The Royalist party now in possession of power planned to bind together its affiliated interests. All the other elements in the nation, including those who had lately ruled and terrified it, drew instinctively together. A large group of villages where modern Birmingham now stands happened to be more than five miles from any "City, Town Corporate or Borough". The nonconformity of the Midlands focused itself there, and can be seen today. Thus from the Restoration there emerged two Englands, each with its different background, interests, culture, and outlook. The lines were being drawn in political life between the Conservative and Radical traditions which have persisted down to our own day. We enter the era of conflict between broad party groups, soon to bear the names of Tory and Whig, which shaped the destinies of the British Empire till all was melted in the fires of the Great War of 1914.

THE COURT OF CHARLES II

This description of Charles II's Court at Whitehall is taken from Arthur Bryant's book, Freedom's Own Island.

The government of this bigoted land rested on triple supports—Crown, Law and People. The Crown was the executive and provided the element of decisive power. Yet it was a carefully tempered power. Its seat was the old Tudor palace of Whitehall. For nearly half a mile it stretched along the river, a warren of galleries, apartments and gardens, the home not only of the King but of the ministers of State, servants high and low, courtiers, chaplains, ladies and all the gilded army which encompassed the throne. One entered it either from the river or "the lane"—that "long dark dirty and very inconvenient passage"—which, spanned by two gateways, linked Charing Cross with Westminster. Its buildings were of all sizes and ages, from Inigo Jones's classic Banqueting Hall to the little octagonal Cockpit.

The centre of this courtly city was the long Stone Gallery, the hub of the Stuart government of Britain. On its walls hung the pictures which Charles I had collected and his enemies dispersed, and which his son had partly reassembled. Here they made a kind of national picture gallery, for the place was open to all comers. Yet few in the crowd that walked continuously up and down the galleries came for the pictures; places, preferment, sightseeing, above all, news, were the business of that place of rumours. "It runs through the galleries", was the prefix which sped the national gossip.

Well it might, for those who waited here saw the outward stir of all that was moving the wheels of State. The velvet curtains across the doors would part and the King himself pass through the crowd, followed by a group of ministers and suitors from Bedchamber or Council Room, still contending for that royal ear whose retention was at once the hardest and most precious achievement of a careerist's life. Here in the Gallery, for a moment, opportunity flitted by.

From the Stone Gallery guarded doors opened into the royal apartments. In the Robe and Council Chambers the principal committees of State met in debate, while in the Withdrawing-room waiting gentlemen warmed their hands before the fire. Beyond was the holy of holies, the Bedchamber. In this great room, with its windows looking onto the tides and shipping of the river, the most secret affairs of State were transacted at all hours of the day "between the bed and the wall".

It was not here, or in his closet, that England saw the King, nor even in the Anteroom where the Foreign Ministers daily awaited his return from the park, but in perfumed banqueting hall and chapel. He dined in state, a little after midday, before a background of tapestry, while the massed lords of the household served him on bended knee and all England came and went in the galleries above to share the pageantry. The mysteries of State were performed against a setting of crimson and gold, with the royal trumpeters and kettledrummers marching in scarlet cloaks faced with silver lace, before fringed hangings, gilt mirrors and a world of gleaming fabric.

For these far-reaching fissures Charles II had no responsibility. He wished to see all religious fervour cooled and abated. Why ill-use people because they would not agree upon the various methods of obtaining salvation? In December 1663, he issued his first Declaration of Indulgence, claiming to exercise a dispensing power inherent in the Crown to relieve Dissenters from the laws enforcing religious conformity or requiring oaths; but the Commons, unconscious that it was what they themselves were doing, protested vehemently against any scheme for "establishing schism by a law". In March 1672 he ran great risks with a second Declaration of Indulgence, which sought to suspend "the execution of all manner of penal laws in matters ecclesiastical against whatsover classes of Nonconformists and Recusants", as the Roman Catholics were called. "Penal statutes in matters ecclesiastical", rejoined the House of Commons severely, "cannot be suspended but by Act of Parliament."

Catherine of Braganza, Charles's forgiving wife, was an intelligent woman who played a significant part in the government of Portugal when she returned there in 1692.

The King submitted as a constitutional sovereign ought to do. Partisans of Parliament should realise that in this crucial period the King's was almost the only modern and merciful voice that spoke.

But Charles II had need of an Act of Indulgence for himself. Court life was one unceasing flagrant and brazen scandal. His two principal mistresses, Barbara Villiers and Louise de Kérouaille, beguiled his leisure and amused themselves with foreign affairs. His marriage with Catherine of Braganza, who brought a rich dowry of eight hundred thousand pounds and the naval bases of Tangier and Bombay, in no way interrupted these dissipations. His treatment of his wife was cruel to an extreme degree; he forced her to accept Barbara as her lady in waiting. The refined, devout Portuguese princess on one occasion was so outraged that the blood gushed from her nostrils and she was borne swooning from the Court. It was with relief that the public learnt that the King had taken a mistress from the people, the beautiful and good-natured Nell Gwyn, who was lustily cheered in the streets as "the Protestant whore". But these were only the more notorious features of a life of lust and self-indulgence.

The King's example spread its demoralisation far and wide, and the sense of relief from the tyranny of the Puritans spurred forward every amorous adventure. The Commonwealth Parliament had punished adultery by death; Charles scourged chastity and faithfulness with ridicule. There can however be no doubt that the mass of the nation did not wish to be the people of God in the sense of the Puritan God. They descended with thankfulness from the superhuman levels to which they had been painfully hoisted. All shrank to a smaller size and an easier pace.

Two personalities of force and capacity, however, Clarendon and Ashley, afterwards Earl of Shaftesbury, swayed the Privy Council. Shaftesbury had plunged into the Revolution in the Short Parliament when he was but eighteen. He had fought on the Roundhead side and worked with Cromwell. As a leader of the Presbyterians he had influenced and aided Monk in bringing about the Restoration. It took him time to rise, but he was still young, and no one understood better the anatomy of the convulsive forces which had devastated the country. Although he had headed the Presbyterians against the Army in the year of anarchy no one knew more about the spirit of the Independents. He was therefore the foremost advocate of toleration in the Council, and no doubt fortified the King in all he did to that end. He was always conscious of the fierce Ironside dogs who now seemed to

England was now isolated, and even her power at sea was uncertain. Both sides bent beneath the financial strain. But other calamities drained the strength of the island. From the spring of 1665 the Great Plague had raged in London. Never since the Black Death in 1348 had pestilence spread such ravages. In London at the climax about seven thousand people died in a single week. The Court retired to Salisbury, leaving the capital in the charge of Monk, whose nerves were equal to every kind of strain. The worst of the plague was over when in September 1666 the Great Fire engulfed the tormented capital. The flames spread with resistless fury for four days.

Wild suspicions that the fire was the work of Anabaptists, Catholics, or foreigners maddened the mob. The King, who had returned to London, acquitted himself with courage and humanity. When the fire was at length stopped outside the City walls by blowing up whole streets, more than thirteen thousand dwelling-houses, eighty-nine churches, and St Paul's Cathedral had been devoured. The warehouses containing the merchandise for months of trade and many warlike stores were destroyed. Yet the fire extinguished the plague, and to later times it seems that the real calamity was not so much the destruction of the insanitary medieval city as the failure to carry through Wren's plan for rebuilding it as a unity of avenues centred on St Paul's. The task of reconstruction was nonetheless faced with courage, and from the ashes of the old cathedral rose the splendid dome of St Paul's as it stands today.

Although the war dragged on till 1667 Charles now sought peace both with France and Holland. Want of money prevented the English battle fleet from keeping the sea, and while the negotiations lingered the Dutch, to

THE DIARY OF SAMUEL PEPYS

Samuel Pepys (1633-1703) was Clerk of the Acts at the Navy Office, and later Secretary to the Admiralty. His diary, which ran from January 1, 1660 to May 31, 1669, gives a vivid picture of Restoration London, particularly of the time of these two great tragedies.

The Great Plague 1665

AUGUST 22ND I walked to Greenwich, in my way seeing a coffin with a dead body therein, dead of the plague, lying in an open close which was carried out last night, and the parish have not appointed any body to bury it; but only set a watch there all day and night, that nobody should go thither or come thence: this disease making us more cruel to one another than we are to dogs.

AUGUST 25TH This day I am told that Dr. Burnett, my physician, is dead of the plague; which is strange, his man dying so long ago, and his house this month open again. Now himself dead. Poor unfortunate man!

AUGUST 28TH I think to take adieu today of the London streets. In much the best posture I ever was in in my life, both as to the quantity and the certainty I have of the money I am worth; having most of it in my hand. But then this is a trouble to me what to do with it, being this day going to be wholly at Woolwich; but for the present I am

resolved to venture it in an iron chest, at least for a while.

AUGUST 30TH Abroad, and met with Hadley, our clerke, who told me the plague encreases much, and much in our parish; for, says he, there died nine this week, though I have returned but six: which is a very ill practice, and makes me think it is so in other places; and therefore the plague much greater than people take it to be.

SEPTEMBER 3RD (Lord's day) 1665. Up; and put on my coloured silk suit very fine, and my new periwigg, bought a good while since, but durst not wear, because the plague was in Westminster when I bought it; and it is a wonder what will be the fashion after the plague is done, as to periwiggs, for nobody will dare to buy any haire, for fear of the infection, that it had been cut off the heads of people dead of the plague. Among those other stories, one was very passionate, methought, of a complaint brought against a man in the town for taking a child from London from an infected house. Alderman Hooker told us it was the child of . . . a saddler, who had buried all the rest of his children, and himself and wife now being in despair of escaping, did desire only to save the life of this little child; and so prevailed to have it received stark-naked into the arms of a friend, who brought it (having put it into new fresh clothes) to Greenwich; where upon hearing the story, we did agree it should be permitted to be received and kept in the town. . . . My Lord Brouncker, Sir J. Minnes and I agreed on some orders for keeping the plague from growing.

spur them, sailed up the Medway, broke the boom which guarded Chatham harbour, burnt four ships of the line, and towed away the battleship *Royal Charles*. In the general indignation and alarm even Cavaliers remarked that nothing like this had happened under Cromwell. Among the Puritans the plague, the fire, and the disaster at sea were regarded as direct visitations by which the Almighty chastised the immorality of the age.

Peace was made on indifferent terms. England's chief gain in the war was New Amsterdam, now renamed New York. But recriminations began. The Court asked how the country could be defended when Parliament kept the King so short of money. Parliament retorted that he had spent too much on his mistresses. Clarendon, expostulating with all sides, was assailed by all. An impeachment was launched against him, and he went into exile, there to complete his noble *History of the Rebellion*, which casts its broad illumination on the times through which he lived. After Clarendon's fall the King was for a while guided chiefly by Arlington, and in his lighter moods by his boon companion Buckingham, son of James I's murdered favourite, a gay, witty, dissolute nobleman. The growing discontents of the Cavalier Parliament at the morals and expense of the Court, however, made it necessary to broaden the basis of the Government, and from 1668 five principal personages began to be recognised as the responsible ministers. There had been much talk of cabinets and cabals; and now, by chance, the initials of these five men, Clifford, Arlington, Buckingham, Ashley, and Lauderdale, actually spelt the word "Cabal".

The dominant fact on the continent of Europe, never realised by Cromwell, was the rise of France at the expense of Spain and Austria. Louis XIV was now in his youthful prime. The French people, consolidated under

The Fire of London 1666

SEPTEMBER 2ND (Lord's day) 1666. Some of our maids sitting up late last night to get things ready against our feast today, Jane called us up about three in the morning, to tell us of a great fire they saw in the City. So I rose, and slipped on my nightgown, and went to her window; and thought it to be on the back-side of Market-lane at the farthest, but being unused to such fires as followed, I thought it far enough off; and so went to bed again, and to sleep. About seven rose again to dress myself, and there looked out at the window, and saw the fire not so much as it was, and further off. By and by Jane comes and tells me that she hears that above 300 houses have been burned down tonight by the fire we saw, and that it is now burning all down Fish-street, by London Bridge. So I made myself ready presently, and walked to the Tower, and there got up on one of the high places, Sir J. Robinson's little son going up with me; and there I did see the houses at that end of the bridge all on fire, and an infinite great fire on this and the other side the end of the bridge. So down with my heart full of trouble to the Lieutenant of the Tower, who tells me that it begun this morning in the King's baker's house in Pudding Lane, and that it hath burned down St. Magnes Church and most part of Fish-street already. So I down to the water-side, and there got a boat, and through bridge, and there saw a lamentable fire. Everybody endeavouring to remove their goods, and flinging into the river, or bringing them into lighters that lay off; poor people staying in their houses as long as till the very fire touched them, and then running into boats, or clambering from one pair of stairs to another. And among other things, the poor pigeons, I perceive, were loth to leave their houses, but hovered about the windows and balconys, till they burned their wings, and fell down.

CHAPTER 13

THE POPISH PLOT

THE MEETING OF PARLIAMENT IN FEBRUARY OF 1673 apprised Charles of his subjects' loathing for the war against the Dutch Protestant Republic. Resentment of Dutch sea trade was overridden by fear and hatred of Papist France and her ever-growing dominance in Europe. Whispers ran through London that the King and his ministers had been bribed by France to betray the freedom and the faith of the island. The secret article in the Dover Treaty had only to be known to create a political explosion of measureless violence. Early in 1673 Arlington seems to have confessed the facts to Shaftesbury. With dexterity and promptitude Shaftesbury withdrew himself from the Government, and became the leader of an Opposition which was ultimately as violent as that of Pym. The growing antagonism of the Commons to France, the fear of the returning tides of Popery, the King's "laxity towards Papists", the conversion of the Duke of York to Rome, all stirred a deep and dangerous agitation throughout the whole country, in which the dominant Anglican forces were in full accord with Presbyterian and Puritan feeling. Everywhere there was the hum of political excitement. Coffee-houses buzzed; pamphlets circulated; by-elections were scenes of uproar. A Bill was forced upon the King for a Test. No man could hold office or a King's commission afloat or ashore who would not solemnly declare his disbelief in transubstantiation, the doctrine which states that the bread and wine of the Communion service change into the actual body and blood of Christ. This purge destroyed the Cabal. Clifford, a Catholic, refused to forswear himself; Arlington was dismissed because of his unpopularity; Buckingham had a personal quarrel with the King. Shaftesbury was the leader of the Opposition. Lauderdale alone remained, cynical, cruel, and servile, master of Scotland.

All eyes were now fixed upon James, Duke of York. His marriage, after the death of his first wife, Anne Hyde, to the Catholic princess Mary of

Gossipmongers discussed news, plotted intrigues, smoked their clay pipes and drank black coffee out of bowls in new Restoration coffee-houses like the one shown here.

Modena had rendered him suspect. Would he dissemble or would he give up his offices? Very soon it was known that the heir to the throne had laid down his post of Lord High Admiral rather than submit to the Test. This event staggered the nation. The Queen was unlikely to give King Charles an heir. The Crown would therefore pass to a Papist king, who showed that for conscience's sake he would not hesitate to sacrifice every material advantage. The strength of the forces now moving against the King and his policy rose from the virtual unanimity which prevailed between the Anglicans and the Dissenters, between the swords which had followed Rupert and the swords which had followed Cromwell. They were all on the same side now, and at their head was the second great Parliamentary tactician of the century, Shaftesbury. This was of all combinations the most menacing to the King.

Dryden has recorded his biased but commanding verdict upon Shaftesbury in lines and phrases which are indelible:

> For close designs and crooked counsels fit,
> Sagacious, bold, and turbulent of wit,
> Restless, unfixed in principles and place,
> In power unpleased, impatient of disgrace . . . ;
> A daring pilot in extremity,
> Pleased with the danger, when the waves went high,
> He sought the storms; but, for a calm unfit,
> Would steer too nigh the sands to boast his wit.
> Great wits are sure to madness near allied,
> And thin partitions do their bounds divide.

The Earl of Shaftesbury was also Baron Ashley, whose surname's initial formed one of the letters of CABAL, the name used to denote the secret council which met in Ham House, Surrey, to determine state policy. This portrait was painted in 1673 by the English artist, J. Greenhill.

The power of the Cavalier Parliament had been made plain in every dispute with the Crown. It had exerted itself in foreign policy, had completely controlled domestic affairs, and had compelled the King to change his advisers by the hard instruments of the Test Act or impeachment. A new departure was now made. Sir Thomas Osborne, a Yorkshire landowner, had gathered great influence in the Commons, and was to a large extent forced upon the King for his own salvation. His policy was the union into one strong party with a popular programme of all those elements which had stood by the monarchy in the Civil War and were now deeply angered with the Court. Economy, Anglicanism, and independence from France were the principal ideals of this party, and Osborne now carried them to the King's Council.

He was very soon raised to the peerage as Earl of Danby, and began an administration which was based on a party organisation possessing a small but effective majority in the House of Commons. In order to rally his followers to the Crown and to break with the Opposition, Danby proposed in 1675 that no person should hold any office or sit in either House without first declaring an oath that resistance to the royal power was in all cases criminal. This was deliberately intended to draw a hard line against the Puritan elements. The plan was to vest the whole Government in the Court party and fight the rest. This design, which Danby pursued by corrupt party management and in unprecedented by-election activity, was countered in the Lords by Shaftesbury and Buckingham; and so vigorous was the opposition of these two ex-ministers that Danby was forced to abandon his new retaliatory Test.

Though he was lured secretly into asking the French monarch for money

James II's first wife, the Protestant Anne Hyde, and her two daughters, Mary and Anne. Each was to become Queen of England and steer the country away from Catholicism. Few people could have foreseen this when Peter Lely began the portrait in 1669. The painting was completed by Benedetto Gennari some ten years later.

a more favourable Parliament. Halifax, fresh from rendering him the highest service, opposed the dissolution. He thought there was still something to be made of the Parliament of 1680. But the King, after a full debate in his Privy Council, overrode the majority. "Gentlemen," he said, "I have heard enough," and for the third time in three years there was an electoral trial of strength. But this was challenging the electors to go directly back on what they had just voted. Again there was no decisive change in the character of the majority returned.

Presently it was learnt that Parliament was to meet in Oxford, where the King could not be bullied by the City of London and Shaftesbury's gangs of apprentices called "White Boys". To Oxford then both sides repaired. Charles moved his Guards to the town, and occupied several places on the roads from London with troops. The Whig lords arrived with bodies of armed retainers, who eyed the Household Cavalry with the respectful hostility of gentlemen upon a duelling-ground. The members came down in parties of forty or fifty, those from London being escorted by armed citizens. A trial of strength impended, and none could tell that it would not take a bloody form. The large majority of the Commons was still resolved upon the Exclusion Bill.

It would seem that the King kept two courses of action open, both of which he had prepared. He had caused Lawrence Hyde, Clarendon's son, the Duke of York's brother-in-law, a competent financier, to examine precisely the state of the normal revenue granted to the Crown for life. Could the King by strict economies "live of his own"? In this calculation his foremost thought was the upkeep of the navy, which he consistently set even in front of his mistresses and his own comfort. Hyde reported that it was impossible to discharge the royal services upon the original grant of customs and excise and such further taxes as Parliament had conceded. With strict economy however the deficit would not be large. Hyde was next employed in negotiating with Louis XIV, and eventually a hundred thousand pounds a year was obtained upon the understanding that England would not act contrary to French ambitions on the Continent. With this aid it was thought the King could manage independently of Parliament. England had now reached a point in its history as low as when King John, in not dissimilar stresses, had made it over as a fief to the Pope. Modern opinion, which judges Charles's actions from the constitutional standpoint, is revolted by the spectacle of a prince selling the foreign policy of his country for a hundred thousand pounds a year. But if present-day standards are to be applied the religious intolerance of Parliament and the party violence of Shaftesbury must also be condemned.

Moreover, the King did not intend to adopt his ignominious policy, which he had almost in his pocket, unless he found no hope in Parliament. He made a show of going to extreme lengths to meet the national fear of a Popish King. James, when he succeeded, should be King only in name. The kingdom would be governed by a Protector and the Privy Council. The accident of the conversion of the heir presumptive to Rome should not strip him of his royalty, but should deprive him of all power. If a son was born to James he would be educated as a Protestant and ascend the throne on coming of age. In default of a son, James's Protestant daughters, Mary and after her Anne, would reign. The Protector meanwhile was to be William of Orange, Mary's husband.

There is no doubt that the King might have agreed to such a settlement, and could then have defied France and made an alliance with the Dutch and the Protestant princes of Germany. But Shaftesbury and all his party were set upon Monmouth for the Crown. Parliament had no sooner met than its hostile temper was apparent. Shaftesbury, still a member of the Privy Council, in a sense part of the Government, held a hard conversation with the King in the presence of many awestruck notables. A paper was handed to Charles demanding that Monmouth should be declared successor. Charles replied that this was contrary to law and also to justice. "If you are restrained," said Shaftesbury, "only by law and justice, rely on us and leave us to act. We will make laws which will give legality to measures so necessary to the quiet of the nation." "Let there be no delusion," rejoined the King. "I will not yield, nor will I be bullied. Men usually become more timid as they become older; it is the opposite with me."

The sitting of the Commons two days later, on March 26, 1681, was decisive. A member unfolded to the House the kind of plan for a Protestant Protectorate during James's reign which the King had in mind. But the Commons passed a resolution for excluding the Duke of York.

Oxford was now a camp in which two armed factions jostled one another. At any moment there might be an outbreak. As James would sacrifice all for his religious faith, so Charles would dare all for the hereditary principle. On the Monday following, two sedan chairs made their way to Parliament. In the first was the King, the crown hidden beneath his feet; in the second, which was closed, were the sceptre and the robes of State. Thus Charles wended his way to the House of Lords, installed in the Geometry School of the university. The Commons were debating a question of jurisdiction arising out of a Crown prosecution for libel, when Black Rod knocked at the door and summoned them to the Peers. Most members thought that this portended some compliance by the King with their wishes. They were surprised to see him robed, upon his throne, and astounded when the Lord Chancellor declared in his name that Parliament was again dissolved.

No one could tell what the consequences would be. Forty years before the Scottish Assembly had refused to disperse upon the warrant of the Crown. But in 1681, Englishmen's respect for law paralysed their action. The King withdrew under a heavy escort of his Guards to Windsor. Shaftesbury made a bid to convert the elements of the vanished Parliament into a revolutionary convention. But no one would listen. Charles had hazarded rightly. On one day there was a Parliament regarding itself as the custodian of national destiny, ready to embark upon dire contention; the next a jumble of members scrambling for conveyances to carry them home.

From this time Shaftesbury's star waned and the sagacious Halifax entered the ascendant. The reaction against the execution of the Catholic lords and others was now apparent. Within two months the King felt strong enough to indict Shaftesbury for fomenting rebellion. This strange man was now physically almost at the last gasp. His health, though not his spirit, was broken. His appearance—he could hardly walk—dismayed his followers. The Middlesex Grand Jury, faithful to his cause, found the evidence insufficient. He was liberated according to law. He fled to Holland, and died at The Hague in a few weeks. He cannot be ranked with the chief architects of the Parliamentary system. As a Puritan revolutionary he understood every move in the party game, but he deliberately stained his

The sedan chair, which originated in Sedan, France, was introduced into England in 1634. It needed two strong bearers to carry it. Some models had a sliding top to accommodate the passenger's wig. This chair can be seen in the Tyrwhitt-Drake Museum, Maidstone, Kent.

PILGRIMS' PROGRESS

THE INFLUENCE OF ENGLISH PURITANISM did not disappear with the fall of the Commonwealth. Indeed, it was given new life and vigour when, rather than submit to the Act of Uniformity of 1662 that followed the Restoration, a large number of Nonconformists—or Dissenters, as they were to call themselves—left the Church of England. And then, in 1678, the great classic of Puritanism, *The Pilgrim's Progress* by John Bunyan was published, providing an inspirational view of a Christian, "he who would valiant be, 'gainst all disaster".

There was no single group of Dissenters, however. They were divided by doctrine and also by attitudes towards Church organisation. In consequence, different denominations, as they came to be called, set up their own chapels for services of worship. Thereafter a new division entered British society—Church versus Chapel.

Among the Dissenters were the Presbyterians, who wanted an official State Church, but without bishops, and this they secured in Scotland. The Congregationalists, the Baptists and the Quakers all disliked any association with the State: they wanted independent congregations of believers. The Baptists practised adult baptism, while the Quakers wore simple, distinctive clothing, had meetinghouses rather than chapels, and objected to all use of physical force.

All these groups were excluded from government office or full participation in the nation's life. Perhaps for this reason many of them prospered financially instead. Certainly, through their sobriety, hard work and their strong family ties, they contributed greatly to Britain's developing commercial and industrial base. Many Dissenters emigrated to the American colonies and forged their independence in the New World.

At the end of the eighteenth century a further group, the Methodists, seceded reluctantly from the Church of England. Thereafter, religious differences were to affect all aspects of nineteenth-century life, political and social as well as spiritual.

THE PILGRIM'S PROGRESS *was begun by John Bunyan (1622–88), a tinker by trade, when he was imprisoned in Bedford gaol for preaching without a licence. His hero, Christian, sets out on a journey of salvation from the City of Destruction to the Celestial City. He nearly perishes in the Slough of Despond but is rescued by Help. Mr Worldly Wiseman tempts him to abandon his quest; Evangelist points to the straight and narrow way leading heavenwards.*

NONCONFORMISTS *objected to ceremonial forms of worship and the rituals of the Church of England. The Quakers in particular favoured simplicity, and based their worship on "the inner light". Pictured above is a Quaker Meeting held in London in about 1737. The Quakers organised self-help and education groups, and charitable work aimed at bringing help to the poor. Many of them put their organising skills to good use in business.*

OPEN-AIR SERMONS, an estimated forty thousand of them, were preached by John Wesley between 1739 and 1791. The saying, "Cleanliness is next to Godliness" comes from one of his sermons. Wesley drew enormous crowds to his inspirational meetings which often began at 5.00 a.m. and were sometimes required by law to be at least five miles from the nearest large town. He was especially successful with the poorer classes to whom he gave the profits of the many books he wrote on religion for the masses. He was interested in medicine, too, and opened dispensaries in London and Bristol. The hymns composed by John's younger brother Charles added to the movement's appeal. Methodism broke with the Church of England in 1791, a year after its founder's death.

RELIGIOUS CONTROVERSY marked the seventeenth century and is satirised in the cartoon above. A Brownist, a Familist, a Papist and an Anabaptist toss a Bible in a blanket. In an age which lacked both cultural and leisure interests for most people, religious discussions assumed immense importance. Later, the question of how people should spend their lives often took precedence over matters of faith. Believers became more practical and less mystical in their approach to life.

BAPTISTS WERE CONVINCED that only adult believers should be christened and their method of administering baptism was by complete immersion. The modern Baptist Church began with the work of John Smyth in the reign of James I. He was an ordained minister of the Anglican Church who changed his beliefs and fled to Holland, where he died in 1612. His chief follower came to England and established a church at Newgate. Pictured above is the Goodshaw Old Baptist Chapel near Rawtenstall in Lancashire.

Sidney Godolphin changed his politics but his talents led William and later Anne to put him in charge of the Treasury. His able financial management helped to fund Marlborough's armies in the War of the Spanish Succession.

power was brief; but the Whig Party owed him their revival in the years which followed.

Step by step the tangle had been cleared. By the private advice of John and Sarah Churchill, Princess Anne, Mary's younger sister, surrendered in favour of William her right to succeed to the throne should Mary predecease him. Thus William gained without dispute the Crown for life. Many honours and promotions at the time of the coronation rewarded the Revolutionary leaders. Churchill, though never in William's immediate circle, was confirmed in his rank of Lieutenant-General, and employed virtually as commander in chief to reconstitute the English army. Created Earl of Marlborough, he led the English contingent of eight thousand men in Flanders when in May 1689 war was formally declared against France.

The British islands now entered upon a most dangerous war crisis. The exiled James, sustained by a disciplined French contingent and large supplies of French munitions and money, landed in Ireland where he was welcomed as a deliverer. He reigned in Dublin, aided by an Irish Parliament, and was soon defended by a Catholic army which may have reached a hundred thousand men. The whole island except the Protestant settlements in the north passed under the control of the Jacobites, as they were henceforth called. While William looked to Flanders and the Rhine, Parliament vehemently drew his attention to Ireland. The King made the time-honoured mistake of meeting both needs inadequately. The defence of Londonderry and its relief from the sea was the one glorious episode of the campaigning season of 1689.

Cracks had appeared in the fabric of the original National Government. The Whigs considered that the Revolution belonged to them. Ought they not then to have all the offices? But William knew that he could never have gained the Crown of England without the help of the High Churchmen, who formed the staple of the Tory Party. Moreover William felt that Whig principles would ultimately lead to a republic. He therefore dissolved the Convention Parliament which had given him the Crown while, as the Whigs said, "its work was all unfinished".

At the election of February 1690 the Tories won.

It may seem strange that the new King should have now turned to the Earl of Sunderland, who had been King James's chief adviser. But James and Sunderland had irrevocably quarrelled. Sunderland was henceforth bound to William's interest, and his knowledge of the European political scene was invaluable to his sovereign's designs. He did not seek office for himself, and the actual government was entrusted to the statesmen of the middle view—the Duke of Shrewsbury, Sidney Godolphin, and Marlborough, and, though now, as always, he stood slightly aloof from all parties, Halifax. All had served King James. Their notion of party was to use both or either of the factions to keep themselves above water and to further the royal service. Of these it was Godolphin during the next twenty years who stood closest to Marlborough. Great political dexterity was combined in him with a scrupulous detachment. He never thrust forward for power, but he was seldom out of office. Awkward, retiring, dreamy by nature, he was yet heart and soul absorbed by the business of government.

William found himself compelled to go in person to Ireland, at the head of thirty-six thousand men. Thus the whole power of England was diverted from the main theatre of the war. The Prince of Waldeck, William's

THE PROTESTANT TRIUMPH

The Revolutions of 1641 and 1688 confirmed that Britain was to stay a Protestant nation. They also ensured that, in spite of political and religious wars abroad, British culture and commerce could thrive.

ST PAUL'S CATHEDRAL, LONDON

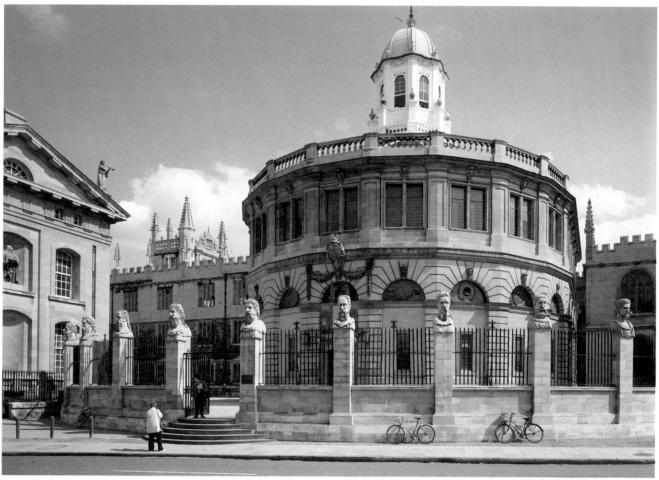

ST PAUL'S CATHEDRAL, LONDON, *(left)* is the fifth church to be built on its site, and it was the first cathedral in England to remain from start to finish under the control of its original architect. Begun in 1675, nine years after the Great Fire, it was completed in 1710. The glory of the cathedral is its magnificent dome, which was constructed in three parts: a central cone-shaped dome being screened both inside and outside by lighter decorative domes. Its creator, Sir Christopher Wren, whose portrait *(right)* by the fashionable court painter Sir Godfrey Kneller can be seen at the National Portrait Gallery, was originally professor of astronomy at London and then at Oxford. He was asked to design the Sheldonian Theatre, Oxford, *(above)* for the public ceremonies of the university. Over the next fifty years he was to design, in London alone, more than thirty churches, Chelsea Hospital, Kensington Palace, Marlborough House, and part of Hampton Court, as well as town halls, chapels, libraries, and private houses throughout the country.

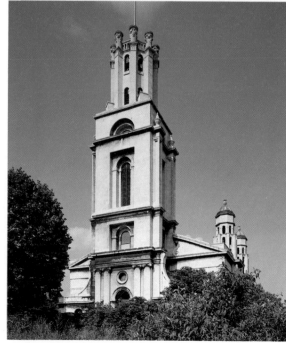

ST GEORGE IN THE EAST, LONDON, *(right)* is an outstanding example of the work of Wren's assistant and successor, Nicholas Hawksmoor. In this and other churches, including St Mary Woolnoth and St Anne Limehouse, Hawksmoor produced Baroque variations on the classical style of his master. The church later acquired stained glass windows by Sir Joshua Reynolds.

HAM HOUSE, GREATER LONDON, (above) originally built as a modest house in 1610, was transformed by Lord Lauderdale, one of Charles II's Cabal, into a flamboyant Baroque mansion. It remains a treasure house of Stuart taste. The Queen's Bedroom (top) was hung with English tapestries for Charles II's wife.

QUEEN ANNE FURNITURE (above) had an elegance and lightness of style which is clearly demonstrated in this walnut bureau-bookcase. The massive Stuart oak designs had given way to more refined continental taste with the arrival of William and Mary from the Netherlands.

"LOUISE DE KÉROUAILLE", National Portrait Gallery, London, (right) was painted by Pierre Mignard, in 1682. She was then Duchess of Portsmouth, and had been Charles II's principal mistress since 1671. An interesting feature of the picture is the pageboy. At that time black servants were very fashionable.

LEVENS HALL, CUMBRIA, an Elizabethan mansion, boasts gardens still laid out to their original design of 1690. Famous for their elaborate topiary (left), they are the work of Guillaume Beaumont, a Frenchman trained by Le Nôtre at Versailles. Beaumont was brought to Levens by Colonel James Grahme, a friend of the exiled James II. Beaumont designed many gardens, but only Levens can still be seen today.

"THE TICHBORNE DOLE", Tichborne Park, Hampshire, (left) painted in 1670 by Van Tilborch, records a distribution of the famous dole that has been distributed by the Tichbornes for some eight hundred years, since an early Tichborne agreed to keep for the poor the harvests of as many acres as his charitable wife could crawl round while a brand remained burning. She completed twenty-three acres.

141

ELM HILL, NORWICH, NORFOLK, (above) the best preserved of several historic streets in Norwich, retains many seventeenth-century buildings typical of urban design of that time.

BLENHEIM PALACE, OXFORDSHIRE, (left) a gift from the nation to the Duke of Marlborough, is England's Versailles, a Baroque monument designed by Vanbrugh and landscaped by "Capability" Brown. "At Blenheim," wrote Churchill, "I took two very important decisions: to be born and to marry. I am happily content with the decisions I took on both these occasions."

DONNINGTON HOSPITAL, NEAR NEWBURY, BERKSHIRE, (right) is a superb example of the almshouses that became a feature of towns in the seventeenth century, when "Hospital" carried its original meaning of a charitable home for the infirm.

CLARENCE HOUSE, THAXTED, ESSEX, (right) is built in the classic Queen Anne style. Thaxted, once the cutlery capital of England, retains fine buildings from almost every one of the last six centuries.

THE ORANGE TREE VASE, Erddig, Clwyd, (far right) is delftware, decorated with the arms of William and Mary. Erddig itself is a late seventeenth-century house, with its domestic wing and outbuildings still kept in working order.

CASTLE HOWARD, NORTH YORKSHIRE, was the first house to be designed by Sir John Vanbrugh. Known until then chiefly as a writer of comedies, he was wise enough to employ, as his assistant at Castle Howard, Nicholas Hawksmoor, formerly clerk of works to Sir Christopher Wren. The grandeur of the overall design was typical of Vanbrugh's style. The Great Hall, its height accentuated by its Corinthian marble pillars, is lit by a many-windowed dome, the first in any private home in England. The rooms now contain pictures by Reynolds, Romney and Gainsborough, and earlier great masters, and the vast stables house a collection of some three thousand costumes spanning three hundred years.

commander in the Low Countries, suffered a crushing defeat at the skilful hands of Marshal Luxembourg in the Battle of Fleurus. At the same time the French fleet gained a victory over the combined fleets of England and Holland off Beachy Head. It was said in London that "the Dutch had the honour, the French had the advantage, and the English the shame." The command of the Channel temporarily passed to the French, and it seemed that they could at the same time land an invading army in England and stop William returning from Ireland.

Queen Mary's Council had to face an alarming prospect. They were sustained by the loyalty and spirit of the nation. The whole country took up what arms they could find. With a nucleus of about six thousand regular troops and the hastily improvised militia, Marlborough stood ready to meet the invasion. However, on July 11, King William gained a decisive victory at the Boyne and drove King James out of Ireland back to France. The appeals of the defeated monarch for a French army to conquer England were not heeded by Louis who had his eyes on Germany. By the winter the French fleet was dismantled, and the English and Dutch fleets were refitted and again at sea. Thus the danger passed.

Late as was the season, Marlborough was commissioned to lead an expedition into Ireland, and in a short and brilliant campaign he subdued the whole of the southern Irish counties. The end of 1690 therefore saw the Irish War ended and the command of the sea regained. William was thus free after two years to proceed in person to the Continent with strong forces and to assume command of the main armies of the Alliance. He took Marlborough with him at the head of the English troops, but gave him no independent scope, and the campaign was indecisive.

The walls of the ancient town of London-derry, Ulster, can be clearly seen in this modern aerial photograph. Northern Ireland supported the Protestant William, while the Catholic south remained loyal to James II.

This portrait of Marlborough in 1712, by Sir Godfrey Kneller, is now in the collection of Earl Spencer at Althorp, Northamptonshire.

Thereafter a divergence grew between the King and Marlborough. When the commands for the next year's campaign were being assigned William proposed to take Marlborough to Flanders as lieutenant-general attached to his own person. Marlborough demurred. He did not wish to be carried round Flanders as a mere adviser, offering counsel that was not taken, and bearing responsibility for the failures that ensued. He asked to remain at home unless required to command the British troops, as in the past year. But the King had offered them to one of his Dutch generals. Many officers loudly expressed their resentment at the favour shown to the Dutch.

At this time almost all the leading men in England resumed relations with James, now installed at Saint-Germain, near Paris. Godolphin, Shrewsbury, Halifax, and Marlborough all entered into correspondence. King William was aware of this. He tolerated the fact that his principal English counsellors were reinsuring themselves against a break-up of his government or his death on the battlefield, and continued to employ them in great offices of State. If he quarrelled with Marlborough it was certainly not because of the family contacts which the general preserved with his nephew, King James's illegitimate son the Duke of Berwick. There was however talk of the substitution of Anne for William and Mary, and the influence of the Churchills with Princess Anne continued to be dominating. A rift between Anne and her sister, Queen Mary, now sharpens the already serious differences between the King and Marlborough. William treated Anne's husband, Prince George of Denmark, with the greatest contempt. Anne, who dearly loved her husband, was infuriated by these affronts.

As often happens in disputes among high personages, the brunt fell on a subordinate. Queen Mary demanded the dismissal of Sarah Churchill from Anne's household. Anne refused with all the obstinate strength of her nature. The two sisters parted in the anger of a mortal estrangement. The next morning at nine o'clock Marlborough, discharging his functions as Gentleman of the Bedchamber, handed the King his shirt, and William preserved his usual impassivity. Two hours later the Earl of Nottingham, Secretary of State, delivered to Marlborough a written order to consider himself as from that date dismissed from the army and all public employment and forbidden the Court. No reasons were given officially. Marlborough took his dismissal with unconcern, but his chief associates, the leading counsellors of the King, were offended. The Queen now forbade Sarah to come to Court, and Anne retorted by quitting it herself. Nothing would induce Anne to part with her cherished friend, and in these fires of adversity links were forged upon which the destinies of England were presently to hang.

CHAPTER 18

CONTINENTAL WAR

NO SOONER HAD KING WILLIAM SET OUT UPON the continental war than the imminent menace of invasion fell upon the island he had left denuded of troops. King James was given his chance of regaining the throne. An army of ten thousand desperate Irishmen and ten thousand French regulars was assembled around Cherbourg. The whole French fleet was concentrated in the Norman and Breton ports.

The Battle of Cape La Hogue was a victory for British seamanship. It dashed James II's hopes of invasion and destroyed Louis XIV's navy.

It was not until the middle of April 1692 that the French designs became known to the English Government, and fevered but vigorous preparations were made for defence by land and sea. As upon the approach of the Spanish Armada, all England was alert. Everything turned upon Admiral Russell. He, like Marlborough, had talked with Jacobite agents: William and Mary feared, and James fervently believed, that he would play the traitor. Russell however plainly told the Jacobite agent that, much as he loathed William's Government, if he met the French fleet at sea he would do his best to destroy it, "even though King James himself were on board." He kept his word. "If your officers play you false," he said to the sailors on the day of battle, "overboard with them, and myself the first."

On May 19–20 the English and Dutch fleets met Admiral Tourville with the main French naval power in the English Channel off Cape La Hogue. Tourville was decisively beaten and the whole apparatus of invasion was destroyed under the very eyes of the former king whom it was to have borne to his native shore.

The Battle of Cape La Hogue broke decisively for the whole of the wars of William and later of Anne all French pretensions to naval supremacy. It was the Trafalgar of the seventeenth century.

On land the campaigns of 1692–95 unrolled in what we know as Belgium. 1692 opened with a brilliant French success. Namur fell to the French armies. But worse was to follow. In August William marched by night with his whole army to attack Marshal Luxembourg. The French were surprised and their advanced troops were overwhelmed. But Luxembourg was equal to the emergency and managed to draw out an ordered line of battle. Eight splendid regiments of English infantry, under General Mackay, charged and broke the Swiss in fighting as fierce as had been seen in Europe in living memory. Luxembourg now launched the Household troops of France upon the British division, already strained by its exertions, and after a furious struggle, fought mostly with cold steel, beat it back. The British lost two of their best generals and half their numbers killed and wounded. William, who was unable to control the battle, shed bitter tears as he watched the slaughter, and exclaimed, "Oh, my poor English!" By noon the whole of the Allied army was in retreat.

These events infuriated the English Parliament. Against great opposition supplies were voted for another mismanaged and disastrous year of war. In July 1693 was fought the great Battle of Landen, unmatched in Europe for its slaughter, except by Malplaquet and Borodino, for over two hundred years. The French were in greatly superior strength. Nevertheless William determined to withstand their attack, and constructed almost overnight a system of strong entrenchments and palisades in the enclosed country along the Landen stream. After an heroic resistance the Allies were driven from their position by the French with a loss of nearly twenty thousand men, the attackers losing less than half this total. In 1694 William planned an expedition upon Brest. Here Tollemache, the British commander, was driven back to his ships with great loss, and presently died of his wounds.

The primitive finances of the English State could ill bear the burden of this European war. William's continental ventures now forced English statesmen to a reconstruction of the credit and finances of the country.

A war government was formed from the Whig Party and possessed in the person of Charles Montagu a first-rate financier. It was he who was responsible for facing this major problem. The first essential step was the creation of some national organ of credit. In collaboration with the Scottish banker William Paterson, Montagu, now Chancellor of the Exchequer, started the Bank of England in 1694 as a private corporation. This institution, while maintaining private joint-stock company methods, was to work in partnership with the Government, and provide the necessary means for backing the Government's credit. Montagu was not content merely to stop here. With the help of the philosopher John Locke, and William Loundes of the Treasury, he planned a complete overhaul of the coinage. Within two years the recoinage was carried out, and with this solidly reconstructed financial system the country was able in the future to bear the burden of European wars. It is perhaps one of the greatest achievements of the Whigs.

At the end of 1694 Queen Mary had been stricken with smallpox, and on December 28 she died, unreconciled to her sister Anne, mourned by her subjects, and lastingly missed by King William. The Crown now lay with

The first home of the Bank of England was Mercers' Hall, shown here as it appeared in 1694 when the Bank was founded by William Paterson.

William alone for life, and thereafter it must come to Anne. A formal reconciliation was effected between William and Anne. This altered the whole position of the Princess, and with it that of the redoubtable Churchills, who were her devoted intimates. Marlborough remained excluded for four more years from all employment; but with his gifts of patience and foresight upon the drift of events he now gave a steady support to William.

In 1695 the King gained one success. He recovered Namur in the teeth of the French armies, an event that enabled the seven-years war to be brought to an inconclusive end in 1696. England and Holland—the Maritime Powers as they were called—and Germany had defended themselves successfully, but were weary of the struggle. Spain was bellicose but powerless. Only the Habsburg Emperor Leopold, with his eyes fixed on the ever-impending vacancy of the Spanish throne, was in earnest in keeping the anti-French confederacy in being, but this "Grand Alliance" began to fall to pieces, and Louis, who had long felt the weight of a struggle upon so many fronts, was now disposed to peace. William was unable to resist the peace movement, but he saw that the quarrel was still unassuaged.

The Treaty of Ryswick in fact was but a truce, yet there were possibilities that it might ripen into a lasting settlement. Many comforted themselves with the hope that Ryswick had brought the struggle against the exorbitant power of France to an equipoise. But the Tories were now in one of their moods of violent reaction from continental intervention. Groaning under taxation, impatient of every restraint, the Commons plunged into a campaign of economy and disarmament. The moment the pressure of war was relaxed they had no idea but to cast away their arms. England came out of the war with an army of eighty-seven thousand regular soldiers. The King considered that thirty-thousand men was the least that would guarantee the public safety. His ministers did not dare to ask for more than ten thousand, and the House of Commons would only vote seven thousand. The navy was cut down only less severely. Officers and men were cast upon the streets or drifted into outlawry in the countryside. England, having made every sacrifice and performed prodigies of valour, now fell to the ground in weakness and improvidence when a very little more perseverance would have made her, if not supreme, at least secure.

The apparent confusion of politics throughout William's reign was largely due to the King's great reluctance to put himself at the disposal of either of the two main party groups. A familiar seesaw pattern of English politics began to emerge. The Whigs were sensitive to the danger of the French aggression in Europe. They understood the deep nature of the struggle, and were prepared to form on many occasions an effective and efficient war government. The Tories, on the other hand, resented the country being involved in continental commitments and voiced the traditional isolationism of the people. The foundation of the Bank of England strongly aroused their suspicions. The Bank had been a Whig creation, supported Government loans, and drew profits from the war. Here was an admirable platform. In 1697 the Whig administration was driven from office upon such themes, and with such a programme Robert Harley, now the rising hope of Toryism, created his power and position in the House of Commons.

This singularly modern figure whom everyone nowadays can understand, born and bred in a Puritan family, originally a Whig and a Dissenter, speedily became a master of Parliamentary tactics and procedure. He

Versailles, near Paris, was a village until Louis XIV built his palace and transferred his court to it in 1682. The grandeur of Mansart's buildings and Le Nôtre's geometric gardens were envied and copied all over Europe. The increasing power of Louis XIV made European war inevitable.

understood the art of "lengthening out" the debates, of "perplexing" the issues, and of taking up and exploiting popular cries. In the process of opposing the Court he gradually transformed himself from Whig to Tory and from Dissenter to High Churchman. Already in 1698 he was becoming virtually the Tories' leader in the House of Commons. He it was who conducted the reckless movement for the reduction of the armed forces. He it was who sought to rival the Whig Bank of England with a Tory Land Bank. All the time however he dreamt of a day when he could step above Parliamentary manoeuvrings and play a part upon the great world stage of war and diplomacy. In the Lords he was aided by Nottingham and the Earl of Rochester who together exploited those unworthy moods which from time to time have seized the Tory Party. They froze out and hunted into poverty the veteran soldiery and faithful Huguenot officers. They forced William to send away his Dutch Guards. They did all they could to undermine the strength of their country. In the name of peace, economy, and isolation they prepared the ground for a far more terrible renewal of the war.

William was so smitten by this wave of abject isolationism that he contemplated an abdication and return to Holland. He would abandon the odious and intractable people whose religion and institutions he had preserved. He would retort to their hatred of foreigners with a gesture of inexpressible scorn. Yet if we reflect on his many faults in tact, in conduct, and in fairness during the earlier days of his reign, the unwarrantable favours he had lavished on his Dutchmen, the injustices done to English commanders, his uncomprehending distaste for the people of his new realm, we cannot feel that all the blame was on one side. His present anguish paid his debts of former years. As for the English, they were only too soon to redeem their follies in blood and toil.

William's distresses led him to look again to Marlborough. The King's life and strength were ebbing, Anne would certainly succeed, and with the accession of Anne the virtual reign of Marlborough must begin. William slowly divested himself of an animosity so keen that he had once said that had he been a private person Marlborough and he could only have settled their differences by personal combat. Anne's sole surviving son, the Duke of Gloucester, was now nine years old, and it was thought fitting to provide the future heir apparent to the Crown with a governor of high consequence and with an establishment of his own. In the summer of 1698 William invited Marlborough to be governor of the boy prince. At the same time Marlborough was restored to his rank in the army and to the Privy Council.

From this time forth William seemed to turn increasingly towards the man of whose aid he had deprived himself during the most critical years of his reign; and Marlborough, though stamped from his youth with the profession of arms, became in the closing years of the reign a powerful politician. While helping the King in many ways, he was also most careful to keep a hold upon the Tory Party, because he was sure that no effective foreign policy could be maintained without its support. Above all, he supported William in his efforts to prevent an undue reduction of the army, and in fact led the House of Lords in this direction. Although the untimely death in 1700 of the little Duke of Gloucester deprived Marlborough of his office, he still remained at the very centre of the political system.

There was now no direct Protestant heir to the English and Scottish thrones. By an Act of Settlement, the House of Hanover, descended from the attractive daughter of James I who had briefly been Queen of Bohemia, was declared next in succession after Anne. The Act laid down that every sovereign in future must be a member of the Church of England. It also declared that no foreign-born monarch might wage continental wars without the approval of Parliament; he must not go abroad without consent; and no foreigners should sit in Parliament or on the Privy Council. Thus were recorded in statute the English grievances against William III. Parliament had seen to it that the House of Hanover was to be more strictly circumscribed than he had been. But it had also gone far to secure the Protestant succession.

Queen Anne bore seventeen children, but only one, William, Duke of Gloucester, survived infancy. But he, too, died in 1700, aged only eleven. This mother and child portrait can be seen in the National Gallery.

CHAPTER 19

THE SPANISH SUCCESSION

NO GREAT WAR WAS EVER ENTERED UPON with more reluctance on both sides than the War of the Spanish Succession. Europe was exhausted and disillusioned. The new-found contacts which had sprung up between William and Louis expressed the heartfelt wishes of the peoples both of the Maritime Powers and of France. But over them and all the rest of Europe hung the long-delayed, long-dreaded, ever-approaching demise of the Spanish Crown. William was deeply conscious of his weakness. He was convinced that nothing would make England fight again, and without England Holland could expect nothing short of subjugation. William therefore cast himself upon the policy of partitioning the Spanish empire, which included Belgium, much of Italy, and a large part of the New World. There were three claimants.

The first was France, represented either by the Dauphin or, if the French and Spanish Crowns could not be joined, by his second son, Philip, the

Duke of Anjou. The second was the Emperor Leopold, who was willing to transfer his claims to his second son by his second wife, the Archduke Charles. Thirdly, there was the Emperor's grandson by his first marriage, the Electoral Prince of Bavaria. The essence of the Partition Treaty of 1698 was to give the bulk of the Spanish empire to the candidate who, if not strongest in right, was at least weakest in power. Louis and William both promised to recognise the Electoral Prince as heir to Charles II of Spain. Important compensations were offered to the Dauphin.

This plan concerted between Louis XIV and William III was vehemently resented by the Emperor and also provoked a fierce reaction in Spain. Spanish society now showed that it cared above all things for the integrity of the Spanish domains and that the question of the prince who should reign over them all was secondary. At the end of the long struggle Spanish sentiment adopted exactly the opposite view.

But now a startling event occurred. In February 1699 the Electoral Prince of Bavaria, the child in whose chubby hands the greatest states had resolved to place the most splendid prize, suddenly died. Why and how he died at this moment did not fail to excite dark suspicions. Now all these elaborate, perilous conversations must be begun over again. By great exertions William and Louis arranged a second Treaty of Partition on June 11, 1699, by which the Archduke Charles was made heir-in-chief. To him were assigned Spain, the overseas colonies and Belgium, on the condition that they should never be united with the Empire. The Dauphin was to have Naples and Sicily, the Milanese, and certain other Italian possessions.

Meanwhile the feeble life-candle of the childless Spanish King, Charles II, burnt low. To the ravages of deformity and disease were added the most grievous afflictions of the mind. The royal victim believed himself to be possessed by the Devil. His only comfort was in the morbid contemplation of the tomb. All the nations waited in suspense upon his failing pulses and deepening mania. He had however continued on the verge of death for more than thirty years, and one by one the great statesmen of Europe who had awaited this event had themselves been overtaken by the darkness of night. Charles had now reached the end of his torments.

But within his diseased frame, his clouded mind, his superstitious soul, there glowed one imperial thought—the unity of the Spanish empire. He was determined to proclaim with his last gasp that his vast dominions should pass intact and entire to one prince and to one alone. The rival

The claimants to the Spanish throne were cousins who, by generations of intermarriage, were descendants of the most powerful royal families in Europe. Marriage between close relatives was encouraged because it kept wealth and power within the family. The policy had disastrous effects: it led to inbreeding which resulted in physical and mental weakness, and finally to a disputed succession which brought Europe into wholesale war.

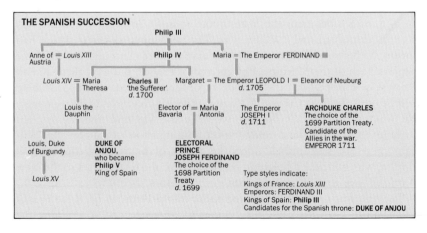

THE SPANISH SUCCESSION

Philip III

Anne of = Louis XIII
Austria

Philip IV

Maria = The Emperor FERDINAND III

Louis XIV = Maria
Theresa

Charles II
'the Sufferer'
d. 1700

Margaret = The Emperor LEOPOLD I = Eleanor of Neuburg
d. 1705

Louis the
Dauphin

Elector of = Maria
Bavaria   Antonia

The Emperor
JOSEPH I
d. 1711

ARCHDUKE CHARLES
The choice of the
1699 Partition Treaty.
Candidate of the
Allies in the war.
EMPEROR 1711

Louis, Duke
of Burgundy

DUKE OF
ANJOU,
who became
Philip V
King of Spain

ELECTORAL
PRINCE
JOSEPH FERDINAND
The choice of the
1698 Partition
Treaty
d. 1699

Louis XV

Type styles indicate:

Kings of France: *Louis XIII*
Emperors: FERDINAND III
Kings of Spain: **Philip III**
Candidates for the Spanish throne: **DUKE OF ANJOU**

interest struggled for access to his death-chamber. In the end he was persuaded to sign a will leaving his throne to the Duke of Anjou. The will was completed on October 7, and couriers galloped with the news from the Escorial to Versailles. On November 1 Charles expired.

Louis XIV had now reached one of the great turning-points in the history of France. Should he stand by the treaty with William, or endorse the will, and defend his grandson's claims in the field against all comers? Would England oppose him? Apart from good faith and solemnly signed agreements upon which the ink was barely dry, the choice, like so many momentous choices, was nicely balanced. On November 8 it was decided to repudiate the treaty and stand upon the will. On November 16 a famous scene was enacted at Versailles. Louis XIV, at his levee, presented the Spanish ambassador to the Duke of Anjou, saying, "You may salute him as your King." The ambassador gave vent to his celebrated indiscretion, "There are no more Pyrenees."

Confronted with this event, William felt himself constrained to recognise the Duke of Anjou as Philip V of Spain. The House of Commons, still in a mood far removed from European realities, eagerly accepted Louis XIV's assurance that, "content with his power, he would not seek to increase it at the expense of his grandson". A series of ugly incidents broke from outside, however, upon the fevered complacency of English politics. A letter from Melfort, the Jacobite Secretary of State at Saint-Germain, was discovered in the English mailbags, disclosing a plan for the immediate French invasion of England in the Jacobite cause. William hastened to present this to Parliament as a proof of perfidy. At about the same time it became apparent that the freedom of the British trade in the Mediterranean was also in jeopardy. But the supreme event which roused all England to an understanding of what had actually happened in the virtual union of the Crowns of France and Spain was a tremendous military operation effected under the guise of brazen legality.

A line of Spanish fortresses in Belgium, garrisoned under treaty rights by the Dutch, constituted the main barrier of the Netherlands against a French invasion. Louis resolved to make sure of these barrier fortresses. During the month of February 1701 strong French forces arrived before all the Belgian cities. The Spanish commanders welcomed them with open gates. They had come, it was contended, only to help protect the possessions of His Most Catholic Majesty. The Dutch garrisons, overawed by force, were interned. Antwerp, Mons, Namur, Leau, Venloo, and a dozen other strongholds, all passed in a few weeks, without a shot fired, into the hands of Louis XIV. All that the Grand Alliance of 1689 had defended in the Low Countries in seven years of war melted like snow at Easter.

Europe was roused, and at last England too. Once more the fighting men came into their own. The armies newly dissolved, the officers so lightly dismissed and despised, became again important. Once more the drums began to beat, and smug merchants and crafty politicians turned to the martial class, whom they had lately abused and suppressed. In June the House of Commons authorised the King to seek allies; ten thousand men at any rate should be guaranteed to Holland. William felt the tide had set in his favour. The parties in opposition to him in his two realms, the Tory majority in the House of Commons and the powerful burgesses of Amsterdam, were both begging him to do everything that he "thought

Louis XIV was enraged by cartoons in the Dutch press depicting the eclipse of the Sun King, as he was known, by a round Dutch cheese.

MEDICAL MATTERS

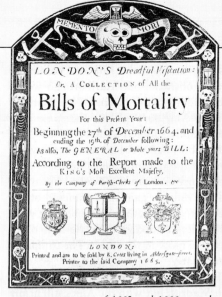

ALTHOUGH ADVANCES MADE in medical knowledge in the seventeenth and eighteenth centuries were not comparable to those made in physics, there was a lively interest in experiment and some significant increase in understanding.

Since the Church was still firmly opposed to human dissection a doctor's anatomical knowledge was sketchy, and his knowledge of the way the body functions was virtually non-existent. Sensible practical use was made of herbal remedies, but otherwise diagnoses and ensuing treatment were primitive. Purgings and bleedings remained common well into the nineteenth century.

The first individual to identify and classify specific diseases was the Swiss-German physician Paracelsus (1493-1541), and the first to understand at least the rudiments of anatomy was Professor Andreas Vesalius (1514-64), at the University of Padua.

In the seventeenth century the most important British medical advance was William Harvey's theory concerning the circulation of the blood, and it was followed in the eighteenth by Edward Jenner's development of a vaccination to prevent smallpox, one of the great scourges of the time. James Lind broke new ground in preventive medicine when he suggested that scurvy, the seaman's disease, could be curbed by a diet of fresh meat and vegetables supplemented with lemon juice.

Although little relief was available for many diseases—some *epidemic*, like the Great Plague of London in 1665, and some *endemic*, like typhus—the growth in society of the idea that cleanliness was next to Godliness was a sign that attitudes were beginning to change. So, too, was a new enthusiasm for the building of dispensaries and hospitals. But, in the absence of basic scientific knowledge, medical attention was bound to be inadequate, and hospitals themselves tended to be centres of contagion as well as of treatment. The connection between dirt and disease was not accepted until the late eighteenth century.

THE GREAT PLAGUE of 1665 and 1666 was the worst of many scourges. Bills of mortality, such as the one above, attempted to provide statistics of its victims. These were probably not completely accurate, but they showed the authorities' concern. The Great Plague died out in the Great Fire of 1666, but other plagues followed. Smallpox, typhus, cholera and tuberculosis claimed their victims in the eighteenth and nineteenth centuries. While vaccination wiped out smallpox, the improvement in hygiene and the purification of water in the nineteenth century helped to combat the other three. There was, however, very little understanding of mental illness until the twentieth century.

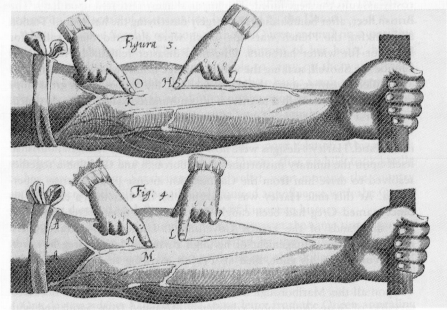

MEDICAL DISCOVERIES, notably William Harvey's brilliant discovery of the circulation of the blood, made the study of anatomy more acceptable. This picture comes from the first edition of Harvey's De Motu Cordis published in 1628. It shows how blood in the veins and arteries of the forearm can flow in only one direction. William Harvey was the first to understand the workings of the ventricle and the aorta, the pumping system of the heart.

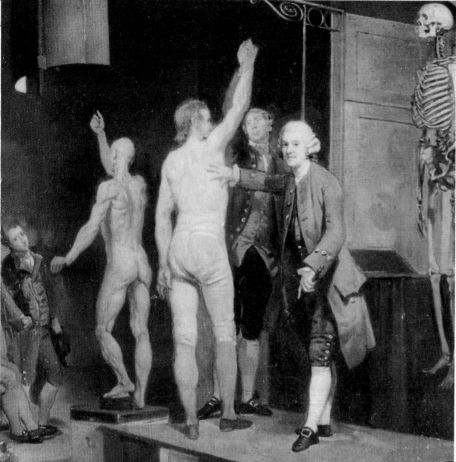

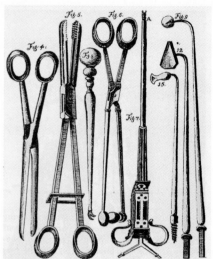

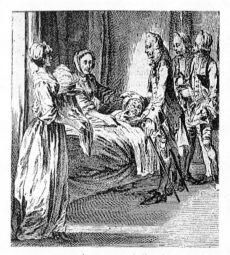

THE FIRST SURGEONS *were barbers who specialised in lancing boils, removing small growths or occasionally performing emergency amputations. Rough and ready surgery had, of course, always been practised in time of war. These surgical instruments were made in the eighteenth century. Sterilisation was not common until World War I.*

ANATOMY, *a subject abhorrent to the medieval Church, was studied more seriously in the eighteenth century. In the picture above, John and William Hunter lecture in anatomy at the Royal Academy. Although more attention was paid to the subject after Harvey's discoveries, no major breakthrough in the care of the human body could yet be made. This would come in the nineteenth century, when advances* in chemistry and bacteriology had brought more accurate diagnosis of disease. The operating theatre shown below was opened in 1822 in St Thomas's Hospital, Southwark, and the first operations were conducted without the use of anaesthetics. The theatre has been restored to its original state and retains authentic details like the box of sawdust near the operating table to catch the blood.

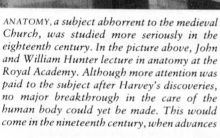

SMALLPOX *was the greatest killer disease of the eighteenth century. It assaulted rich and poor alike, and of those who caught it, one in four died. An old wives' tale held that smallpox never attacked dairymaids, because they had had cowpox. An English country doctor, Edward Jenner, decided to test this idea by taking pus from a girl infected with cowpox and transferring it to two local boys whom he injected with smallpox shortly afterwards. They remained healthy. When Jenner published his findings, the medical establishment was sceptical. However, many, like the novelist Fanny Burney, and the recruits to George Washington's army, were treated.*

ARTS AND LETTERS

I N NO PERIOD OF BRITISH HISTORY was aesthetic taste more subjected to regulation than in the eighteenth century. "Rules" were devised for the composition of music and poetry, for the design of houses and gardens, and even for the painting of pictures. There were rebels of course— William Blake for one—but throughout the century order was generally extolled as civilisation's greatest glory. Essayists like Steele and Addison did much to encourage such thinking, and magazines brought their writings before a wide public. Founded in 1711, the *Spectator* was to be followed in 1731 by the *Gentleman's Magazine*, in which Samuel Johnson, famous for his conversations and his dictionary, for the first time recorded Parliamentary speeches for ordinary citizens to read. Johnson claimed of his dictionary that it was compiled "with little assistance from the learned and without any patronage of the great".

Johnson was a friend of the painter Sir Joshua Reynolds, and of the musician Charles Burney, father of the successful woman novelist Fanny Burney. Patronage might still play an important part in many of the arts, but new readers were emerging who were only too glad to pay for the novels of the writers like Defoe, Fielding, Richardson, and later, Jane Austen.

This was an age, too, of brilliant society hostesses, and of distinguished artistic *salons*. Great private libraries and art collections were founded and learning was no longer confined within the walls of Oxford and Cambridge. Indeed, it was the Scottish universities, Edinburgh in particular, that contributed most to its spread.

Even in an age of aesthetic appreciation, however, of books and wider learning, there were inevitably outsiders. And unashamed ones. Sarah Churchill, Duchess of Marlborough and close confidante of Queen Anne, made herself very clear on the subject: "Books, prithee, don't talk to me about books. The only books I know are men and cards."

THE ROYAL ACADEMY OF ARTS *was founded in 1768 by George III. He chose the original thirty-six members who are shown in "The Life Class at the Royal Academy" (above) by Richard Earlom after a picture by Johannes Zoffany. The Academy's first president, Sir Joshua Reynolds, can be seen positioning the model on the right. Earlom, an engraver who successfully combined the techniques of etching and mezzotint, also sketched the Academy's exhibition of 1777 (below). The public peruse their catalogues of the contemporary paintings lining the walls. Resting on a bench are a bored child and a footsore old lady.*

JOSEPH ADDISON (1672–1719), *who raised essay-writing to an art form, was educated at Charterhouse School with Richard Steele. In 1709 Steele founded* The Tatler *and soon invited Addison to become a contributor. Other journals also offered scope for Addison's literary talents. His portrait (above) is by Michael Dahl and can be seen in the National Portrait Gallery.*

PAMELA or VIRTUE REWARDED, *by Samuel Richardson (1689–1761), is sometimes acclaimed as the first modern novel. It stemmed from a proposal from two printers that Richardson should write a collection of model letters for those unversed in letter writing. The book inspired a whole series of paintings by Joseph Highmore, one of which is seen above.*

THE
LIFE
AND
STRANGE SURPRIZING
ADVENTURES
OF
ROBINSON CRUSOE,
Of *TORK,* MARINER:

Who lived Eight and Twenty Years, all alone in an un-inhabited Ifland on the Coaft of AMERICA, near the Mouth of the Great River of OROONOQUE;

Having been caft on Shore by Shipwreck, wherein all the Men perifhed but himfelf.

WITH

An Account how he was at laft as ftrangely deliver'd by PYRATES.

Written by Himfelf.

LONDON:
Printed for W. TAYLOR at the *Ship* in *Pater-Nofter-Row.* MDCCXIX.

SAMUEL JOHNSON (1709–84), *the author of* The Dictionary of the English Language, *was painted (above) by his close friend, Sir Joshua Reynolds. Apart from writing books and poetry, Johnson, the outstanding critic of his day, founded two literary magazines,* The Rambler *and* The Idler. *He has been immortalised in the fine biography written by his friend, James Boswell.*

FANNY BURNEY (1752–1840), *later Madame D'Arblay, was another close friend of Samuel Johnson and his circle. Her first novel,* Evelina, *was followed by* Camilla *which made her both rich and famous. Her letters and diary give an excellent picture of London culture and society in the years between 1768 and 1840. Her portrait (above) was painted by her cousin, E.F. Burney.*

ROBINSON CRUSOE WAS PUBLISHED *in 1719 when its author, Daniel Defoe (1660–1731), was nearly sixty. It was based on the story of one Alexander Selkirk, who ran away to sea in 1704, was captured by pirates and put ashore on the uninhabited island of Juan Fernandez, from which he was rescued five years later. Defoe knew the facts and added much more from his own imagination.*

The doorway of 10 Downing Street, originally the home of Sir Robert Walpole. He was the first parliamentary leader to be generally referred to as Prime Minister.

"They are ringing their bells now, but soon they will be wringing their hands." Now opened a mighty struggle, at first with Spain only, but later by the family compact between the Bourbon monarchs, involving France. Thus began that final duel between Britain and her nearest neighbour which in less than a century was to see the glories of Chatham, the follies of Lord North, the terrors of the French Revolution and, not least, the rise and fall of Napoleon Bonaparte.

By sure degrees, in the confusion and mismanagement which followed, Walpole's power, as he had foreseen, slipped from him. The operations of the ill-manned fleet failed. The one success, the capture of Portobello, on the isthmus of Panama, was achieved by Admiral Vernon, the hero of the Opposition. Captain Anson's squadron disappeared into the Pacific. It inflicted little damage on the Spaniards, but in a voyage lasting nearly four years Anson circumnavigated the globe, charting as he went. In the course of it he schooled a new generation of naval officers.

Meanwhile, the tide of national feeling ran high. There were riots in London. The Prince of Wales appeared everywhere, to be cheered by opponents of the Government. A new tune was on their lips, with Thomson's resounding words, "Rule, Britannia".

In February 1741 an Opposition member, Samuel Sandys, proposed an address to the King for the dismissal of Walpole. For the last time the old minister outwitted his foes. He had made overtures to the Jacobite group in the Commons, even letting it be supposed that he would countenance a Jacobite Restoration. To the amazement of all, the Jacobites voted for him. The Opposition, in the words of Lord Chesterfield, "broke in pieces". But under the Septennial Act elections were due. Frederick, Prince of Wales spent lavishly in buying up seats, and his campaign brought twenty-seven Cornish seats over to the Opposition. The electoral influence of the Scottish earls counted against Walpole, and when the members returned to Westminster his Government was defeated on an election petition (contested returns were decided by the House on purely party lines) and resigned. It was February 1742. Sir Robert had governed England for twenty-one years.

During the last days before his fall he sat for hours on end, alone and silent, brooding over the past in Downing Street. He was the first Chief Minister to reside at Number Ten. He had accomplished the work of his life, the peaceful establishment of the Protestant succession in England. He had soothed and coaxed a grumbling, irritated country into acquiescence in the new regime. He had built up a powerful organisation, fed and fattened on Government patronage. He had supervised the day-to-day administration of the country, unhampered by royal interference. The sovereign had ceased after 1714 to preside in person over the Cabinet, save on exceptional occasions—a most significant event, though it was only the result of an accident. Queen Anne had always, when in good health, presided on Sunday evenings over her Cabinet meetings at Kensington Palace. The ministers regarded themselves as individually responsible to her and under faint obligations to each other. But George I had been unable to speak English and had to converse with his ministers in French or such dog-Latin as they remembered from Eton. Walpole had therefore created for himself a dominating position in this vital executive committee, "as sole and Prime Minister".

He had kept England at peace for nearly twenty years. Now he went to the House of Lords as Earl of Orford. His obstinate monopoly of political power in the Commons had put all men of talent up against him, and in the end his policy enabled the Opposition to arouse the public opinion he had so assiduously lulled. He was the first great House of Commons man in British history, and if he had resigned before the war with Spain he might have been called the most successful.

CHAPTER 25

THE AUSTRIAN SUCCESSION AND THE "FORTY-FIVE"

THE WAR BETWEEN BRITAIN AND SPAIN, which the Opposition had forced upon Walpole, was soon merged in a general European struggle. Britain had expected to fight naval and colonial campaigns in Spanish waters and in Spanish South America. Instead she found herself engaged in a continental war. Two royal deaths in 1740 set the conflict in motion. East of the Elbe the rising kingdom of Prussia acquired a new ruler, Frederick II, later called the Great, who inherited a formidable army which he fretted to use. It was his ambition to expand his scattered territories and weld them into the strongest state in Germany. Military gifts and powers of leadership, a calculating spirit and utter ruthlessness, were his in equal portion. Almost immediately he had the chance to put them to the test. In October the Habsburg Emperor Charles VI died, leaving his broad domains, though not his Imperial title, to his daughter Maria Theresa. The Emperor had extracted solemn guarantees from all the powers of Europe that they would recognise her accession in Austria, Hungary, Bohemia, and the Southern Netherlands, but these meant nothing to Frederick. He attacked and seized the Austrian province of Silesia, which lay to the south of his own territories. France, ever jealous of the Habsburgs, encouraged and supported him. Thus Europe was plunged into what is termed the War of the Austrian Succession.

In England King George II was much beset by the problems that arose. He correctly measured the ambitions of his nephew, Frederick of Prussia. He was fearful that the next Prussian onslaught might engulf his own estates in Germany, far dearer to his heart than the Kingdom of Great Britain. In London, after Walpole's fall, King George's Government was managed by Henry Pelham, First Lord of the Treasury, and his brother, the Duke of Newcastle, long a Secretary of State. Their great territorial wealth and electoral influence enabled them to maintain Whig dominion over the House of Commons. They were skilled in party manoeuvre, but inexpert in the handling of foreign or military affairs. Newcastle knew much of Europe; by nature, however, he was cautious, and the exercise of patronage at home meant more to him than the conduct of war. George II turned for help and advice therefore, to the Pelhams' rival, Lord Carteret who, under Walpole, had shared the fate of all men who were clever enough to be dangerous, and was dismissed to the Lord Lieutenancy of Ireland. Now by supporting the King's German interests he was able to outbid the Pelhams for the royal favour and was appointed a Secretary of State.

Carteret wanted Hanover and England to preserve and promote a balance of power in Europe. To meet the combination of France, Spain, and

George II came to the throne in 1727. He had no outstanding gifts but Britain progressed and under his rule enjoyed prosperity. During his father's absences in Hanover, he had often deputised as King.

THE ENGLISH SQUIRE

D URING THE EIGHTEENTH century land in England, always a major source of wealth and power for the aristocracy, almost doubled in value. This enabled landowners further to enlarge their holdings: in 1700, peers of the realm owned approximately twenty per cent of the nation's land; by 1800 that figure had increased to twenty-five per cent.

It was the smaller landlords, however, living in closer contact with their tenants, who set the styles of the English squire. In Henry Fielding's novel *Tom Jones*, Squire Western is an attractive example: he could be "a gentleman among stableboys and a stableboy among gentlemen", and he loved foxhunting above all else.

But inevitably not all country squires were like Squire Western. This was a century of large-scale land enclosures, when tenant farmers suffered the miseries of eviction as they found themselves dispossessed by ruthless landlords. Though some squires abused their authority, others recognised that it was a "pity the poor should be deprived of their Right only because they are poor", and tried instead to help their farm labourers.

In general, good or bad, the country squire's main contribution was to accelerate improvements in farming methods on his land. As time passed, a wider range of crops was grown, skilled breeding improved the quality of livestock, and land enclosure, however controversial, made higher crop yields possible.

Innovations made by progressive landowners were imitated by their neighbours, and later writers were to describe this period as one of an "agricultural revolution". Such a description is exaggerated, but it draws attention to the fact that even as industrial cities were coming into existence England's countryside was becoming more able to feed a growing population.

AGRICULTURAL REFORMERS *such as the Cokes and Townshends, Norfolk landowners, developed methods for improving the land and the quality of livestock. Previously, the rotation of cereal crops left a third of the land fallow annually. Now, with the introduction of clover, sainfoin and various root crops, which added nitrogen to the soil, the land could be kept in constant use. The increased yields of hay and turnips also ensured that animals could be fed throughout the winter instead of being slaughtered. The picture (above) shows Thomas Coke of Holkham at one of his sheep inspections. His stock-breeding experiments improved the strains of sheep, cattle and hogs. In the background his great Palladian country house can be seen.*

"FARMER GEORGE" was his subjects' irreverent nickname for George III. On the left, James Gillray cruelly satirises the King's preoccupation with farming, which he evidently felt was demeaning to one of royal rank. Queen Charlotte clutches her husband's arm, while the King terrifies a rustic with questions.

The Godolphin Arabian

ENGLISH THOROUGHBREDS *have been prized and exported since the early eighteenth century. The Godolphin Arabian (above) had an eventful early life. Foaled in 1724, he was presented by the Sultan of Morocco to Louis XV of France. The King sold him, and in 1729 he was found by an English friend of Lord Godolphin's pulling a milk cart in Paris. Brought to Lord Godolphin's Derbyshire stud he became one of three founding sires of the* English Thoroughbred—*the other two were the Byerley Turk and the Darley Arabian. The Thoroughbred strain was the result of crossing earlier breeds of "running horses" with imports of Oriental stock and later with the three Arabians. In the picture above, the foremost animal painter of the day, George Stubbs (1724-1806), shows the characteristically short head, widely spaced eyes, and flared nostrils of the pure-bred Arab.*

JETHRO TULL'S SEED DRILL, *invented in 1701, broke up the soil, drilled orderly trenches and planted seeds by means of pipes attached to a hopper on a small cart, thus doing several jobs at once. It was much less wasteful than the old method of broadcasting seed by hand, and planting grain in straight lines made weeding easier, too. He built his invention from parts of an organ soundboard. The seed drill, one of which is shown in the picture above, still ranks with the later threshing machine and combine harvester as a major breakthrough in agricultural technology. On the right is a portrait of its inventor. Tull wrote his treatise, Horse-hoeing Husbandry, in 1733. It describes his observations on continental farming and expounds the usefulness of his new seed drill.*

frontier forts. Never did a war open with darker prospects. Pitt's hour had come. "I know," he had told the Duke of Devonshire, "that I can save this country and that no one else can." He disavowed Cumberland's surrender, while Frederick, supported by the subsidies which Pitt had spent the eloquence of his youth in denouncing, routed the French at Rossbach and Austrians at Leuthen. Before the year was out it seemed as if Fortune, recognising her masters, was changing sides.

So the great years opened, years for Pitt and his country of almost intoxicating glory. The French were swept out of Hanover; Cape Breton was again taken, and the name of the "Great Commoner" stamped on the map at Pittsburg, Pennsylvania. France's two main fleets, in the Mediterranean and in the Channel, were separately defeated, combined they might have covered an invasion of England. Admiral Boscawen, detailed to watch the Toulon squadron, caught it slipping through the Straits of Gibraltar, destroyed five ships and drove the rest into Cadiz Bay, blockaded and out of action. Three months later, in a high gale and among uncharted rocks and shoals, Admiral Hawke annihilated the Brest fleet. For the rest of the war Quiberon was an English naval station, where the sailors occupied their leisure and maintained their health by growing cabbages on French soil. Between these victories Wolfe had fallen at Quebec, leaving Amherst to complete the conquest of Canada, while Clive and Eyre Coote were uprooting the remnants of French power in India.

It is necessary to examine some of these triumphs at closer hand. In America Pitt faced a difficult and complex task. The governors of the

The drawing for this engraving of the capture of Quebec was made by Wolfe's aide-de-camp after the momentous victory.

English colonies had long been aware of the threat beyond their frontiers. The French were moving along the waterways beyond the mountain barrier of the Alleghanies and extending their alliances with the Indians in an attempt to link their colony of Louisiana in the south with Canada in the north. Thus the English settlements would be confined to the seaboard and their westward expansion would stop.

The New England colonies also lay open to attack down the easy path of invasion, the Hudson valley. A struggle began for a foothold at the valley head. There was little organisation. Each of the colonies attempted to repel Indian raids and French settlers with their own militias. They were united in distrusting the home Government, but in little else. Although there were now over a million British Americans, vastly outnumbering the French, their quarrels and disunion extinguished this advantage. Only the tactful handling of Pitt secured their cooperation, and even so throughout the war colonial traders continued to supply the French with all their needs in defiance of the Government and the common interest.

The year 1756 had been disastrous in America. Oswego, the only English fort on the Great Lakes, was lost. The campaign of 1757 was hardly more successful. The fortress of Louisburg, which commanded the Gulf of St Lawrence, had been taken by an Anglo-Colonial force in the 1740s and returned to France at the peace treaty of 1748 at Aix-la-Chapelle. English troops were now sent to recapture it. They were commanded by an ineffectual and unenterprising officer, Lord Loudon, who prepared to attack by concentrating at Halifax such colonial troops from New England as the colonies would release. This left the Hudson valley open to the French. At the head of the valley were three small forts: Crown Point, Edward, and William Henry. The French, under the Governor of Canada, Montcalm, and his Indian allies, swept over the frontier through the wooded mountains and besieged Fort William Henry. The small colonial garrison held out for five days, but was forced to surrender. Montcalm was unable to restrain his Indians and the prisoners were massacred. The tragedy bit into the minds of the New Englanders. The British were not defending them; while New England was left exposed to the French, the troops which might have protected them were wasting time at Halifax.

Pitt now bent his mind to the American war. Throughout the winter he studied the maps and wrote dispatches to the officers and governors. A threefold strategic plan was framed for 1758. Loudon was recalled. His successor, Amherst, with Brigadier Wolfe, and naval support from Halifax, was to sail up the St Lawrence and strike at Quebec. Another army, under Abercromby, was to seize Lake George at the head of the Hudson valley and try to join Amherst and Wolfe before Quebec. A third force, under Brigadier Forbes, would advance up the Ohio valley from Pennsylvania and capture Fort Duquesne, one of a line of French posts along the Ohio and the Mississippi rivers. Meanwhile, the fleet was so disposed as to stop any reinforcements from leaving France.

A mind capable of conceiving and directing these efforts was now in power at Whitehall, but supervision at a distance of three thousand miles was almost impossible in the days of sail. Amherst and Wolfe hammered at the northern borders of Canada. In July Louisburg was captured. But Abercromby, advancing from Ticonderoga, became entangled in the dense woods; his army was badly beaten and his advance was halted. The

An ally of the British was Joseph Brant, a chief of the Mohawks, (1742–1807) who was painted by Sir George Romney in 1776 when he visited London after fighting for the British in the American wars. He began his career as a soldier when he was only thirteen.

General James Wolfe made his name as a soldier at Dettingen in 1743 and in the Jacobite Rebellion of 1745. By 1759 he had risen to the rank of major general commanding nine thousand men. He was only thirty-two when he conquered Quebec and died a hero.

Pennsylvanian venture was more successful. Fort Duquesne was taken and destroyed and the place renamed Pittsburg; but lack of numbers and organisation compelled the British force to retire at the end of the campaign. Brigadier Forbes gave a bitter description of the affair: "A few of their principal Officers excepted, all the rest are an extream bad Collection of broken Innkeepers, Horse Jockeys, & Indian traders, and that the Men under them are a direct Copy of their Officers, nor can it well be otherwise, as they are a gathering from the scum of the worst people, in every Country. . . ." These remarks reflect the worsening relations and woeful lack of understanding between British officers and American colonists.

There was little enough to show for such efforts, but Pitt was undaunted. On December 29, 1758, further instructions were sent to Amherst. "It were much to be wished," the instructions emphasised, "that any Operations on the side of Lake Ontario could be pushed as far as Niagara, and that you may find it practicable to set on foot some Enterprize against the Fort there, the Success of which would so greatly contribute to establish the uninterrupted Dominion of that Lake, and at the same time . . . cut off the Communication between Canada and the French Settlements to the South." There was also talk about the need of acquiring Indian allies.

Amherst thought little of this. Several months earlier he had written to Pitt that "they are a pack of lazy, rum-drinking people and little good, but if ever they are of use it will be when we can act offensively. The French are much more afraid of them than they need be." Nevertheless, it was fortunate for the British that the Six Nations of the Iroquois, who occupied a key position between the British and French settlements near the Great Lakes, were generally friendly.

According to the new plan, in the coming year the navy would attack the French West Indies, and the invasion of Canada up the St Lawrence would be pushed harder than ever in spite of the bitter experience of the past. Wolfe reported the navy's "thorough aversion" to the task. It was indeed hazardous. But it was to be backed by a renewed advance up the Hudson against the French fort of Niagara on the Great Lakes, the importance of which Pitt had emphasised in his instructions.

The plan succeeded. The year 1759 brought fame to British arms throughout the world. In May the navy captured Guadeloupe, the richest sugar island of the West Indies. In July Amherst took Ticonderoga and Fort Niagara, thus gaining for the American colonies a frontier upon the Great Lakes. In September the expedition up the St Lawrence attacked Quebec. Wolfe conducted a personal reconnaissance of the river at night, and beguiled the officers by reciting Gray's "Elegy": "The paths of glory lead but to the grave." By brilliant cooperation between army and navy Wolfe landed his men, and led them by an unsuspected path, under cover of darkness, up the steep cliffs of the Heights of Abraham. In the battle that followed Montcalm was defeated and killed and the key fortress of Canada was secured. Wolfe, mortally wounded, lived until victory was certain, and died murmuring, "Now God be praised, I will die in peace."

But it needed another year's fighting to gain Canada for the English-speaking world. In September 1760 Montreal fell to Amherst, and the huge province of French Canada changed hands.

The inactivity of the French fleet is a remarkable feature of the war. If

THE AUGUSTAN AGE

Between 1714 and 1760 there were times when the advance of enlightenment seemed to have come to a halt. It was an age of rationalism, materialism and a return to classical styles—an age that contemporaries compared to that of Augustus in ancient Rome.

STOURHEAD, WILTSHIRE

"BROAD QUAY", City Art Gallery and Museum, Bristol, Avon, (above) was painted in about 1735, by an unknown artist. At this time Bristol was one of the major British ports, and its wealth stemmed largely from the slave trade. The heart of Bristol was torn out by the bombing raids of the Second World War, and this picture gives a rare contemporary view of Bristol's buildings in the eighteenth century.

ROYAL CRESCENT, BATH, AVON, (above) was designed by John Wood, whose father had already begun the transformation of Bath from a decaying medieval town to the most elegant of Georgian cities. Number 1 Royal Crescent (above right) is now owned by the Bath Preservation Trust, and has been restored and furnished to illustrate the lifestyle of Bath at the time of Jane Austen's novels.

"CHAIRING THE MEMBER", Sir John Soane Museum, London, (right) is one of a series of paintings in which William Hogarth satirised the corruption of Georgian politics. Hogarth said that he set out to paint "moral subjects . . . which will both entertain and improve the mind." One of the greatest of British painters, he was also the forerunner of the political cartoonists, James Gillray and George Cruikshank.

CHISWICK HOUSE, GREATER LONDON, (left) was designed by Lord Burlington primarily as a home for his art collection. A classic Palladian building, it had a powerful influence on the development of architecture in the early eighteenth century.

"THE THAMES FROM SOMERSET HOUSE TERRACE TOWARDS THE CITY", (above) in The Royal Collection, London, is by the Venetian artist, Canaletto, who worked in London between 1746 and 1756. In this picture we can see Wren's City skyline with its spires, steeples and the dome of St Paul's.

STRAWBERRY HILL, TWICKENHAM, GREATER LONDON, (right) was transformed from a cottage into a "little Gothic castle" by Horace Walpole, in contrast to the generally classical style of Georgian architecture. Here Walpole, son of the first Prime Minister, Sir Robert Walpole, and author of the first "Gothic" novel, The Castle of Otranto attracted a salon of men of letters.

HOLKHAM HALL, NORFOLK, *was designed for Thomas Coke, Earl of Leicester, by Lord Burlington and William Kent in the Palladian style they favoured. The entrance hall (right) is fifty feet high—the full height of the building—and occupies most of the central block. All the rooms have a full measure of eighteenth-century magnificence— much of the sumptuous furniture and decoration being designed by William Kent himself.*

"CHEETAH AND STAG WITH TWO INDIANS", *City Art Gallery, Manchester, (left) by George Stubbs, illustrates Georgian society's interest in the East, which can also be seen in Chippendale's chinoiserie. Stubbs was otherwise known for his pictures of horses based on his remarkable study,* The Anatomy of the Horse.

MILTON ABBAS, DORSET, *(right) is one of several model villages created in the eighteenth century. Here the landowner replaced a complete market town with buildings for his employees, all set conveniently out of sight from his own house, which now is part of a boys' public school.*

"SHEPHERD AND SHEPHERDESS", *City Museum, Plymouth, Devon, (left) were made about 1770, in Plymouth porcelain, one of many styles of pottery that flourished at the time.*

"MR AND MRS ANDREWS", *National Gallery, London, (below) was painted by Thomas Gainsborough shortly before 1750, when he was little more than twenty. It was then the dawn of Britain's golden age of portrait painting. Gainsborough was a countryman whose first love was landscape, and he delighted his wealthy patrons by setting their portraits against backgrounds that reflected the assured prosperity of their lives.*

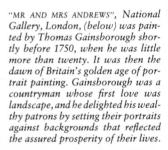

CHIPPENDALE FURNITURE, *was often built by Thomas Chippendale from original designs by Robert Adam. This dressing commode (left) is from Harewood House, West Yorkshire, and the pier glass, with its chinoiserie frame, (far left) from Nostell Priory, West Yorkshire. Chinoiserie is the decorative work produced under the influence of Chinese art motifs.*

CULZEAN CASTLE, STRATHCLYDE, *(above) with its oval staircase (left) and* MELLERSTAIN HOUSE, BORDERS, *with its elegant library (far left) are remarkable monuments to the genius of the Scottish architect, Robert Adam. He created the great Gothic castle of Culzean on a rocky cliff-top, round an original tower house of the sixteenth century.*

"VIEW OF SNOWDON", *Walker Art Gallery, Liverpool, (right) is the best-known work of Richard Wilson, Britain's first great landscape painter. He was to die almost without recognition in 1782, just before the dawn of the Romantic Movement.*

"EXPERIMENT WITH THE AIR PUMP", Tate Gallery, London, (above) by Joseph Wright of Derby, is a fascinating example of how the subject matter of painting expanded in the eighteenth century to include scenes of the Industrial Revolution, capturing the spirit of the age.

COALBROOKDALE, SHROPSHIRE, boasts the first iron bridge (above) to be built in Britain. It was the first use of iron in architecture. It was here too that Abraham Darby pioneered the revolutionary process of smelting iron ore with coke. Ironmaking was at last relieved from its dependence on Britain's dwindling stock of timber.

THE OXFORD CANAL, AT NAPTON LOCK, WARWICKSHIRE, *is an example of a meandering eighteenth-century waterway. It was designed by the pioneer canal-builder, James Brindley—a self-taught engineer who began his career as a millwright. He was commissioned by the Duke of Bridgewater to build the first major canal in Britain, to carry coal from Worsley to Salford. The far longer Oxford Canal was also to bring coal, from the Midlands to the Thames, and it was canals like this (and the later, far straighter, canals of the nineteenth century) that were, until the advent of the railways, to link Britain's industry to the coast, and beyond.*

they had blockaded New York in 1759 while the English ships were gathered at Halifax they could have ruined Amherst's advance on Montreal. If they had attacked Halifax after Wolfe and the English ships had left for the St Lawrence they could have wrecked the whole campaign for Quebec. But now it was too late. In 1761 Amherst dispatched an expedition to Martinique. The capture of yet another great commercial prize was received with jubilation in London. In one of his letters Horace Walpole wrote, "The Romans were three hundred years in conquering the world. We subdued the globe in three campaigns—and a globe as big again."

North America was thus made safe for the English-speaking peoples. Pitt had not only won Canada, with its rich fisheries and Indian trade, but had banished forever the dream and danger of a French colonial empire stretching from Montreal to New Orleans. Little could he know that the extinction of the French menace would lead to the final secession of the English colonies from the British Empire.

Meanwhile, in India the struggle between Britain and France resulted in an even more remarkable development—the growth of the English East India Company into a vast territorial empire.

About the year 1700 probably no more than fifteen hundred English people dwelt in India, including wives, children, and transient seamen. They lived apart in a handful of factories, as their trading stations were called, little concerned with Indian politics. A hundred years later British officials and soldiers in their thousands, under a British governor-general, were in control of extensive provinces. But the Anglo-French conflict would never have spread violently across India if the times had not been ripe for European intervention. The great Empire of the Moguls was disintegrating. For two centuries these Moslem descendants of Tamburlaine had gripped and pacified in Oriental fashion the eighty million inhabitants of the sub-continent. Early in the eighteenth century this formidable dynasty was shaken by a disputed succession. Invaders from the north poured across the frontiers. Delhi was sacked by the Shah of Persia. The Viceroys of the Moguls revolted and laid claim to the sovereignty of the Imperial provinces. In Central India the fierce Hindu fighting tribes of the Mahrattas, bound in a loose confederacy, seized their chance to loot and to raid. The country was swept by anarchy and bloodshed.

Hitherto European traders in India—English, French, Portuguese, and Dutch—had plied their wares in rivalry, but so long as "the Great Mogul" ruled in Delhi they had competed in comparative peace and safety. The English East India Company had grown into a solid affair, with a capital of over a million and a quarter pounds and an annual dividend of nine per cent. The population of Bombay had multiplied more than sixfold since Charles II had leased the city to the Company in 1668, and now exceeded sixty thousand souls. Madras, founded and fortified by the British in 1639, was the chief trading centre on the eastern coast. Calcutta, uninhabited till servants of the corporation built a factory at the mouth of the Ganges in 1686, had become a flourishing and peaceful emporium. The French *Compagnie des Indes*, centred at Pondicherry, had also prospered, though, unlike its British rival, it was in effect a Department of State and not a private concern. Both organisations had the same object, the promotion of commerce and the gaining of financial profit. The acquisition of territory played little part in the thoughts and plans of either nation, and indeed the

English directors had long been reluctant to assume any responsibilities beyond the confines of their trading stations. About 1740, however, events forced them to change their tune. The Mahrattas slaughtered the Nawab, or Imperial Governor, of the Carnatic, the five-hundred-mile-long province on the southeastern coast; threatened Madras and Bombay, and raided the depths of Bengal. It was becoming impossible for the European traders to stand aside. Most of the Dutch had already withdrawn to the rich archipelago of the East Indies; the Portuguese had long since fallen behind in the race; the French and English resolved to stay.

Joseph Dupleix, the French Governor of Pondicherry, had long foreseen the coming struggle with Britain. He perceived that India awaited a new ruler. The Mogul Empire was at an end, and a Mahratta Empire seemed unlikely to replace it. Why then should not France seize this glittering, fertile prize? When the War of the Austrian Succession broke out in Europe Dupleix acted with decision. He proceeded to attack Madras. Its English Governor asked the new Nawab of the Carnatic to enforce neutrality on the French, but omitted to accompany his request with a suitable bribe. Dupleix, on the other hand, promised to hand over the city once it was captured. Thus reassured, the Nawab stood aside, and after a five-day bombardment the town surrendered on September 10, 1746. Some of its British defenders escaped to nearby Fort St David. Among them was a young clerk of twenty-one, named Robert Clive.

Dupleix, victorious, refused after all to surrender Madras to the Nawab and spent the rest of the year repelling his attacks. He then assaulted Fort St David, but news arrived that the war in Europe had ceased and that the peace treaty of Aix-la-Chapelle prescribed that Madras was to be returned to the British in return for the cession of Louisburg to France. Thus ended a dismal and inglorious opening to the great struggle in India.

Clive had watched these events with anger and alarm, but hitherto there had been few signs in his career to mark him as the man who would found the rule of the British in India. The son of a small squire, his boyhood had been unpromising—he had attended no fewer than four schools, and been unsuccessful at all. In his Shropshire market town he had organised a gang of adolescent ruffians who extorted pennies and apples from tradesmen in return for not breaking their windows, and at the age of eighteen was sent abroad as a junior clerk in the East India Company. A difficult and unpromising subordinate, he detested the routine of the counting-house. Twice, it is said, he attempted suicide, and twice the pistol misfired. Not until he had obtained a military commission and served some years in the armed forces of the Company did he reveal a military genius unequalled in the British history of India. The siege of Madras and the defence of Fort St David had given him a taste for fighting. In 1748 a new upheaval gave him the chance of leadership.

Indian pretenders seized the Mogul viceroyalty of the Deccan and conquered the Carnatic. With a few French soldiers and a couple of thousand Indian troops Dupleix expelled them and placed his own puppet on the throne. The British candidate, Mahomet Ali, was chased into Trichinopoly and fiercely besieged. At a stroke France had become master of southern India. It became evident that the East India Company must either fight or die. Clive made his way to Trichinopoly, and saw for himself that Mahomet Ali was in desperate peril. If he could be rescued and placed on the throne

General Joseph-Francois Dupleix raises the siege of Pondicherry. This contemporary engraving is now in the collection of the National Army Museum, Chelsea, London.

all might be well. But how to do it? Trichinopoly was beset by a combined French and Indian army of vast numbers. The English had very few soldiers, and were so short of officers that Clive, still only twenty-five, was given the chief military command.

The direct relief of Trichinopoly was impossible, and Clive at once perceived that his blow must be struck elsewhere. Arcot, capital of the Carnatic, had been stripped of troops; most of them were at Trichinopoly besieging Mahomet Ali. Capture Arcot and they would be forced to come back. With two hundred Europeans, six hundred Indians, and eight officers of whom half were former clerks like himself, Clive set forth. The town fell easily to his assault, and he and his small handful prepared desperately for the vengeance which was to come. Everything turned out as Clive had foreseen. The Indian potentate, dismayed by the loss of his capital, detached a large portion of his troops from Trichinopoly and attacked Clive in Arcot. The struggle lasted for fifty days. Twenty times outnumbered, and close to starvation, Clive's puny force broke the onslaught in a night attack in which he served a gun himself, and the siege was lifted.

This was the end of Dupleix, and of much else besides. By 1752 Clive, after defeating the French and placing Mahomet Ali on the throne, made the Carnatic safe. Next year, newly wed, Clive sailed to England. He was much enriched by the "presents", as they were politely called, which he had received from Indian rulers.

In England Clive used a part of his fortune in an unsuccessful attempt to enter Parliament. In 1755 he returned to India, only just in time, for a new struggle was about to open in the northeast. Hitherto French, Dutch, and English had traded peacefully side by side in the fertile province of Bengal, and its docile, intelligent, and industrious inhabitants had largely escaped the slaughter and anarchy of the south. Calcutta was earning good dividends. Peace had been kept by a Moslem adventurer from the northwest who had seized and held power for fourteen years. But he died in 1756, and the throne passed to his nephew, Surajah Dowlah, young, vicious, violent, and greedy. Fearing, with some justice, that what came to be called the Seven Years' War between Britain and France would reduce him to a puppet, he called on both the European communities to dismantle their fortifications. In May he struck.

Gathering a large army, including guns and Europeans trained to use them, he marched on Calcutta. The small garrison and most of the English civilians fought bravely, but in three days it was all over. A terrible fate now overtook them. A hundred and forty-six Europeans surrendered after the enemy had penetrated the defences under a flag of truce. They were thrust for the night into a prison cell twenty feet square. By the morning all except twenty-three were dead. The victors departed, having looted the Company's possessions. "Little though he guessed it," says Lord Elton, "the dealings of Surajah Dowlah with the British had ensured they would become the next rulers of India. For the tragedy of the Black Hole had dispelled their last wishful illusion that it might still be possible for them to remain in India as traders and no more. There was an outrage to avenge, and at last they were more than ready to fight."

The news reached Madras in August. The Directors gave Clive all their naval power and nearly all their troops. In January 1757, with nine hundred European and fifteen hundred Indian soldiers, he recaptured Calcutta and

This impression of the stifling Black Hole of Calcutta by a later artist probably does not do full justice to the horrors of the scene. In reality, the sheer mass of humanity crammed inside would have made it impossible to give anything like a true picture of conditions inside the cell.

repulsed Surajah Dowlah's army of forty thousand men. The war with France now compelled him to attack Chandernagore, which was in French hands. In March it fell. Then fortune came to Clive's aid. Surajah Dowlah's cruelty was too much, even for his own people. A group of courtiers resolved to depose him and place a new ruler, Mir Jafar, on the throne. Clive agreed to help. On June 23, his army having grown to three thousand men, of whom less than a third were British, he met Surajah Dowlah at Plassey, outnumbered seventeen to one. Battle there was none. Nevertheless it was a trial of strength, on which the fortunes of India turned. For four hours there was a cannonade. Then Surajah Dowlah, sensing treachery in his own camp, ordered a withdrawal. Clive had resolved to let him go, but a junior officer advanced against orders. It became impossible to check the pursuit. The enemy dispersed in panic, and a few days later Surajah Dowlah was murdered by Mir Jafar's son. For the loss of thirty-six men Clive had become the master of Bengal and the victor of Plassey.

Much however still remained to be accomplished. Mir Jafar, who had taken no part in the so-called battle, was placed on the throne, but the province swarmed with Moslem fighting men from the north and was fertile in pretenders. The neighbouring state of Oudh was hostile; the French were still active; and even the Dutch showed signs of interfering. Clive beat the lot. If the English would not rule the country themselves, they must ensure that a friendly local potentate did so. Pitt, who justly appreciated the ability of Clive, had supported him with all the resources at his command, but his influence on events was small. Faced with the difficulties of communication, the distance and the complexities of the scene, he left Clive with a free hand, contenting himself with advice and support.

When Clive sailed once more to England in February 1760 Britain was the only European power left in India. In little more than four years he had brought about a great change upon the Indian scene. The French were still

Robert Clive's meeting with Mir Jafar is dramatically illustrated by the nineteenth-century artist, Francis Hayman. The picture can now be seen in the National Portrait Gallery.

allowed to keep their trading posts, but their influence was destroyed, and nine years later the *Compagnie des Indes* was abolished. Clive had now accumulated a fortune of a quarter of a million pounds. He bought his way into Parliament, as was the custom of the time, and was created an Irish peer. His services in India were not yet over.

Pitt's very success now contributed to his fall. Just as Marlborough and Godolphin had been faced by a growing war-weariness after Malplaquet, so now Pitt, an isolated figure in his own government, confronted an increasing dislike of the war after the great victories of 1759. To the people at large he was the "Great Commoner". This lonely, dictatorial man had caught their imagination. He had broken through the narrow circle of aristocratic politics, and his force and eloquence gained him their support. Contrary to the conventions of the age, he had used the House of Commons as a platform from which to address the country. His studied orations in severe classical style were intended for a wider audience than the place-holders of the Duke of Newcastle. Pitt had a contempt for party and party organisations. He hardly troubled to see his colleagues, except for weekly meetings with Newcastle and the Treasury Secretary to arrange the finances of his strategy, money and troops for Wolfe and Clive, subsidies for Frederick the Great. But his power was transient. There were not only enemies within the Government, stung by his arrogance and his secrecy, but also among his former political allies, the widowed Princess of Wales and her circle at Leicester House. Here the young heir to the throne was being brought up amid the Opposition views of his mother and her confidant, the Earl of Bute. Pitt had been their chosen candidate for the sunshine days when the old King should die. They now deemed him a deserter. They branded his acceptance of office in 1746 as a betrayal. Bute, with his close position at this future Court, was the most dangerous of Pitt's opponents, and it was he who stimulated opinion and the press against the war policy of the minister.

Pitt's position was indeed perilous. He had destroyed France's power in India and North America and had captured her possessions in the West Indies. It seemed as if Britain had achieved everything she desired. All that was left was the detested and costly subsidies to Prussia. Bute found it only too easy to convert the feelings of weariness into an effective opposition to Pitt. Among his colleagues there were some who honestly and patriotically doubted the wisdom of continuing the war, from which Britain had gained more than perhaps she could keep. The war had to be paid for. It was already producing the inevitable consequences. Heavy taxation on the industrial and landed classes was matched by huge fortunes for the stock-jobber and the contractor. It was in vain that Pitt attempted to show that making terms before France was exhausted would repeat the Tory mistakes at Utrecht and only snatch a breathing-space for the next conflict.

In October 1760 George II died. He had never liked Pitt, but had learnt to respect his abilities. The minister's comment was pointed: "Serving the King may be a duty, but it is the most disagreeable thing imaginable to those who have that honour." The temper of George II's grandson, the new ruler, was adverse. George III had very clear ideas of what he wanted and where he was going. He meant to be King, such a King as all his countrymen would follow and revere. Under the long Whig regime the House of Commons had become an irresponsible autocracy. Would not the

An unknown artist painted Robert, Lord Clive, in the uniform of a general in 1764. In the following year Clive returned to Calcutta to reform the civil service and re-establish military discipline there.

THE GRAND TOUR

WITH THE ADVENT of the Age of Enlightenment, British culture inevitably became less insular. Travel to the great European centres of art and learning, cities like Paris, Venice or Vienna, was regarded as essential for an educated man. Also, since the glories of classical Athens and Rome had recently been rediscovered, most journeys included Italy and—for the more adventurous—Greece, which at that time was not an independent country but a reluctant member of the sprawling Ottoman Empire.

The Grand Tour, as it came to be called, was widely undertaken by wealthy young men, accompanied by their tutors and servants, either before going to university or sometimes as an alternative to a college education. In fact, its benefits were so highly regarded that Lady Leicester of Holkham in Norfolk actually offered her great-nephew an annual £650 if he would go on The Grand Tour rather than be "ruined" by a university.

A traveller's pleasures might vary—not all were respectable—but the dangers remained the same, principally those of robbery and death, either on the roads or in the often unprepossessing inns. There were perilous mountains to be climbed also; it was not until the end of the eighteenth century that mountains came to be less feared for their precipices than admired for their grandeur. Beyond them lay all the artistry of the ancient classical world, and there were men who claimed they had never truly seen a statue until they crossed the Alps into Italy.

Generations of young Englishmen were profoundly influenced by The Grand Tour. Some brought back a taste for classical architecture and transformed their ancestral homes. But it was in the fostering of international understanding that the tour was of most value, and when this was made difficult during the French Revolutionary and Napoleonic wars an important broadening cultural force was lost.

THE ITINERARY OF THE GRAND TOUR led through precipitous Alpine passes (above) from Geneva to the Po Valley in Tuscany. The "Short Tour" was confined to Paris and Geneva, then by way of the Alps to Rome and Venice, sometimes returning by ship from Naples. The "Long Tour" included Greece and the Rhine, and could take several years to complete. In the picture below, a rich traveller near Mount Vesuvius, from which smoke rises in the background, is robbed of his coffers and baggage. He had probably visited the newly excavated tourist attraction of Pompeii. The Grand Tour could cost as much as £20,000 and when the Napoleonic Wars closed the Continent to English travellers, more tourists began visiting Wales, Scotland, and British beauty spots instead.

SEEING THE SIGHTS *was—and is—the aim of every tourist. Wonders like the Leaning Tower of Pisa were as popular with travellers in the eighteenth century as they are today. The artist who sketched the picture above has emphasised the slope of the Leaning Tower by drawing the perfectly upright Cathedral of Boschetto and Rinaldo standing next to it.*

TRAVELLERS BROUGHT BACK *art treasures and cultural inspiration of many kinds from their lengthy wanderings. Mereworth Castle, Kent (top) is a copy of Palladio's Villa Rotunda in Vicenza, near Venice. Many other copies were built and the term "rotunda" has since been used to describe these circular buildings. The ornamented tureen (above) was designed by Robert Adam (1728-92) from sketches made in Italy. Adam spent three years in Rome, where he not only gained an education in classical art but met many of the future customers for whom he was to build country houses. One of the finest collections of classical marbles belonged to Charles Towneley, who lived in Italy in his youth and bought statues from Roman villas which were being excavated in the 1750s. The collection (left) was painted in his London home by Johannes Zoffany. The picture is now in the Towneley Museum, Burnley, while the statues are on view in the British Museum.*

The rise of India Stock & Sinking fund of Oppression.

A contemporary cartoonist satirised Warren Hastings as a power-hungry materialist oppressing India. In 1787 he was impeached for various serious crimes, including extortion, but after a controversial trial lasting seven years he was declared innocent of all charges.

without the gratitude of the inhabitants. Unlike many Englishmen in India at this time, he spoke the local languages well. He enjoyed the society of Indians, and had once been rebuked on this account by the formidable Clive. Though proud of his birth and ancestry, consciousness of race, colour, or religion never influenced or distracted him.

In the beginning Hastings was welcomed and honoured in England. His achievements and victories were some compensation for the humiliations and disasters in America, and the Company had much to thank him for. A year before his return, the Prime Minister, Chatham's son the younger Pitt, had passed an India Act making the Board of Control subject to the Cabinet. Hastings had disapproved of this, for though the Governor-General was thus freed from the fetters of the Council at Calcutta imposed by North's ill-conceived measure, patronage passed into the hands of Pitt's friend and adviser, Henry Dundas, appointed President of the Board of Control. Soon after Hastings's return a Parliamentary inquiry into his conduct had been set on foot. No personal charge of corruption could be proved against him, but he was arrogant and tactless in his dealings with the politicians of all parties. Parliament resolved to have his blood. Philip Francis, whom he had wounded in a duel in Calcutta, malignly urged his enemies on. The ancient weapon of impeachment was resurrected and turned against him. The trial opened in Westminster Hall on February 13, 1788. It lasted over seven years. Every aspect and detail of Hastings's administration was scrutinised, denounced, upheld, misunderstood, or applauded. At the end he was acquitted. Though much of the uproar was unfair and uncomprehending, the proceedings proclaimed to the public and the world the support of the British people for Burke's declaration that India should be governed "by those laws which are to be found in Europe, Africa, and Asia, that are found amongst all mankind—those principles of equity and humanity implanted in our hearts, which have their existence in the feelings of mankind that are capable of judging".

The impeachment of Warren Hastings was a turning-point in the history of the British in India. The chief power was no longer to be grasped by obscure, brilliant servants of the Company who could seize and merit it, and the post of governor-general was henceforward occupied by personages distinguished on their own account and drawn from the leading families in England: the Marquis Cornwallis, uncowed by the surrender at Yorktown, the Marquis Wellesley, Lord Minto, the Marquis of Hastings. In effect, though not in name, these men were Viceroys, untempted by the hope of financial gain, impatient of restraint by ill-informed governments in London, and sufficiently intimate with the ruling circles in Britain to do what they thought right and without fear of the consequences. And indeed there had been much for them to do.

The Carnatic, hinterland of Madras, was presided over in 1785 by an Indian Nawab, supported by British arms and British money. The State of Mysore, stretching to the western coast, had been seized from the Moguls by Hyder Ali, and was heartily misgoverned by his son, Tipu Sultan. In the south-central portion of the peninsula the Nizam of Hyderabad ruled feebly over the Deccan. Beyond all these swarmed the Mahrattas, a confederacy of military families, fierce Hindu fighting-men, lightly armed and mounted on swift horses, who could disperse as speedily as they attacked, ancient opponents of the Mahometan Moguls, and avid to found an Indian Empire of their own. Bengal alone lay peacefully in the British grip, precariously shielded from the turmoil by the weak buffer-state of Oudh.

Cornwallis was soon compelled to deal with Tipu. In the last decade of the eighteenth century he marched against him, captured most of Mysore, and made him surrender half his territory. In 1798 Napoleon, victorious in Egypt, and himself seeking an empire in the East, offered help to Tipu, who began to assemble a French-trained army. The struggle between France and England once again loomed over India. There was a danger of naval attack from the French-held island of Mauritius, in the Indian Ocean. The Marquis Wellesley acted with speed and resolution. He offered Tipu what was termed a "subsidiary treaty", and when Tipu preferred to fight, in 1799 he was driven back to his capital and killed. Wellesley then annexed outlying portions of Mysore, and returned the rest to the Hindu potentates whom Hyder Ali had dispossessed. They did not survive for long.

Wellesley now turned his attention to the Carnatic. Its Government was bankrupt and oppressive, and in 1801 he pensioned off the Nawab and made it into the Madras Presidency. In the same year he dealt with Oudh. Here the Nawab, though under British protection, had surrendered his dominions to pillage and exploitation, by his own mutinous troops and by greedy adventurers from Europe. On him also Wellesley imposed a substantial treaty. In return for a guarantee of protection, he ceded most of his territories to the British, except for a small portion round Lucknow, dismissed all Europeans from his service except those approved by the Company, and promised to govern according to the Company's advice.

Lastly Wellesley dealt with the Mahrattas. Some years previously they had captured Delhi, seized the person of the Mogul Emperor, and demanded tribute on his behalf from Bengal. Now they started fighting among themselves. Their chief escaped and appealed to Wellesley, who restored him to his capital at Poona. The rest of them thereupon declared war on the British, and after heavy fighting were defeated at Assaye and elsewhere by Wellesley's younger brother, the future Duke of Wellington. On them also Wellesley imposed a subsidiary treaty, and Orissa and most of the province of Delhi were surrendered to the British. "In seven years," writes a distinguished historian, "he had transformed the map of India and launched his countrymen on a career of expansion which only stopped at the Afghan mountains half a century later." The East India Company however took a different view. The Directors still wanted trade, not conquests, and were so hostile and critical that Wellesley resigned in 1805.

His successor, Lord Minto, was expressly forbidden to take on any new territorial responsibilities. But it was impossible. The pacification which Wellesley had begun must either be completed or perish. The disbanding of local armies which he had imposed on so many Indian rulers let loose a horde of unemployed and discontented soldiery, who formed themselves into robber gangs. Helped by the Mahrattas, who mistook British neutrality for weakness, these gangs began the pillage of Central India. The Marquis of Hastings, appointed governor-general in 1814, was compelled to subdue them with a large force. The Mahrattas, seeing their last chance vanish of succeeding to the Empire of the Moguls, promptly revolted. They too were defeated, their chief was deposed and his Principality of Poona added to the Presidency of Bombay. Against its wishes and almost in spite of itself, the Company was now overlord of three-quarters of India.

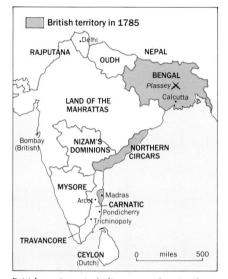

British territory in India appeared insignificant in 1785, but within thirty years the East India Company had acquired nearly three-quarters of the continent.

CHAPTER 32

THE YOUNGER PITT

William Pitt was barely twenty-four years old when George III invited him to become Prime Minister. Pitt overcame strong opposition in Parliament, and won a convincing majority at the fiercely contested General Election of 1784.

THE MARQUIS OF ROCKINGHAM had waited long for his opportunity to form a Government, and when at last it came in March 1782 he had but four months to live. Dark then was the scene which spread around the ambitious island and its stubborn King. Britain stood alone amid a world war in which all had gone amiss. The combined fleets of France and Spain were active in the Channel and had blockaded Gibraltar; Minorca had fallen; Washington's army lay poised before New York, and the American Congress had pledged itself not to make a separate peace. Admiral Rodney indeed regained command of West Indian waters in a great victory off the Saintes, and in September Howe was to relieve Gibraltar from a three-year siege. Elsewhere over the globe England's power and repute were very low. Such was the plight to which the obstinacy of George III had reduced the Empire.

Rockingham died in July, and Lord Shelburne was entrusted with the new administration. He had no intention of following the design which Rockingham and Edmund Burke had long cherished of composing a Cabinet, united on the main issues of the day, which would dictate its policy to the King, and he sought to form a Government by enlisting politicians of the most diverse views and connection. But the entire structure of British politics was ruptured in its personal loyalties by the years of defeat to which King George III had led them, and now, by enlisting the help of the many, the new Prime Minister incurred the suspicion of all. Of great ability, a brilliant orator, and with the most liberal ideas, Shelburne was nevertheless, like Carteret before him, distrusted on all sides. The King found him personally agreeable and gave him full support. But politics were now implacably bitter between three main groups, and none of them was strong enough alone to sustain a Government. Shelburne himself had the support of those who had followed Chatham, including his son, the young William Pitt, who was appointed Chancellor of the Exchequer. But North still commanded a considerable faction, and, smarting at his sovereign's cold treatment after twelve years of faithful service, coveted a renewal of office. A third group was headed by Charles James Fox, vehement critic of North's regime, brilliant, generous-hearted, and inconsistent. Burke, for his part, had no great gift for practical politics, and since the death of his patron, Rockingham, was without influence.

Hostility to Shelburne grew and spread. Nevertheless, by negotiations in which he displayed great skill, the Prime Minister succeeded in bringing the world war to an end on the basis of American Independence. The French Government had only aided the American Patriots in the hope of dismembering the British Empire, and, apart from a few romantic enthusiasts like Lafayette, had no wish to help to create a republic in the New World. Spain had entered the war mainly because France had promised to help her to recapture Gibraltar in return for the use of her fleet against England. But the revolt of the Thirteen Colonies had bred trouble among her own overseas possessions, Gibraltar had not fallen, and she now demanded extensive compensation in North America. Although Congress had promised to let France take the lead in peace negotiations, the American Commissioners in Europe, in direct violation of the Congressional undertaking, signed secret peace preliminaries with England.

Shelburne, like Chatham, had dreamt of preserving the Empire by making generous concessions, but he realised that freedom was the only practical policy. In any case Fox had already committed Britain to this step by making a public announcement in the House of Commons. The most important issue was the future of the western lands lying between the Alleghany Mountains and the Mississippi. Speculators from Virginia and the Middle Colonies had long been active in these regions, and their influence in Congress was backed by powerful men such as Benjamin Franklin, Patrick Henry, and Washington himself. The radical New Englanders, led by Samuel and John Adams, had no direct interest in these western territories, but agreed to press for their complete cession provided the British were made to recognise the rights of the northern colonies to fish off Newfoundland.

Shelburne was by no means hostile to the American desire for the fishery rights and the West. The difficulty was the Canadian frontier. After months of negotiation a frontier was agreed upon which ran from the borders of Maine to the St Lawrence, up the river, and through the Great Lakes to their head. Everything south of this line, east of the Mississippi and north of the borders of Florida, became American territory. This was by far the most important result of the treaty. The only sufferers were the Canadian fur companies, whose activities had till now extended from the province of Quebec to the Ohio; but this was a small price.

On two disputed matters, namely, over the unpaid debts of the American merchants to England accumulated before the war and the security of about a hundred thousand American Loyalists, Shelburne fought hard, but the Americans showed little generosity. South Carolina alone showed an understanding spirit about Loyalist property, and between forty and fifty thousand "United Empire Loyalists" had to make new homes in Canada.

France now made her terms with England. An armistice was declared in January 1783, and the final peace treaty was signed at Versailles later in the year. The French kept their possessions in India and the West Indies. They were guaranteed the right to fish off Newfoundland, and reoccupied

Canadian furs were highly prized in Europe. The three-cornered hats worn by men at this time were made of beaver skin, most of which came from Canada. Indians traded skins with representatives of enterprising fur companies.

A white overseer directs black slaves on a plantation in the West Indies. Sugar and cotton made fortunes for many English gentlemen who returned home with their riches to buy land and a seat in Parliament.

the slave-trade settlements of Senegal on the West African coast. The important cotton island of Tobago was ceded to them, but apart from this they gained little that was material. Their main object however was achieved. England's position in the world seemed to have been weakened.

Spain was forced to join in the general settlement. Her American ambitions had melted away, her one gain in this theatre being the two English colonies in Florida; but this was at the expense of the English retention of Gibraltar, the main Spanish objective. She had conquered Minorca, during the war, and she kept this at the peace. Holland too was compelled by the defection of her allies to come to terms.

Thus ended what some then called the "World War". A new State had come into being across the Atlantic, a great future force in the councils of the nations. England had been heavily battered, but remained undaunted.

Her emergence from her ordeal was the work of Shelburne. In less than a year he had brought peace to the world. That he received small thanks for his services is a remarkable fact. He resigned after eight months, in February 1783. Later he was created Marquis of Lansdowne, and descendants of his under that name have since played a notable part in British politics. Shelburne's Government was followed by a machine-made coalition between North and Fox. It was said that this combination was too much even for the agile consciences of the age. Only five years before Fox had publicly declared that any alliance with North was too monstrous to be admitted for a moment. Yet this was what was now presented to an astonished public. Within nine months this Ministry also collapsed. The immediate cause of its fall was a Bill which Fox drafted with the laudable intention of reforming the government of India. His design was to subject the East India Company to some degree of control by a political board in London. His critics were quick to point out that extensive patronage would be vested in the hands of this political board and opportunities for corruption immeasurably increased. Only close supporters of the Government could hope to benefit. All party groups, except Fox's personal followers, were therefore hostile to the proposal.

The King now seized his chance of regaining popularity by destroying a monstrous administration. George III saw his opportunity if he could find the man. Only one figure stood in the House of Commons free from a wholly discredited process: William Pitt, the son of the great Chatham. He had already held the Chancellorship of the Exchequer during the Shelburne administration. His reputation was honourable and clear. By what was certainly the most outstanding domestic action of his long reign, in December 1783, the King asked Pitt to form a Government. The old Parliamentary machine had failed, and as it broke down a new combination took its place whose efforts were vindicated by the events of the next twenty years.

The revolt of the American colonies had shattered the complacency of eighteenth-century England. Men began to study the root causes of the disaster and the word "reform" was in the air. The defects of the political system had plainly contributed to the secession, and the arguments used by the American colonists against the mother country lingered in the minds of Englishmen. Demand for some reform of the representation in Parliament began to stir; but the agitation was mild and respectable. The main aim of the reformers was to increase the number of boroughs which elected Members of Parliament, and thus reduce the possibilities of Government corruption. There was even talk of universal suffrage and other novel theories of democratic representation. But the chief advocates of reform were substantial landowners, or country clergymen or mature, well-established politicians like Burke, who would all have agreed that Parliament did not and need not precisely represent the English people. To them Parliament represented, not individuals, but "interests"—the landed interest, the mercantile interest, even the labouring interest, but with a strong leaning to the land as the solid and indispensable basis of the national life. The movement in governing circles was neither radical nor comprehensive. It found expression in Burke's Economic Reform Act of 1782, disfranchising certain classes of Government officials who had hitherto played some part in managing elections. No general reform of the franchise was attempted, and when people talked about the rights of Englishmen they meant the sturdy class of yeomen vaunted as the backbone of the country, whose weight in the counties it was desired to increase. The enunciation of first principles has always been obnoxious to the English mind. John Wilkes had made a bold and successful stand for the liberty of the subject before the law, but the whole controversy had turned on the narrow if practical issue of the legality of general warrants. Tom Paine's inflammatory pamphlets had a considerable circulation among certain classes, but in Parliament little was heard about the abstract rights of man. The early reform schemes were mostly attempts to preserve the political power and balance of the rural interest.

Nevertheless the dream of founding a balanced political system on a landed society was becoming more and more unreal. In the last forty years of the eighteenth century exports and imports more than doubled in value and the population increased by over two millions. England was silently undergoing a revolution in industry and agriculture, which was to have more far-reaching effects than the political tumults of the times. Steam-engines provided a new source of power in factories and foundries, which rapidly multiplied. A network of canals was constructed which carried coal cheaply to new centres of industry. New methods of smelting brought a tenfold increase in the output of iron. New roads, with a durable surface, reached out over the country and bound it more closely together. An ever-expanding and assertive industrial community was coming into being. The

Thomas Paine's radical writings influenced the fight for American Independence. Paine emigrated to America in 1774 with letters of introduction to Benjamin Franklin, and soon became involved in the independence struggle. He also influenced people's reactions to the French Revolution. His most famous and provocative book was The Rights of Man (1791).

A CONSUMER SOCIETY

A S INCOMES ROSE during the eighteenth century, demand increased for goods and services of every kind. Some goods, like sugar, which had previously been thought of as luxuries, now became basic requirements, or "decencies". Others, like jewels, which had been thought of primarily as objects of inheritance, now could be obtained by simple purchase. Trading goods came from all over the world—calico and muslins from India, tea and coffee from India, China, Africa and America, wines from Portugal—but most manufactured articles were produced in Britain by enterprising businessmen like Josiah Wedgwood, the great potter, or Matthew Boulton, who made buttons in huge quantities and of all styles before turning to the steam engines for which he is now better known.

Meanwhile, fashionable shops multiplied in London and in large provincial towns like Bristol and Norwich. Some towns, like Bath, became wholly devoted to leisure pastimes. As early as 1736 Brighton was promoting the delights of drinking sea water, and later in the century under the Prince Regent's patronage the town was offering the headier excitement of its bathing beach. George III was very fond of Weymouth.

While the pleasures of the rich were many and varied, the lot of the poor remained grey. William Hogarth made much of social contrasts in his vivid paintings and engravings of the perils both of Gin Lane and of the Rake's Progress.

There were, in fact, many critics of the new society: moralists who objected to extravagance and to the whims of increasingly commercialised fashion; traditionalists, who complained that the poor were being tempted to forget their station in life; and some industrialists, nonconformists who lived simply themselves and ploughed back their profits into their businesses. But far-reaching social change was relentless, and was to accelerate rapidly as the Industrial Revolution progressed.

FASHIONS WERE OFTEN OUTRAGEOUS. Here, a macaroni, or fashionable fop called George Bussy, fourth Earl of Jersey, dresses for the theatre in the 1780s. His hat perches on an immense wig, two beauty spots adorn his face and a buttonhole sprouts from his collar to his eyebrows. His ensemble is a tasteful combination of spots and stripes, embellished with rosettes, ribbons and frills. A dressing-table with a huge mirror holds caskets, phials and brushes to complete his toilette. Although Beau (Richard) Nash, shown right, was large and awkward, he was the unofficial king of manners at Bath, which became the most fashionable health spa. Nash drew up a code of rules for conduct, campaigned against the wearing of swords and duelling and raised £18,000 by subscription for repairing the local roads. From 1705 Nash acted as Master of Ceremonies at Bath and conducted the public balls with legendary panache.

HOUSEHOLD GOODS AND ORNAMENTS *began to be produced in large quantities. In 1769, Josiah Wedgwood set up his pottery at the Etruria works, near Burslem, Staffordshire. The Jasper ware heart-shaped trinket box (above) was a speciality based on classical themes devised by the four Adams brothers, whose ornamental interior designs were widely used in country houses of the period. Jasper ware was a fine white stoneware capable of being coloured right through by metallic oxides. Later Wedgwood pottery received only a surface wash, against which the white reliefs stood out in contrast.*

GAMBLING, DRINKING AND DUELLING *were the pastimes of English gentlemen. They met in London's fashionable new clubs, like Brooks's, opened by a wine merchant in 1778. Thomas Rowlandson's cartoon, (above) dated 1790, is entitled "A Kick-up at a Hazard Table". Possibly an earl has just lost his estate and beggared his family.*

URBAN DEVELOPMENT GAVE NEW SCOPE TO ARCHITECTURE. *Regent Street was built to link the Regent's palace, Carlton House, with Marylebone Park, now Regent's Park. The Prince envisaged a "Royal Mile" to rival the grand boulevards of Napoleon's Paris, but it proved impossible to buy the necessary land to make a straight road. The plan put forward by the architect and surveyor, John Nash, made use of curves, and he added colonnades of cast iron. Speculators invested in sites for shops, banks, houses and hotels, but Nash fought to retain the architectural unity of the site and produced a street of distinction.*

COFFEE DRINKING *became so popular that by 1714 there were five hundred coffee-houses in London and other towns. They were the forerunners of clubs and attracted a clientele who shared similar interests, usually either political or literary. The coffeepot shown above is of Wedgwood Queen's ware decorated with a design of "Rural Lovers" adapted from a painting by Thomas Gainsborough. There were teahouses too—a cup of tea cost about a penny—for tea drinking had also become a popular social habit by the early eighteenth century. Though all classes drank tea, it was the aristocracy who brought its consumption in the home to a fine art.*

Nelson was already a popular hero in 1801, when this picture was painted by Sir William Beechey. It can be seen in the National Portrait Gallery.

British fleet, as he thought, into the waters of the western Atlantic, his ships were ordered to gather. They would then double back to Europe, sail up the Channel, and assure the crossing from Boulogne.

Nelson was lying in wait off the Sardinian coastline in April 1805 when news reached him that Villeneuve was at sea, having slipped out of Toulon on the dark night of March 30 with eleven ships of the line and eight frigates. The fox was out and the chase began. Fortune seemed against Nelson. His frigates lost touch with Villeneuve, and he had first to make sure that the French were not running for Sicily. This done, he headed for Gibraltar. Fierce westerly gales prevented him reaching the Straits until May 4, when he learnt that Villeneuve had passed through more than three weeks before. Six Spanish battleships had come out to join him. Nelson, picking up scattered reports from frigates and merchantmen, pieced together the French design. All his qualities were now displayed to the full. Out of perplexing, obscure, and conflicting reports he fathomed the French plan, and made the momentous decision to sail westward himself. He had ten ships of the line to follow seventeen of the enemy. In stately procession at an average rate of five and a half knots the English pursued their quarry. Villeneuve and his Spanish allies reached Martinique on May 14. Nelson made landfall at Barbados on June 4. News of his arrival alarmed the French admiral, who was promptly out again in the Atlantic by June 8, heading east. Nelson again had to make a crucial decision. Was he right in believing that the French were making for Europe? As he wrote in a dispatch, "So far from being infallible, like the Pope, I believe my opinions to be very fallible, and therefore I may be mistaken that the enemy's fleet has gone to Europe; but I cannot think myself otherwise."

Before leaving the islands Nelson sent a fast sloop back to England with dispatches, and on June 19 it passed Villeneuve's fleet, noting his course and position. The commander of the sloop saw that Villeneuve was heading northeastward for the Bay of Biscay, and raced home, reaching Plymouth on July 8. Lord Barham, the new First Lord of the Admiralty, aged seventy-eight and with a lifetime's naval experience, at once realised what was happening. Villeneuve intended to release the Franco-Spanish squadron blockaded at Ferrol, and, thus reinforced, join with Admiral Ganteaume from Brest. But Ganteaume, in spite of peremptory orders from Napoleon, failed to break out. Admiral Cornwallis's fleet in the Western Approaches kept him in port. Meanwhile, on orders from Barham at the Admiralty, Admiral Calder intercepted Villeneuve off Finisterre, and here in late July the campaign of Trafalgar opened. Calder's action was indecisive, and the French took refuge in Ferrol.

Nelson meanwhile had reached Cadiz on July 18. There he found Collingwood on guard, but no sign of the enemy. Realising that Villeneuve must have gone north, Nelson replenished his fleet in Morocco and sailed for home waters on July 23. On the same day Napoleon arrived at Boulogne. The crisis was at hand, and the Royal Navy gathered at the mouth of the Channel for the defence of the island. Calder joined Cornwallis off Brest on August 14, and on the next day Nelson arrived, bringing the main fleet up to a total of nearly forty ships of the line. Thus was the sea-barrier concentrated against the French. Nelson went on alone with his flagship, the *Victory*, to Portsmouth. In the following days the campaign reached its climax. Villeneuve had sailed again from Ferrol on August 13 in an attempt to join Ganteaume and enter the English Channel, for Napoleon still believed that the British fleets were dispersed and that the moment had come for invasion. On August 21 Ganteaume was observed to be leaving harbour, but Cornwallis closed in with his whole force and the French turned back. Meanwhile Villeneuve, having edged out into the Atlantic, had changed his mind. Well aware of the shortcomings of his ill-trained fleet, desperately short of supplies, and with many sick on board, he had abandoned the great adventure on August 15 and was already speeding south to Cadiz. The threat of invasion was over.

Early in September dispatches reached London telling that Villeneuve had gone south. Nelson, summoned from leave at Merton, was at once ordered to resume his command. Amid scenes of enthusiasm he rejoined the *Victory* at Portsmouth and sailed on September 15. All England realised that her fate now lay in the hands of this frail man. A fortnight later he joined his fleet off Cadiz, now numbering twenty-seven ships of the line. "We have only one great object in view," he wrote to Collingwood, "that of annihilating our enemies." His object was to starve the enemy fleet, now concentrated in Cadiz harbour, and force it out into the open sea and to battle. This involved patrolling the whole adjacent coast. He organised his own ships into blockading squadrons. His energy and inspiration roused the spirit of his captains to the highest pitch. To them he outlined a new and daring plan of battle. To gain a decisive victory, he was resolved to abandon the old formal line of battle, running parallel to the enemy's fleet. He would break Villeneuve's line, when it came out of port, by sailing at right angles boldly into it with two main divisions. While the enemy van

THE BATTLE OF TRAFALGAR

A seaman aboard HMS Royal Sovereign *wrote home with this account of the victory at Trafalgar and Nelson's death, on October 21, 1805.*

Honoured Father,
This comes to tell you I am alive and hearty except three fingers; but that's not much, it might have been my head. I told brother Tom I should like to see a greadly battle, and I have seen one, and we have peppered the Combined rarely: and for the matter of that, they fought us pretty tightish for French and Spanish. Three of our mess are killed, and four more of us winged. But to tell you the truth of it, when the game began, I wished myself at Warnborough with my plough again; but when they had given us one duster, and I found myself snug and tight, I set to in good earnest, and thought no more about being killed than if I were at Murrell Green Fair, and I was presently as busy and as black as a collier. How my fingers got knocked overboard I don't know, but off they are, and I never missed them till I wanted them. You see, by my writing, it was my left hand, so I can write to you, and fight for my King yet. We have taken a rare parcel of ships, but the wind is so rough we cannot bring them home, else I should roll in money, so we are busy smashing 'em, and blowing 'em up wholesale.

Our dear Admiral Nelson is killed! So we have paid pretty sharply for licking 'em. I never sat eyes on him, for which I am both sorry and glad; for, to be sure, I should like to

have seen him—but then, all the men in our ship who have seen him are such soft toads, they have done nothing but blast their eyes and cry, ever since he was killed. God bless you! chaps that fought like the devil, sit down and cry like a wench. I am still in the *Royal Sovereign*, but the Admiral [Collingwood] has left her, for she is like a horse without a bridle, so he is in a frigate that he may be here and there and everywhere for he's as *cute* as here and there one; and as bold as a lion, for all he can cry!—I saw his tears with my own eyes, when the boat hailed and said my Lord was dead. So no more at present from your dutiful son;

Sam

"England expects every man will do his duty." Nelson's lieutenants on HMS Victory *prepare to raise the signal.*

was thus cut off and out of touch his centre and rear would be destroyed. After his conference with his captains Nelson wrote, "All approved. It was new, it was singular, it was simple. It must succeed." In a mood of intense exhilaration the fleet prepared for the ordeal ahead. Meanwhile Villeneuve had received orders to sail for Naples in support of Napoleon's new military plans. On the morning of October 19 a frigate signalled to Nelson's flagship, "Enemy ships are coming out of port." On receiving this message Nelson led his fleet to the southeast to cut off the enemy from the Straits and force them to fight in the open sea. At daybreak on October 21 he saw from the quarterdeck of the *Victory* the battle line of the enemy, consisting of an advance squadron of twelve Spanish ships under Admiral Gravina and twenty-one French ships of the line under Villeneuve. It was seven months since the escape from Toulon, and the first time Nelson had seen his foes since war had begun again in 1803.

The British fleet lay about ten miles west of the enemy, to the windward, and at six in the morning Nelson signalled his ships to steer east-northeast for the attack in the two columns he had planned. The enemy turned northward on seeing the advancing squadrons, but the clumsy seamanship of his men convinced Villeneuve that flight was impossible, and he hove to in a long sagging line to await Nelson's attack. Nelson signalled to Collingwood, who was at the head of the southern column in the *Royal Sovereign*, "I intend to pass through the van of the enemy's line, to prevent him getting into Cadiz." Nelson went down to his cabin to compose a prayer. "May the Great God whom I worship grant to my country, and for the benefit of Europe in general, a great and glorious Victory. . . . For myself, I commit my life to Him who made me, and may His blessing light upon my endeavours for serving my country faithfully." The fleets were drawing nearer and nearer. Another signal was run up on the *Victory*, "England expects every man will do his duty." When Collingwood saw the flutter he remarked testily, "I wish Nelson would stop signalling, as we all know well enough what we have to do," but when the message was reported to him cheers broke out from the ships.

A deathly silence fell upon the fleet as the ships drew nearer. Each captain marked down his adversary, and within a few minutes the two English columns thundered into action. The roar of broadsides, the crashing of

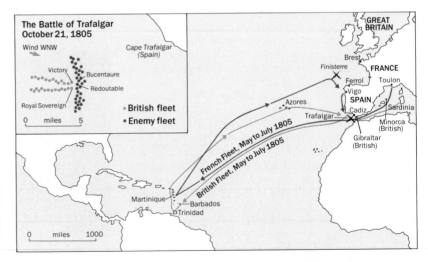

This map shows how Nelson pursued the French Admiral Villeneuve all the way to Martinique, and back to the coast of Spain. The insert demonstrates how he eventually cut the French line of battleships off Cape Trafalgar.

REGENCY

The end of the eighteenth century saw huge changes in Britain brought about by war on the Continent and by the Industrial Revolution at home. Yet it is from the Prince Regent, who patronised the arts and set the style for civilised society, that the period takes its name.

THE ROYAL PAVILION, BRIGHTON, SUSSEX

CHARLOTTE SQUARE, EDINBURGH, LOTHIAN, (above) is part of the elegant "New Town" planned originally by James Craig in 1767. The Square itself was designed by Robert Adam in 1791. Number 7 (left) is furnished and decorated in period style, and gives a vivid impression of what life was like "upstairs and downstairs" in the reign of George III.

THE PROMENADE, CHELTENHAM, GLOUCESTERSHIRE, (left) is one of many fine terraces in a town graced by some of Britain's finest Regency architecture and cast-iron work.

THE ROYAL PAVILION, BRIGHTON, SUSSEX, was originally built as a classical mansion by Henry Holland in 1787, when the patronage of the Prince Regent established Brighton as England's most fashionable resort. In 1815 it was transformed into an oriental palace by Nash. The Banqueting Hall (right), with its one-ton chandelier, and Nash's own drawing of the kitchen (above), illustrate the scale and extravagance of this fantastic pleasure dome.

PARK CRESCENT, LONDON, (left) was built by John Nash in 1812, as part of his grandiose plan for the development of what is now Regent's Park. Of his design for a garden city only his terraces were completed.

JANE AUSTEN'S HOUSE, CHAWTON, HAMPSHIRE, (above) is now a museum to the great novelist of the Regency Age. She lived here with her mother and sister from 1809 to 1817. She wrote many of her novels at Chawton, including Emma and Mansfield Park.

GRASMERE, CUMBRIA, was both inspiration and home to the first great poet of the English Romantic Movement, William Wordsworth. During his life he lived in various houses round the lake (right), writing some of his finest work in Dove Cottage (below). Here he worked alongside his sister Dorothy, whose room is shown (below right). Next to the cottage there is now a museum devoted to him and the other lakeland poets—especially Samuel Taylor Coleridge—who were frequent visitors there.

"BEATRICE ADDRESSING DANTE", Tate Gallery, London, (right) is a fine example of the work of the supreme individualist of eighteenth-century art, William Blake. He belonged to no movement, pursuing his own interpretation of religion and morality in visionary pictures and deceptively simple poems.

"COUNTESS SPENCER AND HER DAUGH-
TER", ALTHORP, NORTHAMPTON-
SHIRE, (above) is one of a number
of portraits by Sir Joshua Reynolds
of the Princess of Wales's ancestors.
Reynolds was the most successful
artist of his age, and the first President of the Royal Academy.

"THE PLUMB-PUDDING IN DANGER",
(above) a satirical cartoon by James
Gillray, illustrates William Pitt and
Napoleon carving up the world in
1805. Gillray and Cruikshank gave
their cartoons a style that established them as important works of art.

BUCKLERS HARD, HAMPSHIRE, (above) once a shipyard, is now the home of a maritime museum. Among the ships built there was Nelson's favourite flagship, the Agamemnon.

"ADMIRAL LORD NELSON", National Portrait Gallery, London, (left) was painted by L.F. Abbott in 1797, shortly after Nelson's famous victory at Cape St Vincent. His last flagship, the Victory (right) is now preserved in the Royal Dockyards, Portsmouth, Hampshire.

"WATERLOO", by William Allan, (above) depicts the Duke of Wellington directing the famous battle of 1815, mounted on his horse Copenhagen. This picture now hangs in Apsley House, London. Once the Duke's home, it now houses a museum devoted to his memory. Wellington's portrait (far left) is by Goya, the finest portrait painter of his day. The painting of "Napoleon on board Bellerophon", by Charles Eastlake, (left) is from the National Maritime Museum, Greenwich, Greater London, and illustrates the fallen conqueror on his way to exile in St Helena.

masts, the rattle of musketry at point-blank range rent the air. The *Victory* smashed through between Villeneuve's flagship, the *Bucentaure*, and the *Redoutable*. The three ships remained locked together, raking each other with broadsides. Nelson was pacing as if on parade on his quarterdeck when at 1.35 p.m. he was shot in the shoulder by a bullet from the masthead of the *Redoutable*. His backbone was broken, and he was carried below amid the thunder of the *Victory* guns. The battle was still raging. By the afternoon of October 21, 1805, eighteen of the enemy ships had surrendered and the remainder were in full retreat. Eleven entered Cadiz, but four more were captured off the coast of Spain. In the log of the *Victory* occurs the passage, "Partial firing continued until four-thirty, when a victory having been reported to the Right Hon. Lord Viscount Nelson, K.B. and Commander in Chief, he then died of his wound."

The victory was complete and final. The British fleet, under her most superb commander, like him had done its duty.

Napoleon meanwhile was attracted to other fields. When Villeneuve failed to break through into the Channel, the Emperor made a sudden change of plan. He determined to strike at the European coalition raised against him by Pitt's diplomacy and subsidies. In August 1805 the camp at Boulogne broke up, and the French troops set out on their long march to the Danube.

The campaign that followed wrecked Pitt's hopes. In the month of Trafalgar the Austrian General Mack surrendered at Ulm. Austria and Russia were broken at the Battle of Austerlitz. Napoleon's star had once more triumphed, and for England all was to do again.

A personal sorrow now darkened Pitt's life. The House of Commons by the casting vote of the Speaker resolved to impeach his close colleague, Dundas, for maladministration in the Admiralty. The decisive speech against Dundas was made by none other than Wilberforce. The scene in the House of Commons was poignant. Pitt's eyes filled with tears as he listened to Wilberforce attacking his other greatest friend. After the adverse decision the Opposition crowded round him to see how he took it; but, encircled by his supporters, he was led from the House. It was this disgrace, rather than the news of Austerlitz, which finally broke the spirit and energy of the Prime Minister. In January 1806 he died. Wilberforce has written a valediction for his friend.

"For a clear and comprehensive view of the most complicated subject in all its relations; for the fairness of mind which disposes a man to follow out, and when overtaken to recognise, the truth; for magnanimity which made him ready to change his measures when he thought the good of the country required it, though he knew he should be charged with inconsistency on account of the change; for willingness to give a fair hearing to all that could be urged against his own opinions, and to listen to the suggestions of men whose understanding he knew to be inferior to his own; for personal purity, disinterestedness, integrity, and love of his country, I have never known his equal."

"In an age", runs the inscription on his monument in Guildhall, " when the contagion of ideals threatened to dissolve the forms of civil society he rallied the loyal, the sober-minded, and the good around the venerable structure of the English monarchy."

This is a fitting epitaph.

"The Death of Nelson" by A.W. Devis. Before he died, news was brought to Nelson that fourteen or fifteen enemy ships, from a total of thirty-three, had been taken or destroyed by the British fleet. Nelson commented, "That is well, but I had bargained for twenty." The final score was, in fact, eighteen.

CHAPTER 35

THE EMPEROR OF THE FRENCH

WILLIAM PITT'S SUCCESSORS WERE STAUNCH in the prosecution of war, but even less adept at it than he. The three years after his death were uncheered by fortune. England's military strength was wasted in unfruitful expeditions to the fringes of the Mediterranean coastline. One small victory was won at Maida, in the Kingdom of Naples. There the rush of French attack was first broken by steady British infantry. Accounts of the battle reached Sir Arthur Wellesley, now home from India, and fortified his views on how to meet the French in the field. But Maida was of no strategic consequence. Thanks to the fleet, however, the sea lanes of the world remained open, and in Europe the important islands of Sicily and Sardinia were kept from Napoleon's grasp.

In 1806 and 1807 there was a brief ministry of "All the Talents" under Lord Grenville. The talent was largely provided by the Whigs, now in office for the first time since 1783, but over twenty years of divorce from power had had an insidious and lowering effect upon the party. Their organisation and their programme dissolved in the perplexed bickering of their leaders. The renewal of the European conflict quenched the hopes of Parliamentary Reform, upon which they had taken their stand in the early 1790s. They hoped to lift some of the restrictions upon Roman Catholics, for they were much oppressed by the problem of Ireland. But in this they failed. The Government's tenure of office was redeemed only by Fox's abolition of the slave trade, a measure which ranks among the greatest of British achievements, and from which Pitt had always shrunk. It was Fox's last effort. For forty years his warm-hearted eloquence had inspired the Whigs. Almost his whole Parliamentary life was spent in Opposition. He died as Secretary of State, nine months after Pitt had gone to the grave.

In 1807 the Whigs fell. They were succeeded by a mixed Government of Tory complexion under the nominal leadership of the Duke of Portland. Its object was to hold together the loyalties of as much of the nation as it could command. In this it was remarkably successful. New figures were appearing in the Tory ranks, trained by Pitt in the daily business of government. George Canning, Spencer Perceval, Viscount Castlereagh, were reaching out for power. Politics centred on the conduct of the War Office and these restless spirits soon impelled the Government to discard the strategies of William Pitt. Active participation in the military and naval struggle for Europe became the order of the day.

Speed was essential, for Napoleon was reaching the height of his career. At Austerlitz he had struck down Russia and Austria. He was already master of the Netherlands, Italy, and the states of the Rhine. At Jena, a year later, he had broken Prussia. The Tsar was still in the field, but in June 1807 the Russian army was defeated on the Eylau River. There followed the reconciliation of Napoleon and Alexander. On a raft upon the Niemen, with their armies gathered on either bank, the two Emperors met and embraced. Peace was made between them. And not only peace, but alliance. Alexander, estranged from England by the paltry support he had received, yielded himself to Napoleon's spell. The two potentates planned Europe according to their common interests. When he reviewed the French army and at Napoleon's side watched the Old Guard march past, Alexander was struck by the scars which many of these veterans bore. "And where are the soldiers who have given these wounds?" he exclaimed to Ney. "Sire, they are dead."

The Franco-Russian Alliance, signed at Tilsit on July 7, was the culmination of Napoleon's power. He dominated all Europe. His brothers reigned as kings at The Hague, at Naples, and in Westphalia. His stepson ruled northern Italy in his name. Spain lent itself to his system, trusting that worse might not befall. Denmark and Scandinavia made haste to obey. Only Britannia remained unconquered, mistress of the oceans, ruled by her proud, stubborn aristocracy, facing this immense combination alone, sullen, fierce, and almost unperturbed. Some anxious merchants and manufacturers complained of the British blockade, which materially affected their interests. They stirred up Whig politicians to denounce it. But the Government was founded on land, not trade, and turned a deaf ear. Nevertheless Britain owed much of the power that was to bring her victory to her growing industrial supremacy. Industry knew this. The seeds were now sown for a crop of post-war troubles in which industry was to demand a greater share in the councils of the nation. But for the time being patriotism healed all, or nearly all.

It was against this contumacious land that Napoleon now directed his whole strength. To venture upon salt water, except for cruiser raids on commerce, was to be sunk or captured. The British blockade wrapped the French Empire and Napoleon's Europe in a clammy shroud. No trade, no coffee, no sugar, no contact with the East, or with the Americans! And no means of ending the deadlock! Napoleon had believed that the marshalling of all Europe under his hands would force England to make terms. But no response came from the island, which throve upon seaborne trade, and whose ruling classes seemed to take as much interest in prizefighting and foxhunting as in the world crisis.

Napoleon crowned himself Emperor on December 2, 1804. He took the crown from the hands of the Pope and set it on his own head. Jacques-Louis David's fine painting is in the Louvre, Paris. Napoleon's mother can be seen in the background, looking on with pride.

SOCIETY AND INDUSTRY

AT THE BEGINNING of the eighteenth century the word "industry" was used simply to describe a quality possessed by hard-working people. By the end of the century, however, it was being used to describe a whole new sector of the economy—the world of mines, workshops and factories. British society was becoming subject to the new routines of the "factory system". The British environment changed also: one area of the Midlands even became known as the "Black Country". The growth of large industrial cities with no Members of Parliament to represent their interests was to lead to much-needed reforms in the nineteenth century.

The Industrial Revolution grew directly out of British enterprise and inventive genius. New and more efficient techniques for the production of iron and coal made available plentiful resources of steam power, while the introduction of power-driven machinery for spinning and weaving cotton transformed the textile industry.

Successful industrialisation depended upon the ability of the employers to "discipline" a new and inexperienced labour force—a significant part of which now consisted of women and children. Although there were many examples of benevolent management, in general hours were long and working conditions could be appalling. In most manufacturing communities the gospel of service to the god of steam was preached as fervently as the gospel of service to Christ.

During the early stages of the Industrial Revolution there was a widespread belief that it would improve the lot of every citizen. But this optimism could not last, and industrialisation soon acquired passionate critics. It brought greater national prosperity, however, and in time a share of this new wealth filtered down to ease the lives of even the most unfortunate factory workers.

THE INDUSTRIAL REVOLUTION transformed large parts of the British landscape as factory towns sprang up where, before, all had been rural peace. The Severn Gorge was one of the first industrial centres. Its development dates back to 1709 when the ironmaster, Abraham Darby, discovered a process of smelting iron ore with a flux of lime at high temperatures. Instead of charcoal he used coke, which was more readily available. His innovations prepared the way for cast-iron bridges, boats, locomotives, cylinders and aqueducts. Coalbrookdale in the Severn Gorge (above) was an ideal industrial site because, as its name suggests, it was near accessible coal seams. Supplies of iron ore and lime were also nearby, as was a navigable river. The Iron Bridge, built there in 1779, was the focus for a whole complex of industrial sites. These are now open to the visitor, and sound and light recordings explain the various processes used at Coalbrookdale. Fine local porcelain is on display at the Coalport China Museum (left), and visitors can see the original workshops.

THE FIRST RAILWAYS, *known originally as wagonways, were constructed to carry coal from the mines to the nearest large towns. The first passenger railway was opened between Stockton and Darlington in 1825. In the picture (above), a steam locomotive of about 1814 hauls coal along a three-and-a-half-mile track from Middleton Colliery to Leeds. Pithead winding machinery and a steam pump can be seen in the background.*

THE FIRST WELL-KNOWN CANAL, *completed in 1761 by the Duke of Bridgewater and James Brindley, connected the seven miles between Worsley, where the Duke had extensive coal mines, and Manchester, where coal was in short supply. Barton Bridge, shown below, is an aqueduct built by Brindley to carry the canal over the River Irwell. Brindley and the Duke went on to construct a canal between Manchester and Liverpool, enabling food and raw materials to reach Lancashire more easily than by road, thus lowering their price.*

THE FIRST TEXTILE MILLS *were built in hilly districts near running water to power the new machinery invented throughout the eighteenth century. The most famous of the new businessmen was Sir Richard Arkwright. His portrait (top) was painted in 1790 by the school of Joseph Wright of Derby. One of these inventions, the water-frame machine patented by Arkwright in 1769, led to the construction of a great mill at Cromford, Derbyshire. Most later mills are associated with Lancashire and woollen mills with Yorkshire. In Scotland, Robert Owen developed the New Lanark Mills (above). He was a philanthropic industrialist who introduced social and welfare reforms, building houses and schools for workers and their families. Most textile workers were not treated so well.*

A STOPPAGE to a STRIDE over the GLOBE

A massive Napoleon straddles the globe while a puny John Bull hacks at his boot. Gillray's cartoon emphasises the stupendous odds faced by the British in the Napoleonic Wars.

Grave and threatening news was now conveyed to London from the raft where the two Emperors had met upon the River Niemen. An English secret agent reported that an arrangement had been reached whereby Napoleon was to seize the Danish fleet and gain control of the entrance to the Baltic. This was to be a preliminary to a joint invasion of England with the help of the Russians. The Cabinet acted with praiseworthy decision. Admiral Gambier was immediately ordered to procure, by force if necessary, the surrender of the Danish fleet. After a heavy action in the harbour of Copenhagen the Danes yielded to this humiliation. This act of aggression against a neutral state aroused a storm against the Government in Whig circles. But events vindicated the promptitude and excused the violence of their action. Two days after the British fleet left home waters, Napoleon had informed the Danish minister in Paris that if England were to refuse Russian mediation in the Great War Denmark would be forced to choose sides. Had the British Government not acted with speed the French would have been in possession of the Danish navy within a few weeks.

At the War Office Castlereagh was busy attempting to reorganise the regular army. Thirty thousand men were drawn from the local militia, and formed into regular regiments, and provision was made to raise forty-four thousand recruits for the militia to take their place in home defence.

Powerless at sea, Napoleon realised that to destroy his one outstanding rival he must turn the weapon of blockade against the island. English goods must be kept out of the markets of Europe by an iron ring of Customs guards stretching from the borders of Russia round the coasts of Europe as far as the Dardanelles. It was a land blockade of sea-power. The weakest link in the immense barrier of French troops and Customs officers was the Peninsula of Spain. To complete this amazing plan it was essential to control not only Spain, but also Portugal, the traditional ally of Britain, whose capital, Lisbon, was an important potential base for the British fleet.

The crucial point therefore lay in the Peninsula. Canning, in charge at the Foreign Office, displayed the energy of youth. An English squadron sailed to the Tagus, collected the Portuguese ships, and packed off the Portuguese royal family, Government, and society to the safety of Brazil. A few days later General Junot entered the Portuguese capital, and the following day Napoleon declared war on the country he had just occupied.

Napoleon, insatiable of power, and seeking always to break England and her intangible blockade, also resolved to seize the Spanish Crown. He enticed King Charles IV of Spain and his son Ferdinand into a trap at Bayonne, and under the threat of a firing squad compelled them to sign documents of abdication. He placed his own brother Joseph on the throne of Spain as a vassal of the French Empire. "Spanish opinion bends to my will. Tranquillity is everywhere re-established," he wrote. But, happily for human freedom, things are not so easy as that. As soon as the Spaniards realised what had happened and that their country was practically annexed to France they rose everywhere in spontaneous revolt. Between May 24 and 30, 1807, in every hamlet and village throughout the Peninsula they took up what arms they could find. Nothing like this universal uprising of a numerous, ancient race and nation, all animated by one thought, had been seen before. The tiny province of Asturias, on the Biscayan shore, separated by the mountains from the rest of Spain, knowing nothing of what the rest were doing, drove out the French governor, seized the arsenal with booty of a hundred thousand muskets, constituted itself an independent government, declared war upon Napoleon at the height of his greatness, and sent their envoys to England to appeal for aid. The envoys landed at Falmouth on the night of June 6, and were conveyed by the Admiralty to Canning. Canning understood. From that moment the Peninsular War began. For the first time the forces unchained by the French Revolution, which Napoleon had disciplined and directed, met, not kings or Old World hierarchies, but a whole population inspired by religion and patriotism.

The character of the warfare darkened. In Germany and Italy and elsewhere there had been pillage and rough deeds, but the armies had given quarter and the inhabitants had remained spectators. Now, in Spain, the French troops found as they marched the corpses of their stragglers and wounded, often horribly mutilated, sometimes bearing signs of torture. It was with a chill that they realised they were at grips with a foe who, though incompetent in a set battle, neither gave nor sought mercy. Moreover, this foe lay everywhere. In July King Joseph wrote to Napoleon from Madrid, "No one has told the truth so far. The fact is that there is not a single Spaniard who is for me except the few who came here with me." The Emperor was very slow to measure the force of the Spanish revolt. He could not understand a people who preferred misgovernment of their own making to rational rule imposed from without. Now, at the end of July, news reached him of an event in Spain, grave in itself, and menacing to the whole structure of his power.

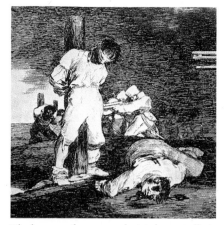

The horrors of war were depicted repeatedly in drawings and paintings by the Spanish artist, Francisco Goya (1746–1828). One of his most powerful themes was the execution of deserters and prisoners.

General Dupont, withdrawing to Madrid from Cordova, had been entangled and brought to a standstill at Baylen, in Andalusia. In the burning summer he had to fight for water, and, not gaining it, surrendered to the Spanish insurgents with twenty-two thousand French soldiers. This was a new event in Europe since the Revolutionary wars began. The capitulation of Baylen compelled the evacuation of Madrid. The French army, carrying King Joseph with them, withdrew to the northeast behind the Ebro. General Junot, in Portugal, whose people had likewise risen, was isolated by hundreds of miles of hostile country and by the salt seas where Britain ruled, and from which she could strike. Napoleon felt in every nerve and fibre the tremor which ran through Europe and jarred the foundations of his Imperial throne. This country, which he had expected to incorporate in his Empire by a personal arrangement with a feeble government, by a trick, by a trap, without bloodshed or expense, suddenly became his main military problem. He resolved to conquer. He reached out to Germany and drew the flower of his armies to the south.

But meanwhile the English had struck a shrewd blow. Canning and his colleagues decided to send an army to the Peninsula to aid the Spanish insurgents. But as the juntas of Galicia and Andalusia were not as yet willing to accept foreign troops, the expedition was sent to Portugal, and in July 1808 disembarked north of Lisbon at the Mondego River. This small British army consisted of thirty thousand well-equipped men. At the head of the first troops to land appeared Sir Arthur Wellesley, whose conduct of the Mahratta war in India had been distinguished. The younger brother of the Governor-General of India, he was a Member of Parliament and actually held office at this time as Chief Secretary to the Lord Lieutenant of Ireland. He immediately took the field. At the combat at Roliça Junot received a sharp repulse. At Vimiero this was repeated on an even larger scale, for here, the French columns of assault were broken by the reserved fire of the "thin red line", which now began to attract attention. General Junot therefore retreated upon Lisbon.

Wellesley was superseded in the moment of victory by the arrival of Sir Harry Burrard, who later in the same day made over his command to Sir Hew Dalrymple. Wellesley's wish to seize the pass of Torres Vedras and thus cut Junot's line of retreat was frustrated by his seniors. The French commander now offered to evacuate Portugal if the British would carry him back to France. The Convention of Cintra was signed, and punctiliously executed by the British. Junot and twenty-six thousand Frenchmen were landed from British transports at Rochefort. Wellesley, in dudgeon, remarked to his officers, "We can now go and shoot red-legged partridges." There was a loud and not unnatural outcry in England at Junot being freed. A military court of inquiry exonerated the three commanders, but only one of them was ever employed again.

He was the one that mattered:

> Sir Arthur and Sir Harry,
> Sir Harry and Sir Hew,
> Sing cock-a-doodle doodle,
> doodle-doodle-doo
>
> Sir Arthur was a fighting cock,
> But of the other two
> Sing doodle-doodle-doodle,
> doodle-doodle-doo.

Napoleon had now moved a quarter of a million of his best troops into Spain. While the Grand Army was gathering behind the Ebro he organised a mighty display. At Erfurt thirty-eight princes and rulers assembled at the Emperor's call. When Tsar Alexander arrived Napoleon sought to inflame his mind with schemes of a Franco-Russian march to Constantinople and beyond along the historic route to India. Alexander was still fascinated by Napoleon's personality. He liked to dream of world conquest with him. But he was also vexed by the large garrisons Napoleon kept on the Oder. All passed off with pomp and splendour. Alexander and Napoleon kissed before the august circle. But Erfurt was only a hollow echo of Tilsit.

The moment had now come for Napoleon to take command on the Ebro. An avalanche of fire and steel broke upon the Spanish juntas, who, with ninety thousand raw but ardent volunteers, had nursed a brief illusion of freedom regained. The Emperor advanced upon Madrid, driving the Spanish army before him in a series of routs in which the French cavalry took pitiless vengeance. He astonished his personal staff by his violent energy. Always with the leading troops, he forced the fighting. In December he entered Madrid, and replaced Joseph, who had hitherto followed with the baggage train, upon the stolen throne. But the Spanish people were undaunted, and all around the camps of the victorious invaders flickered a horrible guerrilla.

A new English general of high quality had now succeeded the commanders involved in the Convention of Cintra. Sir John Moore advanced from Lisbon through Salamanca to Valladolid. He had been lured by promises of powerful Spanish assistance, and he tried by running great risks to turn Spanish hopes into reality. His daring thrust cut or threatened the communications of all the French armies, and immediately prevented any French action in the south of Spain or against Portugal. But Napoleon, watching from Madrid, saw him as prey. At Christmas 1808, with fifty thousand men, with Ney, Soult, and the Old Guard, he marched to intercept and destroy him. On foot with his soldiers Napoleon tramped through the snows of the Guadarrama. He moved with amazing speed. Moore, warned in time, and invoking amphibious power, dropped his communications with Portugal and ordered his transports to meet him at Corunna, on the northwest tip of Spain. It was a race; but when the French horse crossed the Rio Seco they were hurled back, and their general captured by the cavalry of the English rearguard. Moore had already passed Astorga and was halfway to his haven.

At Astorga the Emperor sat down on the parapet of a bridge to read dispatches brought from the capital. After a few moments he rose, and stood absorbed in thought. Then, ordering up his travelling coach, he handed over the pursuit of the British to Soult, and, without offering any explanation to his officers, set off for Valladolid and Paris. He had been warned of an intrigue, or even plot, against him by Talleyrand and Fouché, his Minister of Police. Besides, there was now no chance of cutting off the British. The pursuit had become a chase. Soult and Ney could have it.

The retreat of the British through the rugged, snowbound hill country was arduous. The French pressed heavily. Scenes of mass drunkenness where wine stores were found, pillage, stragglers dying of cold and hunger, and the army chest of gold flung down a precipice to baffle capture darkened the British track. But when, at Lugo, Moore turned and offered battle, his army showed so firm a posture that for two days Soult, although already superior, awaited reinforcements. It was now resolved to slip away in the night to Corunna, where the army arrived on January 14, 1809. But the harbour was empty. Contrary winds had delayed the fleet and transports. There would be a battle after all. On the sixteenth Soult assaulted Moore with twenty thousand against fourteen thousand. When darkness fell the pursuers had had enough. But both Sir John Moore and his second-in-command, Sir David Baird, had fallen on the field.

Moore died like Wolfe and Nelson, in the hour of victory. By daring, skill, and luck he had ruptured Napoleon's winter campaign and had drawn the Emperor and his finest army into the least important part of Spain, thus affording protection and time for movements to get on foot in all the rest of the Peninsula. He had escaped Napoleon's amazing forward spring and clutch. His army re-embarked unmolested. His campaign had restored the military reputation of Britain, which had suffered increasing eclipse since the days of Chatham; he had prepared the way for a new figure, destined to lead the armies of Europe upon the decisive field.

The return of the Emperor to Paris recalled his servants to their treacherous allegiance. He had now to face war with Austria. For this purpose he made demands upon the manhood and youth of France, already drained by so many years of glory. He drew the class of 1810 to the colours; he compelled the leading families to send their sons to the military colleges from the age of sixteen upwards. He brought some troops back from Spain, and in April, having a flow of life filling his ranks or training on behind him to the number of two hundred and forty thousand men, he marched against Austria. High authorities consider that the opening phase of the

Volunteer soldiers were sketched by Thomas Rowlandson in many drawings which detailed the uniforms worn by different regiments.

The Austrians defeated the French at the battle of Essling, but Napoleon quickly recovered and reconquered them at the decisive Battle of Wagram.

campaign of 1809 in the Danube valley ranks among the finest examples of military genius. In what has been called the Battle of the Five Days he unfolded a single theme of war, each day was marked by a fresh and fruitful victory. The centre of the long Austrian front was pierced, and its fragments retreated with heavy losses. For the second time he entered Vienna at the head of his troops.

But he had not yet disposed of the Austrian army. When he attempted to cross the Danube at Aspern-Essling a sudden rise of the river broke his bridges and he narrowly escaped a decisive defeat at the hands of the Archduke Charles, ablest of the Austrian commanders. In the wooded island of Lobau he lay crouched for six weeks while he gathered reinforcements from every quarter of his Empire. Meanwhile the Tsar, nominally his ally, trembled upon the verge of coming in against him. On July 4 Napoleon sallied out from his island and forced the passage of the Danube in the immense Battle of Wagram. Nearly four hundred thousand men fought on this field, and forty thousand fell. Europe was stunned. The Tsar Alexander hastened to send his congratulations, and Austria submitted again to the conqueror's sword.

CHAPTER 36

THE PENINSULAR WAR AND THE FALL OF NAPOLEON

WHEN THE BRITISH SAILED AWAY FROM CORUNNA, no organised forces remained in Spain to hinder Napoleon's marshals. Everywhere Spanish armies were defeated, and only the implacable guerrilla continued. In the opening months of 1809 the French were again free to move their armies where they pleased in the Peninsula. Soult now entered Portugal and established himself at Oporto. What was left of the original British expedition still occupied Lisbon, and by successive reinforcements was raised to a strength of thirty thousand men. These, conjoined with an equal number of Portuguese, organised under a British general, Beresford, were sufficient to keep Soult inert for several months, during which he distracted himself with an intrigue to become king. The Government in London were divided in counsel upon what ought to be done. Should they resume a major campaign in the Peninsula or strike at the Netherlands? They decided to split their effort and make an attempt in both quarters. An expedition was mounted to seize the Dutch island of Walcheren, at the mouth of the Scheldt, and occupy Antwerp. It proved a costly diversion. Few observers were then convinced that effective success could be won in distant Spain and Portugal. These doubts were not shared by Arthur Wellesley. In April he was re-appointed to take command in Lisbon. He was to spend the next five years in the Peninsula, and return to London in triumph by way of the capital of France.

Wellesley reached Lisbon before the end of the month. He could choose between attacking Soult at Oporto or re-entering Spain to engage one or other of the numerous French marshals whose corps were widely spread throughout the Peninsula. He decided first to clear Portugal. By a swift and secret march he reached the Douro, passed a division across it by night in boats and barges, and surprised Soult and his army in the town. With very small loss he compelled the Marshal to abandon the whole of his artillery, his wounded, and the bulk of his baggage. The discomfiture of Soult constituted a brilliant achievement for the new British general and paved the way for further action.

Arthur Wellesley, first Duke of Wellington, was painted by Sir Thomas Lawrence in 1814, a year before his great victory at Waterloo.

Wellesley now resolved to penetrate the centre of Spain along the valley of the Tagus, and, joining the Spanish army under Cuesta, to engage Marshal Victor. Soult, his troops re-organised and re-equipped, was moving to join Victor, who would give him a decisive superiority. Wellesley's position at Talavera, a hundred miles southwest of Madrid, became precarious, and his soldiers were near starvation. Marshal Victor conceived himself strong enough to attack without waiting for the arrival of Soult. On July 27, 1809, the armies engaged. The French were fifty thousand strong. Wellesley had twenty thousand British and twenty-four thousand Spaniards, but these latter, though brave, could not be counted upon for serious work in a set battle. Their strength lay in harassing operations. Victor's attacks were repulsed with heavy loss after fierce mass-fighting with the bayonet. The English Guards, elated by the defeat of the French column in their front, were drawn from their place in the line by the ardour of pursuit. The British centre was open, and a French counter-stroke caused widespread disorder. But Wellesley had brought the 48th Regiment to the scene, who, in perfect array and discipline, advanced through the retreating soldiery, and, striking the French column on the flank, restored the day. A wild cavalry charge by the 23rd Light Dragoons, in which half the regiment fell, cut deeply into the enemy's flanks. Marshal Victor accepted defeat and withdrew towards Madrid. The ferocity of the fighting may be judged from the British losses. Nearly 6,000 men out of Wellesley's total of 20,000 had fallen, killed or wounded; the French had lost 7,500 and twenty guns. The Spaniards claimed to have lost 1,200 men.

Wellesley was in no condition to pursue. He could no longer place any reliance upon the cooperation of his Spanish allies. They engaged the enemy in their own free way, which was certainly not his. Like Moore before him, he had run enormous risks, and had been saved only by the narrowest of margins. He withdrew unmolested along the Tagus back to Portugal. Not only had he established the reputation of a highly skilful and determined general, but the fighting quality of the British had made a profound impression upon the French. In England there was unwonted satisfaction. Wellesley was raised to the peerage as Viscount Wellington. Nelson was gone; Pitt was gone; but here at last was someone to replace them.

At home the failing health of the Duke of Portland, the titular. head of the Government, now increased the rivalry of Canning and Castlereagh for the succession to the premiership. A duel was fought between them, in which Canning was wounded. Both resigned office, and so did Portland. Spencer Perceval, hitherto Chancellor of the Exchequer, took over the Government. He was an unassuming figure, but an adroit debater, and in the conduct of the war a man of considerable resolution. Wellington's cause in Spain was favoured by the new administration. Perceval appointed as his Foreign Secretary the Marquis Wellesley, who steadfastly stood up for his younger brother in the Cabinet. The new War Minister, Lord Liverpool, was also well disposed. The Government did their best to satisfy Wellington's requirements, but, faced with the Whig Opposition and the Tory rebels in the Commons, they were continually obstructed by petty issues. In 1810 the King's renewed illness provoked a fresh crisis. George, Prince of Wales, became Regent, but he did not send for his former friends, the Opposition Whigs, as they had fondly hoped. To his credit he decided to trust his father's ministers. By frugal finance Perceval was able to maintain supplies and nourish the armed forces. The three years of his Government were marked by quietly growing efficiency.

These were testing years for Wellington. Failure would have been disastrous to Britain, and to the patriots in Spain and Portugal; it would also have liberated large numbers of French troops for the reinforcement of

THE ENGLISH AT TABLE

This description of the eating habits of the English in the early nineteenth century is taken from Arthur Bryant's The Age of Elegance.

In one of his outbursts against the social changes that were destroying the England of his youth Cobbett [William Cobbett, 1763–1835, author of *Rural Rides*] declared that, though no theologian, he loved any religion that gave men plenty to eat and drink. In this he spoke for his country. The English ate as though eating were an act of grace; the very sick were prescribed beefsteaks and port. They ate more than any people in the world, because they grew more. A Hampshire farmer at his wedding dinner fed his guests from his own land on beef, fowls, a gammon of bacon and a sucking pig, a green goose, river-fish, plum pudding, apple pie, cheese-cakes, custards, home-brewed beer, homemade wine and syllabub. The English enjoyed the best of everything. Their seas afforded harvests as rich as their fields; cross-Channel passengers, wind-bound off the Kentish coast, would borrow lines from the captain and fill their baskets with whiting, mackerel and gurnet.

Every part of the island had its peculiar delicacies: Lincolnshire acelet and collared eel, Norfolk dumpling, Oxford John, Pegwell Bay shrimps, Solomon Gundy, Banbury cake, and the cheeses—Stilton, and Cheddar, Double Gloucester, Blue Vinney, Lancashire Leigh, Wensleydale—which were among England's regional glories. There seemed so much to eat that many found it hard to stop eating. A Yorkshire squire at a single sitting absorbed a plateful of haddock, another of veal, two of tongue, three of mutton, two of roast pig, a wing of duck, and half the tail of a lobster.

After the salads and cheeses the servants set on the table, with oranges and nuts, the brandy-primed sherries, ports, marsalas and madeiras in which Englishmen delighted. Except in Scotland and the exotic little world of the higher aristocracy, clarets were little drunk by men; such thin, washy stuff was thought unworthy of gentlemen. There were better things to crown a festive evening: broiled bones and a bowl of punch of "Bishop", that noble concoction of steaming port and roasted lemons so loved of the higher Anglican clergy. Those who survived would top up, before retiring, with a night-cap of hot brown brandy or a glass of Hollands gin with a lump of sugar in it. It was not surprising that bulging veins, mottled noses and what was politely termed a full habit were common among the English upper and middle classes.

The gluttony of the middle classes is evident in Thomas Rowlandson's picture, "A Two O'Clock Ordinary".

Napoleon's ventures elsewhere. All this was not lost upon the English commander. For the time being caution must be his policy. "As this is the last army England has," he drily wrote, "we must take care of it." The French had always bent every effort to driving the British into the sea. In 1810 they were massing for a fresh attempt. Wellington was resolved that no hasty evacuation would be forced upon him. All the previous winter he had been perfecting a series of fortified lines around Lisbon on the heights of Torres Vedras. This was to form his final bastion, and on these defences he gradually fell back.

The ablest of Napoleon's marshals, Masséna, now headed the French army of Portugal. Having overwhelmed Spanish resistance, Masséna advanced across the frontier with eighty thousand men. The British numbered about twenty-five thousand, and their Portuguese allies the same. In September there was a stiff battle at Busaco. The French were badly mauled and beaten. Wellington's withdrawal nevertheless continued. Suddenly the forward flow of the French came to a halt. Ahead of them rose the formidable lines of Torres Vedras, manned by the undefeated British, and all around extended a countryside deliberately laid waste. Masséna saw before him a prospect of bleak, hungry months, with no hope of successful assault. This was the hinge of the whole campaign.

The French paused and dug into winter quarters. Wellington hovered about them, determined, as he put it, "to force them out of Portugal by the distresses they will suffer". So it turned out. In the following spring Masséna gave up. He retreated into Spain, leaving behind him seventeen thousand dead and eight thousand prisoners.

Portugal was now free, and Wellington's successes strengthened the position of the Government at home. Rejoicing in London and Lisbon, however, was mingled with a certain impatience. Wellington himself was

Marie Louise of Austria married Napoleon in 1810 when she was nineteen, and bore him a son during the following year. The boy, who was briefly King of Rome, was held virtually a prisoner in Austria from 1815 until his death from tuberculosis in 1832. Marie Louise remarried twice after Napoleon's death in 1821.

unperturbed by cries for haste. Nothing could shake him, and he kept his own counsel. Before he ventured into the recesses of Spain, he must have in his hands the frontier fortresses of Badajoz and Ciudad Rodrigo, which guarded the roads to Madrid. Two French armies confronted him. Masséna, later replaced by Marmont, held the northern front. Soult lay to the south. They and their fellow marshals elsewhere in Spain commanded some quarter of a million men, of whom about a hundred thousand faced Wellington. They were much hampered by the incessant guerrilla. They could no longer count on living off the country, as French armies had hitherto done all over Europe; and they were in constant receipt of angry instructions from their Emperor in Paris, based on fancy rather than on fact. For the genius of Napoleon, grappling with the problems of his continental empire, failed him in his conduct of the distant, remorseless Spanish struggle.

Wellington had gauged precisely the size and scope of the task before him. A war of manoeuvre unfolded in 1811 within the Spanish frontiers, and both the French armies blocking his advance were separately met and defeated at Fuentes d'Oñoro and Albuera. These were violent battles. Of Fuentes, which lies to the west of Ciudad Rodrigo, Wellington admitted, "If Boney had been there we should have been beaten." But Napoleon was enmeshed in diplomacy and preparations for war elsewhere. Besides, he had just solemnised his second marriage. The Corsican's bride was a daughter of the proud house of Habsburg, the Archduchess Marie Louise. She gave him a long-desired son and heir, but little happiness.

The battles of Fuentes and of Albuera, which was fought by Wellington's lieutenant, Beresford, were not decisive, but the British remained masters of the field. As Wellington wrote to Lord Liverpool, "We have certainly altered the course of the war in Spain; it has become to a certain degree offensive on our part." This was a typical understatement. In fact Wellington was already laying his plans for the day when he would drive the French back over the Pyrenees. Amid the snows of January 1812 he was at last able to seize Ciudad Rodrigo. Four months later Badajoz fell to a bloody assault. The cost in life was heavy, but the way was opened for an overpowering thrust into Spain. Wellington and Marmont manoeuvred about one another, each watching for the other to make a mistake. It was Marmont who erred, and at Salamanca Wellington achieved his first victory on the offensive in the Peninsular War. King Joseph Bonaparte fled from Madrid, and the British occupied the capital amid the pealing of bells and popular rejoicing. But there was still Soult to be dealt with. Coming up from the south, the French marshal wheeled round Wellington's flank. His forces outnumbered the British by nearly two to one, and he was careful to offer no opening for promising attack. Wellington fell back once more on the Portuguese frontier. In the year's campaign he had shattered one French army and enabled the whole of southern Spain to be freed from the French. But meanwhile heavier shadows from the east were falling upon Napoleon's Empire. It was the winter of the retreat from Moscow.

All through the spring of 1812 the Emperor had been gathering forces on a scale hitherto unknown in Europe, and as the summer came he drew them eastward from all his dominions. For two years past his relations with Russia had been growing more and more embittered. The amiable days of Tilsit were forgotten, and the Emperors who had sworn friendship on the raft in the River Niemen were now foes. Napoleon determined to get his blow in first, and to make it a shattering one. Although his generals and ministers were reluctant and apprehensive a kind of delirium swept the martial classes of the Empire. The idea of a campaign larger than any yet conceived, more daring than the deeds of Alexander the Great, which might lead to the conquest of all Asia, took possession of the fighting men.

Many voices had warned Napoleon of the hardships and difficulties of campaigning in Russia. Nor did he disregard their advice. He had assembled what seemed for those days abundant transport and supply. In June 1812 he crossed the Niemen and headed straight for Moscow, some five hundred miles to the east. He was confronted by two main Russian armies totalling two hundred thousand men. His plan was to overwhelm them separately and snatch at the old Russian capital. He confidently expected that the Tsar would then treat for peace. All the other sovereigns of Europe in similar circumstances had hastened to bow the knee. But Russia proved a different proposition. Defence, retreat, and winter—on these resources the Russian high command relied. Napoleon had studied the amazing Russian campaigns of the great Swede, King Charles XII. He thought he had profited by his reading. In the twentieth century another more ruthless dictator was to study Napoleon's errors. He too thought he had marked the lesson. Russia undeceived them both.

Before Napoleon the Russian armies fell back, avoiding the traps he set for them and devastating the countryside through which the French had to pass. At Borodino, some sixty miles west of the capital, the Russians turned at bay. There in the bloodiest battle of the nineteenth century General Kutusov inflicted a terrible mauling on Napoleon. Both the armies engaged, each of about a hundred and twenty thousand men, lost a third of their strength. Kutusov withdrew once more, and Moscow fell to the French. But the Russians declined to sue for peace. As winter drew near, it was forced on Napoleon's mind that Moscow, burnt to a shell by accident or by design, was untenable by his starving troops. There was nothing for it but retreat through the gathering snows—the most celebrated and disastrous retreat in history. Winter now took its dreadful toll. Rearguard actions sapped the remaining French strength. Out of the huge Grand Army launched upon Russia only twenty thousand straggled back to Warsaw.

"Boney Hatching a Bulletin, or Snug Winter Quarters" is a Cruikshank cartoon satirising the plight of the French army during the retreat from Moscow. Most of the soldiers are buried in snow while Bonaparte dictates a reassuring message to his subjects. Finally he exclaims, "Tell anything but the truth."

This affectionate contemporary cartoon by Paul Pry is entitled "A Wellington Boot, or The Head of the Army."

On December 5 Napoleon abandoned the remnant of his armies on the Russian frontier and set out by sleigh for Paris. Whatever salvaging could be done he left to his marshals. For himself he was insensible of disaster. He still put trust in his star. If he had failed to extend his Empire to the east, he could yet preserve it in the west. By tremendous efforts he would raise new forces and fight again. In the spring of 1813 he once more took the field, but reluctant support was all he could get, and even his marshals began to waver. Germany rose in the hour of his downfall. The spirit of nationalism, diffused by French armies, sprang up to baffle and betray the master of Europe. Coalitions were formed, backed by the finances of Britain. Napoleon was offered the chance of an honourable peace. Thinking that fate could be reversed by genius in battle, he rejected it. One by one his hesitant allies dropped away. Sweden, ruled by the French Marshal Bernadotte, abandoned him. The Tsar was resolved upon a march for the Rhine. Central Europe, so long subservient to France, joined the Russian thrust. A series of gigantic engagements were fought in Saxony and Silesia. At last in the three-day battle of Leipzig in October all Napoleon's foes closed in upon him. Nearly half a million men were involved on each side. In this Battle of the Nations Napoleon was overwhelmed and driven westward to the frontiers of France. The Allies gathered on the borders of their enemy for the first time since 1793. The great Revolutionary and Imperial adventure was drawing to a close.

On the southern front Wellington's achievement also surpassed all expectations. Issuing from his frontier bastions in May 1813, he flourished his cocked hat. "Farewell, Portugal!" he exclaimed. "I shall never see you again." Nor did he. He once more bundled King Joseph Bonaparte out of Madrid. He cleared the whole north of Spain and herded the retreating French into the old mountain kingdom of Navarre. At the battle of Vitoria on June 21 he routed Marshal Jourdan and drove his forces over the Pyrenees. News of this victory heartened the Tsar and the Allied armies of Europe in Saxony. For the first and only time the success of British arms was greeted by a Te Deum sung in Russian. By the spring of 1814 Wellington was on French soil and had occupied Bordeaux. In early April he sought out and defeated his old antagonist, Soult, at Toulouse.

For Napoleon the end had already come. In the south the front had crumpled; to the east Prussians, Russians, and Austrians were reaching into the heart of France. Napoleon was never more brilliant in manoeuvre than during his brief campaign of 1814. But the combined strength of Europe was too much for him. The forces of opposition to his rule in France openly rose against him. Fouché and Talleyrand, long conspiring in doubt, now put it to themselves that France could only be saved by deserting her Emperor. At the end of March Marshal Marmont, defending Paris, gave up and surrendered the capital. On April 3 Napoleon abdicated and retired to the island of Elba. The long, remorseless tides of war rolled back, and at the Congress of Vienna the powers prepared for the diplomatic struggle of the peace.

Britain was represented at Vienna by Castlereagh. In 1812 the Prime Minister, Perceval, had been shot dead by a madman in the lobby of the House of Commons. Perceval's colleague, Lord Liverpool, took over the administration, and remained in power for fifteen years. Castlereagh rejoined the Government as Foreign Secretary, an office he was to hold until his death. The war Governments of Perceval and Liverpool, Canning and Castlereagh, had borne the burden with courage and increasing skill. Castlereagh was now to take an influential part in the reconstruction of Europe. His voice was foremost in proposing a just and honourable peace. Castlereagh believed in the balance of power. There were five great powers in Europe. His object was to concert their interests. Harmony between them was too much to expect. But at least it might be arranged that the jars of international life should not lead inevitably to war.

Castlereagh's principal colleagues at Vienna were Metternich, the Austrian Chancellor, and Talleyrand, the spokesman of France. Metternich's desire was to put back the clock to pre-Revolutionary days. The supple Talleyrand had served in turn the Revolution, Napoleon, and now the Bourbons; his aim was to salvage for France all that he could from the ruins of the Imperial adventure. Between them Castlereagh held the advantage of disinterestedness.

The most urgent problem was the government of France. Napoleon had gone, but who was to replace him? It was Talleyrand who persuaded the five powers to restore the Bourbons in the person of Louis XVIII, brother of the executed king. Louis represented at least a tradition, a fragment of the political faith of France; above all, he represented peace. He was himself a man of mildness and accommodation. The years of exile had not soured him. The main social changes of the past twenty-five years were tacitly accepted; the system of government and administration created under Napoleon was continued by his successors, with the added novelty of the beginnings of a Parliamentary constitution.

A politic moderation was displayed in the terms offered to the defeated enemy: no indemnity, no occupation by Allied troops, not even the return of the art treasures which had been looted from the galleries of Europe. The foreign conquests of the Emperor were surrendered, but the essential unity of France remained untroubled and the territory over which Louis XVIII ruled was slightly more extensive than that of Louis XVI. The reason for this moderation is not difficult to comprehend. To disrupt France would add too much weight to one or other of the Continental powers. Besides, it would kindle a flame of vengeance in the hearts of all Frenchmen.

The British were principally concerned with the colonial settlement. Many conquests were returned, yet the Peace of Paris, which was the outcome of the Congress, marks another stage in the establishment of the new Empire which was replacing the lost American colonies. The captured French colonies were surrendered, with the exception of Mauritius, Tobago, and St Lucia. The Dutch recovered their possessions in the East Indies. Sir Stamford Raffles, who had governed with singular success the rich island of Java, saw this British prize given back to its former owners. It was not until some years later that he founded the trading settlement which is now the city of Singapore. At the price of three million pounds sterling Britain acquired part of Guiana from the Dutch. The Government however was most concerned with those possessions which had a strategic value as ports of call. For that reason it held on to Malta, and the key of the route to India, the Cape of Good Hope. Dutch Ceylon was kept, and Danish Heligoland, which had proved a fine base for breaking the Continental system. These gains were scattered and piecemeal, but, taken together, they represented a powerful consolidation of the Imperial structure.

On the Continent the main preoccupation of the powers was to draw a *cordon sanitaire* around France to protect Central Europe from the infections and dangers of revolution. In the north was established a precarious and uneasy union of Calvinist Holland and Catholic Belgium in the Kingdom of the Netherlands—a union which lasted only until 1830. In the south the King of Sardinia regained Piedmont and Savoy, with the old Republic of Genoa as a further sop. Throughout the rest of Italy the authority of Austria stretched unchallenged. At Naples for a while Marshal Murat was left in possession. But not for long. Soon the Bourbons were restored, and over them Austrian influence also reigned supreme.

So much for Western Europe. The root trouble lay in the east. Russia wanted Poland, Prussia wanted Saxony. Left to themselves each might have

THE PRESS GANG

Better pay and conditions in the merchant navy made it almost impossible to find crews for naval service. During the eighteenth century recruitment was done by press gangs. This account of his kidnap and imprisonment was written by Robert Hay, twenty-two-year-old merchant seaman who was captured just after his vessel had docked.

I was when crossing Towerhill accosted by a person in seamen's dress who tapped me on the shoulder enquiring in a familiar and technical strain "What ship?" I assumed an air of gravity and surprise and told him I presumed he was under some mistake as I was not connected with shipping. The fellow, however, was too well acquainted with his business to be thus easily put off. He gave a whistle and in a moment I was in the hands of six or eight ruffians who I immediately dreaded and soon found to be a press gang. They dragged me hurriedly along through several

These press-ganged recruits seem more at home in the alehouse than in battle.

streets amid bitter execrations bestowed on them, expressions of sympathy directed towards me, and landed me in one of their houses of rendezvous.

In a short time I was conducted before the Lieutenant, who told me I might as well make a frank confession of my circumstances, it would save time and insure me better treatment. I therefore acknowledged that I had been a voyage to the West Indies and had come home Carpenter of a ship. "I am glad of that, my lad," said he, "we are very much in want of Carpenters. Step along with these men and they will give you a passage on board."

By midday I was securely lodged on board the *Enterprise* and sent down into the great cabin, in various parts of which tables were placed covered with green cloth, loaded with papers and surrounded with men well dressed and powdered. Such silence prevailed and such solemn gravity was displayed in every countenance that I was struck with awe and dread.

A short sketch of what had passed between the press officer and myself had been communicated to the examining officer, for when I was ushered into his presence he thus addressed me:

"Well, young man, I understand you are a carpenter by trade."

"Yes, sir."

"Are you willing to join the King's Service?"

"No, sir."

"Why?"

"Because I get much better wages in the merchant service and should I be unable to agree with the Captain I am at liberty to leave him at the end of the voyage."

"As to wages," said he, "the chance of prize money is quite an equivalent and obedience and respect shown to your officers are all that is necessary to insure you good treatment. Take my advice, my lad," continued he, "and enter the service cheerfully. If you continue to refuse you will be kept as a pressed man and treated accordingly."

He said no more, but making a motion with his hand I was seized by two marines and thrust down among five or six score of miserable beings, who like myself had been kidnapped, and immured in the unwholesome dungeon of a press room.

accepted the demands of the other, but this was far from agreeable to either France or Austria. Castlereagh, as fearful of the expansion of Russia as Metternich was of Prussia, took sides against so sweeping a settlement. An alliance between Britain, France, and Austria was formed to resist these pretensions, if necessary even by war. War did not prove necessary. Russia consented to swallow the greater part of Poland, with many professions from the Tsar that Polish rights and liberties would be respected. He did not live up to his promises. Prussia, grumbling, accepted two-fifths of Saxony as well as the Rhineland. This compromise was reached only just in time. For while Congress danced at Vienna and the statesmen of Europe replotted the map, Napoleon was brooding and scheming in his new retreat at Elba. Long before the wrangling of the powers had ended he again burst upon the scene.

CHAPTER 37

THE WAR OF 1812

THE CONFUSED AND TUMULTUOUS ISSUES of European politics reached America in black and white. Debate on the French Revolution had raged throughout the country. Controversy however had become less theoretical and much more vehement as soon as American commercial interests were affected, and the European war revived the old sinister issues of embargo, blockade, and impressment. The British were entitled by the customs of the time to impress British subjects who happened to be serving in American ships; but they also made a practice of impressing American citizens and many sailors whose nationality was doubtful. Also, in retaliation for Napoleon's Berlin Decrees, establishing a continental blockade of Britain, Orders in Council were issued in London imposing severe restrictions on all neutral trade with France and her allies. United States commerce was hard hit by both these belligerent measures.

The unofficial trade war with the United States told heavily upon England too. The loss of the American market and the hard winter of 1811–12 brought widespread unemployment and a business crisis. Petitions were sent to Parliament begging the Government to revoke the Orders in Council. After much hesitation Castlereagh announced in the House of Commons that the Government had done so. But it was too late. The Atlantic crossing took too long for the news to reach America in time. On June 18, 1812, Congress declared war on Great Britain.

The root of the quarrel, however, lay rather in the problems of the western frontier. The seaboard states, and especially New England, wanted peace. Their main concern was America's foreign trade, which had already gravely diminished. War with Britain would bring it to a stop. But American domestic politics had brought to power representatives of the west and southwest, men who were hungry for land, and this could be had only from the Indians or from the British Empire. They had no conception of affairs in Europe; they cared nothing about Napoleon's designs. The prime aim and object was to seize Canada and establish American sovereignty throughout the whole northern continent. Through their influence President James Madison was won over to a policy of war.

During the war against America in 1812 the British were able to conscript troops from among the Indians. George Catlin's nineteenth-century drawings of American Indians record a way of life that was about to be destroyed by contact with European settlers and armies.

On paper the forces were very unequal. The population of the United States was now seven and a half millions, including slaves. In Canada there were only five hundred thousand people, most of them French. But there were nearly five thousand trained British troops, about four thousand Canadian regulars, and about the same number of militia. The Indians could supply between three and four thousand auxiliaries.

The American regular army numbered less than seven thousand men, and although with great difficulty over four hundred thousand state militia were called out few were used in Canada. Nor was this all. The Seven Years' War had shown that Canada could only be conquered by striking up the St Lawrence, but the Americans had no sufficient navy for such a project. They were therefore forced to fight an offensive war on a wide frontier, impassable at places, and were exposed to Indian onslaughts on their columns. Their leaders had worked out no broad strategy. If they had concentrated their troops on Lake Ontario they might have succeeded, but instead they were forced to make half-hearted and uncoordinated thrusts across the borders.

The first American expedition ended in disaster. The ablest British commander, General Isaac Brock, supported by the Indian Confederacy, drove it back. By August the British were in Detroit, and within a few days Fort Dearborn, where Chicago now stands, had fallen. The American frontier rested once more on a line from the Ohio to Lake Erie. The remainder of the year was spent on fruitless moves upon the Niagara front, and operations came to an inconclusive end.

The war at sea was more colourful, and for the Americans more cheering. They had sixteen vessels, of which three surpassed anything afloat. These were 44-gun frigates, the *Constitution*, the *United States*, and the *President*. They fired a heavier broadside than British frigates, they were heavily timbered, but their clean lines underwater enabled them to outsail any ship upon the seas. Their crews were volunteers and their officers highly trained. A London journalist called them "a few fir-built frigates, manned by a handful of bastards and outlaws". This phrase was adopted with glee by the Americans, who gloried in disproving the insult. The British fleet on the transatlantic station included eleven ships of the line and thirty-four frigates. Their naval tradition was long and glorious, and, with their memories of Trafalgar and the Nile, the English captains were confident they could sink any American. But when one English ship after another found its guns out-ranged and was battered to pieces, the reputation of the "fir-built frigates" was startlingly made. The American public, smarting at the disasters in Canada, gained new heart from these victories. Their frigates within a year had won more successes over the British than the French and Spaniards in two decades of warfare. But retribution was at hand. On June 1, 1813, the American frigate *Chesapeake* sailed from Boston harbour with a green and mutinous crew to accept a challenge from HMS *Shannon*. After a fifteen-minute fight the *Chesapeake* surrendered. Other American losses followed, and command of the ocean passed into British hands. American privateers however continued to harry British shipping.

These naval episodes had no effect on the general course of the war, and if the British Government had abandoned impressment a new campaign might have been avoided in 1813. But they did not do so, and the Americans set about revising their strategy. Canada was still their main objective. By land the Americans made a number of raids into the province of Upper Canada, now named Ontario. Towns and villages were sacked and burnt, including the little capital which has since become the great city of Toronto. The war was becoming fiercer. During the winter of 1812–13 the Americans had also established a base on Lake Erie, and stores were laboriously hauled over the mountains to furnish the American commander, Captain Perry, with a flotilla for freshwater fighting.

In the autumn Perry's little armada sailed to victory. A strange amphibious battle was fought in September 1813. Negroes, frontier scouts, and militiamen, aboard craft hastily built of new green wood, fought to the end upon the still waters of the lake. The American ships were heavier, and the British were defeated with much loss. "We have met the enemy," Perry reported laconically, "and they are ours." Thus the United States were established on the southern shore of the Great Lakes and the Indians could no longer outflank their frontier. But the invasion of Upper Canada on land had been

The capture of the American frigate Chesapeake *by HMS* Shannon *on June 1, 1813, is recorded in this painting by J. Whitcombe.*

a failure, and the year of 1813 ended with the Canadians in possession of Fort Niagara.

Hitherto the British in Canada had lacked the means for offensive action. Troops and ships in Europe were locked in the deadly struggle against Napoleon. Moreover the British Government was anxious not to irritate the New England states by threatening them from the north. Indeed, the British forces were almost entirely fed from the New England ports. But by the spring of 1814 a decision had been reached in Europe, and the British could at last send adequate reinforcements. They purposed to strike from Niagara, from Montreal by way of Lake Champlain, and in the south at New Orleans, with simultaneous naval raids on the American coast. The campaign opened before Wellington's veterans could arrive from the Peninsula. The advance from Niagara was checked by a savage drawn battle at Lundy's Lane, near the Falls. But by the end of August eleven thousand troops from Europe had been concentrated near Montreal to advance by Burgoyne's old route down the Hudson valley. In September, under Sir George Prevost, they moved on Plattsburg, and prepared to dispute the command of Lake Champlain. They were faced by a mere fifteen hundred American regulars, supported by a few thousand militia. All depended on the engagement of the British and American flotillas. As at Lake Erie, the Americans built better ships for freshwater fighting, and they gained the victory. This crippled the British advance and was the most decisive engagement of the war. Prevost and his forces retired into Canada.

At sea, in spite of their reverses of the previous years, the British were supreme. More ships arrived from European waters. The American coast was defenceless. In August, the British general Ross landed in Chesapeake Bay at the head of four thousand men. The American militia, raw and untrained, retreated rapidly, and on August 24 British troops entered the Federal capital of Washington. President Madison took refuge in Virginia.

So hasty was the American withdrawal that English officers sat down to a meal cooked for him and his family in the White House. The White House and the Capitol were then burnt in reprisal for the conduct of American militiamen in Canada. Washington's home on the Potomac was spared and strictly guarded by the British.

In December the last and most irresponsible British onslaught, the expedition to New Orleans, reached its base. But here in the frontier lands of the southwest a military leader of high quality had appeared in the person of Andrew Jackson, who as an early settler in Tennessee had won a reputation in warfare against the Indians.

Andrew Jackson's successful years in the army were followed by a distinguished career in politics. He became the seventh President of the United States in 1829.

Eight thousand British troops landed at New Orleans under Sir Edward Pakenham, who had commanded a division at Salamanca. The swamps and inlets in the mouth of the Mississippi made an amphibious operation extremely dangerous. All men and stores had to be transported seventy miles in rowboats from the fleet. Jackson had entrenched himself on the left bank of the river. His forces were much inferior in numbers, but composed of highly skilled marksmen. On the morning of January 8, 1815, Pakenham led a frontal assault against the American earthworks—one of the most unintelligent manoeuvres in the history of British warfare. Here he was slain and two thousand of his troops were killed or wounded. The only surviving general officer withdrew the army to its transports. The Americans lost seventy men, thirteen of them killed. The battle had lasted precisely half an hour.

Peace between England and America had meanwhile been signed on Christmas Eve, 1814. But the Battle of New Orleans is an important event in American history. It made the career of a future president, Jackson, and it created a legend that the Americans had decisively won the war. In fact, at the peace negotiations both sides agreed upon the status quo.

The war however was a turning point in the history of Canada. Canadians took pride in the part they had played in defending their country. Their growing national sentiment was strengthened, and the results of the peace were solid and enduring. Henceforward the world was to see a three-thousand-mile international frontier between Canada and the United States undefended by men or guns.

CHAPTER 38

ELBA AND WATERLOO

IN THE NEW YEAR OF 1815 peace reigned in Europe and in America. In Paris a stout, elderly, easygoing Bourbon sat on the throne of France, oblivious of the mistakes made by his relations, advisers, and followers. His royalist supporters, more royal than their king, were trying the patience of his newfound subjects. The French people, dreaming of Imperial glories, were ripe for another adventure. At Vienna the powers of Europe were still by no means in accord on many details of the map of Europe which they had met to redraw. After the exertions of twenty years of warfare they felt they had earned leisure enough to indulge in haggling, bargains, and festivity. A sharp and sudden shock was needed to recall them to their unity of purpose. It came from a familiar quarter.

Napoleon kills time during his exile on Elba by gaming with his mother. He draws a number 18 and tucks it into his hat. A year later he was to meet his defeat at Waterloo on June 18, 1815.

Napoleon had for nine months been sovereign of Elba. He kept about him the apparatus of Imperial dignity. He applied to the iron mines and tunny fisheries of his little kingdom the same probing energy that had once set great armies in motion. He still possessed an army. It included four hundred members of his Old Guard, a few displaced Polish soldiers, and a local militia. He also had a navy, for which he devised a special Elban ensign. His fleet consisted of a single brig and some cutters. To these puny armaments and to the exiguous Elban budget he devoted his attention. He would henceforth give himself up, he had told the people of Elba, to the task of ensuring their happiness. At Porto Ferrajo, his capital, he furnished a palace in the grand manner. He played cards with his mother and cheated according to his recognised custom. He entertained his favourite sister and his faithful Polish mistress. Only his wife, the Empress Marie Louise, and their son were missing. The Austrian Government took care to keep them both in Vienna.

A stream of curious foreign visitors came to see the fallen Emperor, many from Britain. One of them reported, perhaps not without prejudice, that he looked more like a crafty priest than a great commander. The resident Allied Commissioner on Elba, Sir Neil Campbell, knew better. As the months went by, close observers became sure that Napoleon was biding his time. Through spies he was in touch with many currents of opinion. He perceived that the restored Bourbons could not command the loyalty of the French. In February 1815 he saw, or thought he saw, that the Congress of Vienna was breaking up. The Allies were at odds and France, discontented, beckoned to him. Of all this conjunction of circumstances Napoleon took lightning advantage. On Sunday night, February 26, he slipped out of harbour in his brig, attended by a small train of lesser vessels. At the head of a thousand men he set sail for France. On March 1 he landed near Antibes. The local band, welcoming him, played the French equivalent of "Home, Sweet Home".

The drama of the Hundred Days had begun, and a bloodless march to Paris ensued. Royalist armies sent to stop the intruder melted away or went

The house in which Napoleon lived for nine months on Elba afforded a peaceful environment in which to plan his future military strategies.

over to him. Marshal Ney, "the Bravest of the Brave", who had taken service under the Bourbons, boasted that he would bring his former master back to Paris in an iron cage. He found he too could not resist the Emperor's call. Other marshals who had turned their coats now turned them again. Within eighteen days of his landing Napoleon was installed in the capital. The Bourbons ran for cover, and found it at Ghent. Meanwhile the Emperor proclaimed his peaceful intentions, and at once started shaping his army. He bid for support by promising liberal institutions to the French people. In fact he dreamt of restoring all the old forms of Empire as soon as he had behind him the consolidation of military victory. But the mood of France had changed since the high noon of Austerlitz, Jena, and Wagram. There was enthusiasm, but no longer at the topmost fighting pitch. The army and its leaders were not what they had been. The frightful losses of the Russian campaign and of Leipzig could not be made good. Since 1805 a hundred and forty-eight French generals had fallen in battle. Of those that remained only half were now loyal to Napoleon. While Napoleon himself abounded in self-confidence, the flashing military judgment of earlier years was dimmed. The gastric ulcer from which he had long suffered caused him intermittent pain. Yet the Emperor remained a formidable figure and a challenge to Europe.

The powers at Vienna acted with unaccustomed speed and unanimity. They declared Napoleon an outlaw. They set about marshalling their forces. The British Government realised that they would have to bear the brunt of a whirlwind campaign. It would take time for Russia and Austria to muster their strength. Prussia was the only main ally then in readiness. There was no time to lose. Wellington recommended the immediate transport of an army to the Netherlands, to form bases for a march on Paris and prepare for a clash upon the frontiers. Within a month of the escape from Elba, Wellington took up his command at Brussels.

The state of his army did not please the Duke. Many of his best troops from the Peninsula had gone to America, including his Chief of Staff, Sir George Murray. With great difficulty the British Government had collected six regiments of cavalry and twenty-five battalions of infantry, consisting partly of Peninsular veterans and partly of untrained boys. The biggest deficiency was in artillery. On the conclusion of the Peace of Paris in 1814 the British Cabinet had ordered the wholesale discharge of gunners and drivers, and the shortage was now serious. But there were, as in all European wars, the continental allies and auxiliaries. The King of Great Britain was still King of Hanover. Hanoverian troops, on their way home through the Netherlands, were halted and joined the new army. Wellington, at a loss for numbers, tried to persuade the Portuguese to send a few battalions. He had taught them the arts of war, and he was proud of his "fighting cocks", as he called them. But his efforts were in vain. The Dutch and Belgian troops put under his command by the King of the Netherlands looked unreliable. Their countries had for twenty years been occupied by the French, and the sympathies of their rank and file would probably waver towards Napoleon. There were contingents also from Nassau and other German provinces. As the summer drew near Wellington assembled a mixed force of eighty-three thousand men, of whom about a third were British. He bluntly cursed, as was his habit, the quality of his untried troops, while bending all his endeavours to train and transform them. The main support for his new adventure must be Marshal Blücher. The Prussians had a force of a hundred and thirteen thousand men, but nearly half of them were untrained militia. They lay in eastern Belgium.

Wellington, with his staff, planned a large-scale advance into France. He did not propose tamely to await a Napoleonic onslaught. In his calm, considering way, he worked it all out. Based upon Brussels, he took up a line between Maubeuge and Beaumont, with the Prussians on his left holding the position between Philippeville and Givet. As it happened, the Emperor seized his usual initiative.

Napoleon could not afford to waste a day. Nor did he do so. His two main enemies stood on his northeastern frontier within a few days' march of his capital. He must strike immediately at his gathering foes. The moral value of victory would be overwhelming, and the prestige of the British Government would be shaken. His admirers in London, the pacific Whigs, might replace the Tories and proffer a negotiated peace. Louis XVIII would be driven into permanent exile and the Belgian Netherlands restored to French rule. This achieved, he could face with equanimity the menaces of Austria and Russia. Such were his hopes while he applied his intense power of will to rousing the exhausted French nation. Five corps of about a hundred and twenty-five thousand men were organised on the frontier fortress line. The protection afforded by these fortresses, behind which he

THE FUTURE GEORGE IV

A more favourable view than was usual is taken of the future George IV by Dr Burney in a letter to his daughter, the writer Fanny Burney.

July 12, 1805

Your brother, Dr Charles, and I, have had the honour last Tuesday of dining with the Prince of Wales at Lord Melbourne's, at the particular desire of HRH. He is so good-humoured and gracious to those against whom he has no party prejudice, that it is impossible not to be flattered by his politeness and condescension. I was astonished to find him, amidst such constant dissipation, possessed of so much learning, wit, knowledge of books in general, discrimination of character, as well as original humour. He quoted Homer in Greek to my son as readily as if the beauties of Dryden or Pope had been under consideration. And as to music, he is an excellent critic; has an enlarged taste—admiring whatever is good in its kind, of whatever age or country the composers or performers may be; without, however, being insensible to the superior genius and learning necessary to some kinds of music more than others.

The conversation was general and lively, in which several of the company, consisting of eighteen or twenty, took a share, till towards the heel of the evening, or rather the *toe* of the morning; for we did not rise from table till one o'clock, when Lady Melbourne being returned from the opera with her daughters, coffee was ordered; during which HRH took me aside and talked exclusively about music near half an hour, and as long with your brother concerning Greek Literature. He is a most excellent mimic of well-known characters; had we been in the dark any one would have sworn that Dr Parr and Kemble were in the room.

George, Prince of Wales hid a refined nature beneath a coarse exterior. Hoppner's flattering portrait of him was painted in 1795.

could build up at leisure, gave Napoleon the impetus in the opening phases of the campaign, for Wellington was obliged to quarter his troops upon a possible defence line of forty miles.

During the early days of June tension was heightening. It was plain, or at least predictable, that Napoleon would attempt to rout Wellington's and Blücher's armies separately and piecemeal. But where would he land his first blow? Wellington waited patiently in Brussels for a sign of the Emperor's intention. He and his great opponent were to cross swords for the first time. They were both in their forty-sixth year.

Quietly on June fifteenth, Napoleon crossed the Sambre at Charleroi and Marchiennes, driving the Prussian forward troops before him to within twenty-five miles of Brussels. He had struck at the hinge of the allied armies. The capture of Brussels would be a great forward stride. Possession of a capital city was always a lure for him, and a source of strength.

Liaison between the British and Prussians was mysteriously defective and hours passed before the news reached Wellington. Military intelligence was confusing and contradictory. There were no British troops on the Waterloo–Charleroi road, which was held thinly by a Dutch-Belgian division. On the night of the fifteenth, while the French armies massed to destroy the Prussians, the Duchess of Richmond gave a ball in Brussels in honour of the Allied officers. Wellington graced the occasion with his presence. He knew the value of preserving a bold, unruffled face. Amid the dancing he reflected on the belated news which had reached him. At all costs the French advance upon Brussels must be held. Wellington resolved to concentrate on the stategic point of Quatre-Bras. In the early hours of the morning of the sixteenth Picton's brigade rumbled down the Brussels road to join the Dutch troops already covering this dangerous ground lying open between the British and Prussian array.

For the French everything depended upon beating the Prussians before forcing Wellington northwestward to the coast. Napoleon had in mind the vision of a shattered British army grimly awaiting transports for home in the Flemish ports. At Corunna and Walcheren such things had happened before. Leaving Ney with the French left, the Emperor swung with sixty-three thousand men and ninety-two guns to meet the main Prussian army, centred in Ligny. Realising that so far only a small force held the position at Quatre-Bras, he ordered Ney to attack, and then meet him that evening in Brussels. At two o'clock in the afternoon of the 16th the French went into action on a two-mile front. Wellington himself arrived to take command with a force of seven thousand men and sixteen guns. The brunt of the battle fell upon Picton's leading brigade. After having marched for twelve hours from Brussels these Peninsular veterans steadily pressed on. In vain the French cavalry swirled round them while the Allied Dutch and Belgian infantry were edged from the field. There was little tactical manoeuvre in the fierce struggle which swayed backwards and forwards on that June afternoon at the crossroads on the way to Brussels. It was a head-on collision in which generalship played no part, though leadership did. Wellington was always at his coolest in the hottest of moments. In this battle of private soldiers the firepower of the British infantry prevailed. Out of thirty thousand men engaged, by nightfall on their side the Allies lost four thousand six hundred; the French somewhat less. But Ney had not gained his objective. Brussels was not in his grasp.

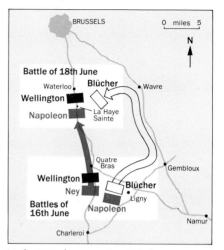

In the Waterloo campaign Napoleon separated Wellington from Blücher, his Prussian ally, and defeated the latter at Ligny on June 16. Napoleon assumed that Blücher would retreat to Namur and sent French troops after him, but he went to Wavre instead, and was able, therefore, to come to Wellington's aid when on June 18 he faced the massed French armies at La Haye Sainte, just south of Waterloo.

This picture shows the Marquis of Anglesey in action. He subsequently lost a leg at Waterloo, turned to Wellington and said, "By God! I have lost my leg." The Duke's laconic reply is reputed to have been, "Have you, by God?"

On the French side the staff work had hardly been creditable. Napoleon had gained the advantage at the opening of the campaign, but he had not intended that both wings of his army should be in action at once. He seems to have departed from his original plan. At Ligny however he won a striking success. Marshal Blücher was out-generalled, his army split in two, battered by the magnificent French artillery, and driven back on Wavre. Again liaison between the Allied armies broke down. Wellington had no immediate information of the outcome at Ligny, nor of the subsequent movements of the Prussians. His main body had gathered round the village of Quatre-Bras by the time he learnt of the Prussian defeat. Napoleon decided in the small hours of June 17 to send Marshal Grouchy with thirty-three thousand men to pursue the Prussians while he flung his main weight against Wellington. The crisis of the campaign was at hand.

There seems no doubt that in the opening days Wellington had been surprised. As he confessed at the time, Napoleon's movements had "humbugged" him. Years later, when he read French accounts of Quatre-Bras, he declared with his habitual frankness, "Damn them, I beat them, and if I was surprised, if I did place myself in so foolish a position, they were the greater fools for not knowing how to take advantage of my faults." Immediately after the opening battle his methodical mind was in full command of the situation. His plan was to fall back upon a prepared position at Mont St Jean. There he would accept battle, and all he asked from the Prussians was the support of one corps.

Wellington himself had inspected this Belgian countryside in the autumn of 1814. He had noted the advantages of the ridge at Waterloo. So had Marlborough a century earlier, when his Dutch allies had prevented him from engaging Villeroi there. His unfought battle was now to unroll. Throughout the night of June 16 and 17 a carefully screened retreat began, and by morning the Waterloo position, a line of defence such as Wellington had already tested in the Peninsula, was occupied. Upon the French must be forced the onus of a frontal attack. A line of fortified farms and rolling slopes made up the Allied front, held by sixty-three thousand men and a hundred and fifty-six guns. The French troops failed to harass the retreat. Their staff work had again gone awry. Napoleon was unaware of what had happened at Quatre-Bras, and there was an imminent danger that the Prussians would fall back and unite with Wellington. That was indeed their intention. Blücher and his Chief of Staff, Gneisenau, who was the brain of the Prussian army, were retiring northwest from Ligny in the direction of Brussels. Marshal Grouchy, misinformed or misjudging, thought they were moving northeast towards Liège, a costly mistake for the French. Meanwhile Napoleon, furious to hear of Wellington's skilful withdrawal, pounded in his carriage down the Brussels road with his advance guard in a desperate attempt to entrap the British rear. The mercy of a violent storm slowed up progress. The English cavalry galloped for safety through the thunder and torrential rain. An angry scene took place upon the meeting of Napoleon and Ney, who was greeted with the words from the Emperor, "You have ruined France!" As Napoleon reached the ridge of Waterloo and saw the British already in their positions he realised how complete had been their escape.

Late in the morning of June 18 the French attacked both flanks of the Allied position, of which the key points were the fortified chateau of

Hougoumont on the right and the farm of La Haye Sainte in the middle. Napoleon promised his staff they would sleep that night in Brussels. And to Soult, who raised some demur, he said, "You think Wellington a great general because he beat you. I tell you this will be a picnic." Then seventy thousand French troops and two hundred and twenty-four guns were concentrated for the decisive assault. The battle swayed backwards and forwards upon the grass slopes, and intense fighting centred in the farm of La Haye Sainte, which eventually fell to the French. At Hougoumont, which held out all day, the fighting was heavier still. In the early afternoon a terrific artillery barrage was launched upon Wellington's infantry as preparation for the major cavalry advance of fifteen thousand troopers under Ney. Under the hail of the French guns Wellington moved his infantry farther back over the ridge of Waterloo to give them a little more shelter. On seeing this Ney launched his squadrons in a series of attacks. Everything now depended upon the British muskets and bayonets. Anxiously Wellington looked eastward for a sign of the Prussians. They were on their way, for Blücher was keeping faith. But the French cuirassiers were upon the Duke. They never reached the infantry squares. As one eye-witness wrote: "As to the so-called charges, I do not think that on a single occasion actual collision occurred. I many times saw the cuirassiers come on with boldness to within some twenty or thirty yards of a square, when, seeing the steady firmness of our men, they invariably edged away and retired. Sometimes they would halt and gaze at the triple row of bayonets, when two or three brave officers would advance and strive to urge the attack, raising their helmets aloft . . . but all in vain, as no efforts could make the men close with the terrible bayonets and meet certain destruction."

No visible decision was achieved. Napoleon, looking through his glasses at the awful melee, exclaimed, "Will the English never show their backs?" "I fear," replied Soult, "they will be cut to pieces first." Wellington too had much to disturb him. Although the Prussians had been distantly sighted upon the roads in the early afternoon, they were slow in making their presence felt upon the French right. But by six o'clock in the evening Ney's onslaughts had failed and Blücher and his Prussians were beating relentlessly upon the wing. They drew off fourteen thousand men from the forces assailing Wellington.

The French made a final effort, and desperate fighting with no quarter raged again round the farms. The Imperial Guard itself, with Ney at its head, rolled up the hill, but again the fury of British infantry fire held them. The long-awaited moment to counterattack had come. Wellington had been in the forefront of danger all day. On his chestnut, Copenhagen, he had galloped everywhere, issuing brusque orders, gruffly encouraging his men. Now he rode along his much-battered line and ordered the advance. "Go on, go on!" he shouted. "They will not stand!" His cavalry swept from the ridge and sabred the French army into a disorganised mass of stragglers. Ney, beside himself with rage, a broken sword in his hand, staggered shouting in vain from one band to another. It was too late. Wellington handed over the pursuit to the Prussians. In agony of soul Napoleon followed the road back to Paris.

Late that night Blücher and Wellington met and embraced. *"Mein lieber Kamerad,"* said the old German Field-Marshal, who knew not a word of English, *"quelle affaire!"*, which was about all the French he could

This side drum was used at Waterloo by the First Foot Guards who distinguished themselves by defeating Napoleon's reserve regiment of Imperial Guards, whom he considered invincible. The Prince Regent subsequently honoured the First Foot Guards by appending the name "Grenadier" to their regimental title. (In each regiment, the grenadiers were the elite troops, tall, strong men entrusted with throwing grenades.)

command. This brief greeting was greatly to Wellington's laconic taste. It was a story he delighted to repeat in later years. The Duke rode back to the village of Waterloo. The day had been almost too much even for a man of iron. Only the power and example of his own personality had kept his motley force together. The strain had been barely tolerable. "By God!" as he justly said, "I don't think it would have been done if I had not been there." As he took tea and toast and had the casualty lists read to him he broke down and wept.

Letters of congratulation poured in to the Duke in the days that followed. Metternich, the Austrian Chancellor, conveyed his appreciation of what he cautiously called the "brilliant opening of the campaign". In fact it was all over. Blücher and his Prussians marched steadily and uneventfully upon Paris. Napoleon had reached his capital three days after the battle. He had a momentary surge of hope. He would fight again in France a campaign like that of 1814. But no one shared his optimism. On June 22 he abdicated and retired to Malmaison. Fouché headed a provisional government and set about treating with the Allies and with Louis XVIII. There was nothing else to be done. On July 6 Blücher and Wellington entered the capital. One of the Duke's first tasks was to restrain the Prussians from resentful vengeance. Their army in 1806 had been thrashed by the French, their country mutilated and their garrison towns occupied. They nourished a bitterness which the Duke did not share. When Blücher proposed to blow up the Bridge of Jena over the Seine, named after the celebrated Prussian defeat, Wellington posted British sentries to prevent him. Two days after the Allies' arrival, Louis XVIII appeared.

His second restoration was largely of Wellington's making. Most French-

The meeting of Wellington and Blücher after Waterloo is shown in this fresco by Daniel Maclise. It is in the Royal Gallery at the Palace of Westminster.

men and many of the Allies would have preferred a monarchy under the Duke of Orleans, a regency for Napoleon's young son, or a constitutional republic. Wellington had no high regard for the Bourbons, but he was convinced that France under their shaky rule would no longer have the power to disturb the peace of Europe. Louis XVIII was no grand monarch and could never aspire to become one. Wellington, like many great soldiers when victory is complete, looked forward to an age of tranquillity. Laurels and bay had been won; it was time to cultivate the olive.

Napoleon left Malmaison at the end of June. He made for Rochefort, on the Biscay coast, narrowly evading capture on the way by Blücher's Prussians. Had they taken him they would have shot him. He had thoughts of sailing for America, and he ordered a set of travel books about the transatlantic continent. Perhaps a new empire might be forged in Mexico, Peru, or Brazil. The alternative was to throw himself upon the mercy of his most inveterate foe. This is what happened. Captain Maitland in the *Bellerophon* was cruising off Rochefort with orders to prevent any French ships from putting to sea. With him Napoleon entered into negotiation. Maitland offered him asylum on his ship. He could not forecast what the British Government would decide to do with his eminent hostage. Nor did he make any promise. Napoleon hoped he might be kept in pleasant captivity in some English country house or Scottish castle. Marshal Tallard and other French generals a century earlier had enjoyed their forced residence in England. The ex-Emperor wrote a flattering letter to the Prince Regent, whom he addressed as "the strongest, the stubbornest, the most generous of my foes". When the Prince read this missive it must have helped to convince him that he and not his generals had really won the war. On this matter he did not need much convincing. The *Bellerophon* anchored in Torbay, and curious Devonshire crowds gazed upon the "Corsican ogre", while Lord Liverpool and the Cabinet deliberated in London. Newspapers clamoured that Napoleon should be put on trial. The Government, acting for the Allies, decided on exile in St Helena, an island about the same size as Jersey, but very mountainous, and far away. Escape from it was impossible. On July 26 the Emperor sailed to his sunset in the South Atlantic. He never permitted himself to understand what had happened at Waterloo. The event was everybody's fault but his own. Six years of life in exile lay before him. He spent them with his small faithful retinue creating the Napoleonic legend of invincibility which was to have so powerful an effect on the France of the future.

The Congress of Vienna had completed its work in June. It remained for the emissaries of the powers to assemble in Paris and compose a new peace with France. The task took three months. The Prussians pressed for harsh terms. Castlereagh saw that mildness would create the least grievance and guard best against a renewal of war. In this he had the hearty support of Wellington, who now exerted a unique authority throughout Europe. The second Treaty of Paris, concluded in November, was somewhat stiffer than that of 1814. Together with the loss of certain small territories, France was to pay an indemnity of seven hundred million francs and to submit to an Allied army of occupation for three years. In the moderation of the settlement with France the Treaty had its greatest success. Wellington took command of the occupying army. For the next three years he was practically a great European power in himself. Castlereagh, with his sombre cast of

European statesmen met at the Congress of Vienna to discuss matters of peace. The chief foreground figures in this portrayal are Metternich and Castlereagh (seated, left to right). Wellington stands on the far left, Talleyrand is seated on the far right.

mind, thought the Treaty would be justified if it kept the peace for seven years. He had built better than he knew. Peace reigned for forty years between the great powers, and the main framework of the settlements at Vienna and Paris endured until the twentieth century.

So the scene closes on a protracted peacemaking after the longest of the world wars. The impetus of the French Revolution had been spread by the genius of Napoleon to the four quarters of Europe. Ideals of liberty and nationalism, born in Paris, had been imparted to all the European peoples. In the nineteenth century ahead they were to clash resoundingly with the ordered world for which the Congress of Vienna had striven. If France was defeated and her Emperor fallen, the principles which had inspired her lived on. They were to play a notable part in changing the shape of government in every European country, Britain not excepted.